2023年江苏高校“青蓝工程”中青年学术带头人经费资助项目
苏州市职业大学科技处经费资助项目
明基友达公益基金会江南文化研究基金经费资助项目

苏州发展研究丛书

苏州外文史料译编

（第二辑）

主　编　卞浩宇
副主编　孟祥德　徐　冰　蔡　骏
参　编　严　佳　余利霞　戴　莉　吴悦茜
　　　　徐舟涟　骆碧筠　孙　丹

苏州大学出版社
Soochow University Press

图书在版编目(CIP)数据

苏州外文史料译编. 第二辑 / 卞浩宇主编. --苏州：苏州大学出版社，2023.12
(苏州发展研究丛书 / 王国平主编)
ISBN 978-7-5672-4678-2

Ⅰ.①苏… Ⅱ.①卞… Ⅲ.①苏州-地方史-史料-汇编-英、汉 Ⅳ.①K295.33

中国国家版本 CIP 数据核字(2024)第 022008 号

Suzhou Waiwen Shiliao Yibian(Di-er Ji)
书　　名：苏州外文史料译编(第二辑)

主　　编：卞浩宇
责任编辑：沈　琴
装帧设计：吴　钰

出版发行：苏州大学出版社(Soochow University Press)
社　　址：苏州市十梓街 1 号　**邮编**：215006
印　　刷：苏州工业园区美柯乐制版印务有限责任公司
邮购热线：0512-67480030
销售热线：0512-67481020

开　　本：710 mm ×1 000 mm　1/16　**印张**：17　**字数**：305 千
版　　次：2023 年 12 月第 1 版
印　　次：2023 年 12 月第 1 次印刷
书　　号：ISBN 978-7-5672-4678-2
定　　价：85.00 元

图书若有印装错误，本社负责调换
苏州大学出版社营销部　电话：0512-67481020
苏州大学出版社网址　http://www.sudapress.com
苏州大学出版社邮箱　sdcbs@suda.edu.cn

苏州发展研究丛书

编 委 会

序　言

苏州是首批国家历史文化名城，是吴文化的重要发祥地之一，有“人间天堂”的美誉。从 2 500 多年前建城至今，任凭风吹雨打、时光流转，苏州保留了中国城市最完整的肌理，勾勒着承载诗意栖居的都市梦想。历史赋予生命，活力创造未来。苏州的名片不仅是“人家尽枕河”的江南好景，更是依托强有力的工业基础而迅速崛起的现代化强市。改革开放以来，从“小康构想”印证地到“勾画现代化目标”地，“强富美高”美好蓝图正一步一个脚印在苏州大地化为美好现实。站在全面建设社会主义现代化国家的新起点，一向敢为人先的苏州人再次拿出当年创造“三大法宝”的魄力，努力将全面小康阶段的“曾经先发”变为现代化新征程上的“再度领先”。

“苏人以为雅者，则四方随而雅之。”苏州是一座被文化浸润的城市，长江文化、运河文化、吴文化、古城文化、江南文化等在此交会融通。历史给苏州留下的不仅是园林文化、精致文化，更是一种追求卓越、胸怀天下的文化。追溯历史，放眼全国，苏州是一种独特的文化现象，中国式现代化的重要特征在苏州都有更为集中的体现，苏州理应成为中国区域经济、社会和文化研究中一个独具魅力、独领风骚的重要研究对象。党的二十大报告指出，要推进文化自信自强，铸就社会主义文化新辉煌。“全面建设社会主义现代化国家，必须坚持中国特色社会主义文化发展道路，增强文化自信，围绕举旗帜、聚民心、育新人、兴文化、展形象建设社会主义文化强国，发展面向现代化、面向世界、面向未来的，民族的科学的大众的社会主义文化，激发全民族文化创新创造活力，增强实现中华民族伟大复兴的精神力量。”站在“两个一百年”奋斗目标的历史交汇点，把苏州城市发展作为一门学科来探索和打造，是一个城市增强历史自觉、坚定文化自信的体现。文化自信是一种态度，是苏州的信心和决心；文化自强是一种行动，是推进中国式现代化的重要支撑。近年来，苏州全力推进文化自信自强，增强历史责任、时代责任，高标准高质量推进苏州地域文明探源工程，加强太湖流域文明、史前文化、吴越文化等研究力度，扎实做好“苏州全书”编纂等工作，着力填补苏州历史研究缺环，进一步发扬光大苏州优秀传统文化，为推动中华文化更好走向世界做出更大贡献。

对苏州发展的研究，应当立足于苏州在中华文明发展历程和世界城市发展史中的地位和贡献，突出城市文脉、城市品质、城市精神、城市叙事的一体建构，从根本上回答苏州何以成为苏州、苏州将成为什么样的新苏州等重大命题。当前，要把文献开发研究摆在突出位置，编纂汇聚分散在世界各地有关苏州的文献，再通过出版向世界各地传播苏州历史文化，钩沉文献原著的全貌，探寻我们的精神原乡，重建文化高地的辉煌。

当前，苏州社科界各路“大军”都在为推动城市文化的基础性工程建设群策群力、添柴加薪。作为苏州唯一的市属公办本科院校，苏州城市学院责无旁贷、奋勇争先。苏州城市学院在建校伊始就成立了苏州发展研究院，旨在就深入挖掘、传承、保护、利用苏州历史文化资源方面做出自己的努力和贡献，为城市的数字化转型、城市更新和创新发展进一步集智汇力、建言献策。为此，苏州城市学院苏州发展研究院隆重推出“苏州发展研究丛书”，近期主要包括苏州历史文化与当代苏州研究系列、苏州文献史料编研系列，希望能为讲好苏州故事、展现苏州风采而绵绵用力、久久为功。

聚沙成塔、集腋成裘，我们期待大家的共同参与！

是为序。

芮国强

2022 年 11 月

目录

Notes on the History of Suchow

苏州历史摘录

（潘慎文著 卞浩宇、严佳译）

《苏州历史摘录》（“Notes on the History of Suchow”）作者系美国监理会来华传教士潘慎文（A. P. Parker, 1850—1924）。潘慎文 1875 年来华，1876 年被派到苏州协助曹子实办学，此后执掌苏州博习书院、上海中西书院数十年，为中国早期现代化运动培养了大批人才。潘慎文还曾担任基督教中国教育会第二任会长，亲自编写和组织出版了一大批近代教科书，推动了近代中国教育的发展。

《苏州历史摘录》是潘慎文于 1882 与 1883 年间发表在《教务杂志》（*The Chinese Recorder and Missionary Journal*）上的系列文章，共计六篇。在文中，潘慎文向西方读者较为详细地介绍了苏州的建城史、众多的古城门、周边的名胜古迹，以及苏州历史上的诸多重要人物和精彩故事，引人入胜。尽管潘慎文在第六篇篇末注明“未完待续”，但很可惜，此后《教务杂志》上再也没出现续篇，着实令读者感到遗憾。

NOTES ON THE HISTORY OF SUCHOW I

By Rev. A. P. Parker

This so called "History" is a bulky work of 150 volumes of over fifty pages each. I have read and noted parts of it which may perhaps be of interest to the readers of the Recorder. I shall not attempt a consecutive history of the city, but will notice only a few of the more prominent points of interest that I have been able to glean from the Book.

This gives, in unconnected portions, the principal facts (and fancies too) in relation to the men and things that for more than two milleniums have played their parts in unceasing succession in the history of this great city. There is no attempt made at giving the history of Suchow in this work. It is simply a collection and records and annals—in a word the archives of Suchow.

The first two volumes contain a record of the visits of several emperors to the city, and their sayings and doings while here, together with various Imperial Autographs that had been bestowed upon men whom the emperor had met, or places he had visited.

Not until the fourth volume is reached is any record found of the time when the city began to be, and then only in a very meagre and unsatisfactory manner is the record made. It is only here and there as one wades through this great mass of tedious details that the principal facts of the history are found.

These annals are the work of many hands. According to the preface, the first topographical history of Suchow was written in the Sung dynasty, about A.D. 900, by Fan Wên Kung (范文公)[1], a name held in great reverence by the people of this city and surrounding country. His grave is situated about six miles west of the city and is visited every year on the 11th day of the 3rd moon by many people, who go there to burn incense, and pay respect to the illustrious dead.

The History was twice revised and reprinted during the Ming dynasty, once each in the reigns of K'ang Hi and K'ien Lung, about A.D. 1690-1749. The last and best edition was produced in 1824, in 150 volumes (卷) and was the joint work of a number of Suchow scholars under the leadership of Sung Jü Ling (宋

[1] 本书外文原文中的注均为原作者所加。

苏州历史摘录（1）

潘慎文

这本所谓的“史书”[1]是一部包含150卷、每卷超过50页的鸿篇巨制。我在阅读过程中记录了一些内容，也许会令我们杂志的读者产生兴趣。我并不打算完整地介绍苏州历史，而只是关注那些从书中搜集而来的令我产生浓厚兴趣的内容。

在这里，我们向读者呈现出这座城市在连续两千多年中发生的重要事件（也有故事）以及与其相关的人和物，各部分之间并无关联。我们这里不打算讲苏州历史。这里只是历史记载的一个集合——换句话说，只是苏州的历史档案。

这部史书的前两卷主要记录了几位皇帝游历苏州的经过，以及他们在此期间的言行，还有这些皇帝赐给他们所遇见之人或在所游览之地的各种亲笔题字。

一直读到该书的第四卷，我才发现有关苏州建城的一些记录，但这些记录仅只言片语，难以令人满意。只有从大量枯燥的细节中慢慢搜寻，方能从中找到一些散落的历史事实。

这部史书由多位学者共同执笔完成。据该书前言介绍，苏州首部地形史约公元900年由宋朝的范文公[2]所撰。范文公在苏州及周边地区声名远扬，受人敬重。他的墓地位于苏州城西六英里[3]处，每年农历三月十一日，大批民众前往焚香叩拜，以表达对这位逝去先贤的敬意。

这部史书在明朝[4]曾先后经历两次修订和重版，大约在公元1690—1749年，一次在康熙年间，一次在乾隆年间。最后一版于1824年完成，

[1] 即宋如林所修《苏州府志》。
[2] 此处应为范文穆公，即范成大。此处指范成大晚年撰《吴郡志》，故潘慎文所记时间亦有误。
[3] 英里，一种英制长度单位，1英里约1 609米。
[4] 应为清朝，疑为作者误。

如林). A new edition bringing the history down to the end of the reign of Tung Chi (同治) 1874 and including the dire experiences of the devoted city during the T'ai P'ing Rebellion, is now being published under the auspices of the Fu T'ai.

The city is more than 2,300 hundred years old. The first wall was built under the supervision of Wu Tz Sü (伍子胥) by order of Hoh Lü (阖闾) prince of Wu in the reign of King Wang of the Cheu dynasty, B.C. 513-496.

In the first volume, actually the fourth, which treats of the principal changes that have befallen the city, it is stated that the country in which Suchow is situated belonged originally to the Yang Chen District in the time of the Great Yü (大禹) of the Hia dynasty, B.C. 2205. In the period embraced in the Spring and Autumn Annals (春秋时) Suchow was the capital of the kingdom of Wu (吴).

When T'ai Pêh (太伯) and Chung Yung (仲雍) the elder sons of T'ai Wang (太王) of the Cheu fled from their younger brother who had been appointed successor to their father's dominions, they went south and settled in a region of country called King Man (荆蛮), and named the country—which they seemed to have ultimately conquered and ruled—Ken Wu (句吴)[1]. T'ai Pêh dwelt in Mei Li (梅里) about twenty miles north of the city of Hoh Lü. The elder son of Sheu Mung, who was a descendant of the nineteenth generation from T'ai Pêh, moved still further south and settled on or near the place where, four generations later, Hoh Lü built the city of Suchow.

There is still a town in existence some twenty miles north of Suzhou, called Mei Li (梅里), which is supposed to be identical with the Mei Li of T'ai Pêh's time.

The History states that Hoh Lü had frequent conversations with his minister, Wu Tz Sü as to the best methods of strengthening his kingdom and securing the safety and prosperity of his people. Among other plans proposed by Wu Tz Sü to this end, one of the most important was the founding of a new city and stronghold for the seat of government. The king agreed to the necessity of this movement, and commissioned Wu Tz Sü to select a site and proceed with the building of the city, which he accordingly did.

There is a village some eight or ten miles north-east of Suchow called "Prospect City" (相城), which derives its name from the alleged fact that it was the site originally "prospected" and selected by Wu Tz Sü for the contemplated

[1] 句 has the sound of 钩 probably derived from the pronunciation of the aborigines.（原注："句"发音与"钩"相同，大概是源自当地人的发音。）

共计150卷，由宋如林任总主编，众多苏州学者共同协助完成，这也是最好的一个版本。而新版则将历史写到1874年同治皇帝统治结束，内容还包括了在太平天国期间苏州所经历的悲惨遭遇。目前，在抚台的资助下，新书正在出版印刷之中。

苏州已有2 300多年历史。在周敬王统治期间，吴王阖闾（公元前513—公元前496年）[1]命伍子胥监督建造了苏州首座城墙。

该书第一卷，记录了苏州城历经的主要变化。据记载，公元前2205年，苏州所在地属于夏朝大禹统治时期的扬州地区。在春秋时期，苏州成为吴国都城。

太伯[2]和仲雍皆为周太王之子，周太王将王位传给他们的弟弟季历。为避开季历，太伯和仲雍向南出走，最终在一个叫作荆蛮的地方落脚，并将此处——后来他们最终统治了这个地区——更名为句吴。太伯定居梅里，位于阖闾大城[3]以北20英里处。太伯的第十九代后裔寿梦的长子[4]，又将居住地向南迁徙，最终定在了其四代之后的阖闾建造的苏州城或其附近。

如今仍有一处叫作梅里的地方，就在苏州北20英里处，据说就是当年太伯所居住的梅里。

据记载，阖闾经常与大夫伍子胥商谈，探讨如何更好地增强国力，确保臣民安全、富足。在伍子胥所提的众多建议中，最为重要的一条就是建立一座新城，使之成为都城所在地。阖闾认同此项提议的必要性，并命令伍子胥择地建城，随后伍子胥奉命行事。

苏州城东北八到十英里处有座村庄叫“相城”，据说被称为“相城”，是因为伍子胥最初是在此“相其地”并考虑在此建造吴国都城苏州城。但由

[1] 吴王阖闾在位期间应为公元前514—公元前496年。
[2] 即泰伯。
[3] 即苏州。
[4] 即诸樊。

city of Suchow, the capital of Wu. But for some now unknown reason this site was abandoned for the one which the city now occupies.

The name of the city, as at first built, seems to have been Hoh Lü city (阖闾城). The name Su was derived from a very high tower, built by the son and last successor of Hoh Lü in or near the city, and named by him "Beautiful Su Tower" (姑苏台). This tower was named from the Ku Su Mountain (姑苏山). This tower is said to have been so high that from the top of it a man could be seen at a distance of 100 miles. It was built by Fu Ch'a, Hoh Lü's son, principally as a pleasure resort. An artificial lake, a pleasure garden and other accessions were built in connections with it, and here Fu Ch'a abandoned himself to pleasure in the society of the beautiful Si Shi. This female beauty had been sent to him as a snare by the crafty king of Yueh. The latter unable to withstand the power of either of Hoh Lü, or his son, resorted to stratagem. Soon after, Fu Ch'a's accession to his father's dominions, the king of Yueh selected one of the most beautiful women of his kingdom, and after training her in all the female accomplishments of the time, sent her as a present to Fu Ch'a. The device was only too successful. Fu Ch'a gave himself up to dissolute enjoyment, notwithstanding the brave remonstrances of the faithful Wu Tz Sü. Ruin gradually stole unawares upon his army and kingdom, and he was ere long completely crushed by the wily king of Yueh and his kingdom overthrown. It would be tedious and unprofitable to tell of the many vicissitudes through which the city has passed since it was founded. It has been the scene of many fierce struggles, and in its earlier history passed frequently from one to another of the three kingdoms that then held this part of China, each new ruler changing its name, and sometimes also changing the names of its gates. The name Su (苏) seems to have become permanently attached to the city in the reign of K'ai Hwang of the Sui dynasty, about A. D. 590, at which time the kingdom of Wu was finally overthrown and the country added to the dominions of K'ai Hwang.

The city has long been noted as the abode of wealth and luxury, and as one of the principal literary centres of China. The well-known saying: "Above is heaven, below are Su and Hang" (上有天堂下有苏杭), indicates what a paradise each of the cities, Suchow and Hangchow, is in the estimation of the Chinese.

Dr. William, in his *Middle Kingdom* says that Suchow is situated on islands in the Great Lake, and contains a population of 2,000,000 inhabitants. I do not

于某些未知原因，伍子胥最终选择他处建造苏州城。

苏州在最初建城之时叫作阖闾城。“苏”这个字来自一座高台，这座高台由阖闾之子，也是吴国最后一位国君夫差所建，位于苏州城附近，夫差为其取名“姑苏台”。而“姑苏台”之名则来自“姑苏山”。据说，这座高台相当之高，即便距离高台一百英里之外的人都能够看得见站在台上之人。夫差修建姑苏台主要供其游玩之用。姑苏台四周建有人工湖泊、游乐花园以及其他一些配套设施。夫差和美女西施在这里纵情享乐。西施是狡猾的越王进献给夫差的一位美女，这其实是一个圈套，因为越王无法抵抗无论是来自阖闾还是来自夫差的攻势，不得已而使用计谋。夫差继承王位后不久，越王就在国内挑选了一位最美丽的女子，在对其进行全方位训练之后，将其作为礼物送给夫差。这一计谋极其成功，夫差很快就放纵自己，沉溺于享乐之中，完全不听对其忠心耿耿的伍子胥的劝谏。不知不觉中，夫差慢慢失去了对军队和国家的掌控，不久以后他就被狡猾的越王彻底打败，他的统治也被推翻。自苏州城建成之后，苏州历经风波，如今再讲述这些岁月沧桑，既令人感到乏味又毫无实际意义。在苏州发生过很多场激战，在其早期历史中，苏州被三个王国轮番统治。每一个新的统治者都会更换苏州的名称，有时还会更改城门的名称。大约公元590年，隋朝开皇年间，“苏”这个名称才最终和这座城市永久地联系在一起。也正是在此期间，吴国统治最终被推翻，苏州也被并入隋朝版图。

苏州长久以来被看作财富和奢侈的聚集地，也是中国重要的文学中心之一。众所周知的一句俗语“上有天堂，下有苏杭”表明，在中国人的心目中，苏州和杭州代表了人间天堂。

卫三畏博士在他的《中国总论》一书中提到，苏州坐落在太湖群岛之上，共有人口 2 000 000 人。我不知道他是从哪里获得这样的信息的。很显然，

know where he could have got his information. He certainly could not have visited the city himself.

The city is situated some ten miles east of the eastern shore of the Great Lake. It is possible that the numerous small lakes surrounding the city at various distances may have led early visitors to believe that the land on which the city is built, consisted of islands, while the fact is that the numerous small lakes are separate and independent bodies of water, each having a different name. As to the population it is hardly probable that there were ever two millions. It is the common opinion among the natives that during the T'ai P'ing rebellion seven-tenths of the population were destroyed or driven away. And yet notwithstanding the rapid recuperation and growth that has been going on for fifteen years since the rebellion was suppressed a recent census shows that the present population cannot be more than 300,000, including the suburbs. It is not probable therefore that in its palmiest days it ever contained more than 1,000,000 inhabitants.

In a future communication I may tell something of the places of interest in and about the city, its temples, pagodas, noted hills, &c., and of the men and women who have had a prominent place in its history.

NOTES ON THE HISTORY OF SUCHOW II

By Rev. A. P. Parker

The city is an oblong square lying nearly north and south, something over four miles long by over two miles wide. The wall is nearly thirty feet high, having an embankment on the inside twenty feet wide at the base, and wide moats on both the inside and outside. As originally built by Wu Tz-sü, in the 6th year of King Wang of the Cheu, the circumference of the city, or length of the city wall, was forty-seven *li* and 1262 feet, equal to fifteen and one half miles. There were eight land gates, representing the eight winds of heaven (以象天八风), and eight water gates, representing the eight diagrams of the earth (以象地八卦). It is recorded that when Wu Tz-sü, set about the founding of the city he "prospected the ground, tasted the water, observed the heavens and planned the earth" (相土尝水象天法地), and after taking the result of these somewhat extensive and complicated observations, he selected the site and built the great city. It is a matter of some speculation as to what was the nature of these seemingly

他并没有亲自到过苏州。

苏州位于太湖东畔以东约十英里处。大概是由于苏州周边湖泊众多，因此早期的游客误以为苏州是建在群岛之上的，而事实上，这些湖泊都是独立的水域，每个湖泊都有自己的名字。就苏州人口而言，不太可能达到两百万。当地人普遍认为，在太平天国运动期间，有十分之七的人口被杀害或驱逐。尽管如此，在太平天国被镇压之后的十五年间，最新的人口普查显示，苏州人口包括郊区在内不到 300 000 人。因此，即便在最繁荣时期，苏州人口也应该不超过 1 000 000 人。

在接下来的文章中，我打算介绍一些苏州城内和周边的名胜古迹，包括寺庙、宝塔和著名的山丘等，此外，还有在苏州历史上占有重要地位的人物。

苏州历史摘录（2）

潘慎文

苏州城整体为南北走向，呈长方形，长 4 英里有余，宽 2 英里多。城墙高达 30 英尺左右，内有堤岸一座，堤岸底部宽 20 英尺[1]，城墙内外均有宽阔的护城河。周敬王六年，伍子胥建造苏州城，整个城墙周长为 47 里[2] 1 262 英尺，相当于 15.5 英里[3]。苏州城内共有八个陆地城门，以象天八风；八个水城门，以象地八卦。据记载，当伍子胥着手兴建苏州城时，他曾相土尝水、象天法地。经过一系列纷繁复杂的观测之后，伍子胥根据

[1] 英尺，英美制长度单位，1 英尺等于 12 英寸，合 0.304 8 米。

[2] 里，长度单位，1 里合 500 米。

[3] 此处两种单位换算相差了 1 000 多米，潘慎文计算有误。

comprehensive observations. But the ominous jingle of the characters in the sentence indicate, too plainly to be mistaken, that the famous Tz-sü employed geomancers and astrologers to assist him in selecting a site for the proposed city.

Inside the main city were two smaller cities (城).One was called the Small City of Wu, and was ten li—over three miles—in circumference. In the beginning of the Ming dynasty only the south gate of this "Small City" remained—with its watch tower which was used as the office of the night patrol. It was completely demolished in the reign of Kia Tsing A. D. 1522.

The second inner city was called "Wu Tz-sü City", and was nine li and 1620 feet—about three and one half miles—in circumference.

Outside of the main city and surrounding the whole, was another wall or defence (郭), nearly sixty-nine li—twenty-three miles—in circumference. There are no traces of either of these outer or inner walls remaining at the present day.

Of the original eight gates, six remain open, the other two having been walled up. The Ch'ang (阊) Gate was so named to represent the Gate of Heaven (阊阖) through which blows the cool Western Breeze (阊阖风). The Sü (胥) Gate was named for Wu Tz-sü, under whose superintendence the city was built. The Pan (盘) Gate took its name from the appearance of the water in the canal or lake near the gate, a strong eddy or whirlpool in which led to the belief that a dragon was "coiled up" (盘) under the water. Hence it is call Coil Gate.

The following legend is connected with the Ts'i (齐) Gate: —Hoh Lü, king of Wu having conquered the king of Ts'i, took the daughter of the latter for a wife for his son. She, being quite young, soon became very homesick, and wept day and night till she fell ill. Hoh Lü, in order to comfort her, opened a gate in the north side of the city and built a tower over it, to which the young lady might go at pleasure, and look toward her native land. Hence the gate was named "The Gate for Looking toward Ts'i" (望齐门).

The Liu (娄) Gate was named after the district Liu Hien, through which flowed the Liu river. The name of this district was long ago changed. The Fung (葑), commonly called Fu, Gate is said by some to have been named for the Fung mountain (封山)— the original 封 being afterwards changed to 葑 . Others give a different origin for the name, but there is no certainty about it.

In the eleventh month of the 10th year of K'ai Hwan of the Sui, A. D. 592, nearly two years after the imperial forces had conquered the kingdom of Chên (陈) of which Wu formed a part, the natives of Wu rose in rebellion, headed by

观测结果择地建造苏州城。至于这些看似全面的观测，其本质到底为何，不得而知。为避免出错，赢得好兆头，伍子胥还专门聘请了风水先生和占星师协助其寻找合适的建城地点。

苏州主城内还有两座小城，一座叫作“吴城”，周长 10 里——约 3 英里多。明代初期，“吴城”仅留下南城门——城门上的瞭望台作为巡夜办公场所。公元 1522 年，明嘉靖年间，该城门被完全拆除。

第二座内城被称作“伍子胥城”[1]，周长 9 里 1 620 英尺——大约 3.5 英里[2]。

主城之外还有一处城墙，或称作“郭”，环绕主城，周长大约 69 里——约 23 英里。如今，无论是内城墙还是外城墙都未留下遗迹。

在苏州最初的 8 个城门中，如今有 6 个仍然开放，另外 2 个已被围墙围了起来。阊门之所以称为阊门，是因为它代表了阊阖，阊阖风从中吹过。胥门是为了纪念伍子胥，苏州城正是在其监督之下建成的。盘门得名源自城门附近河内水流的样貌，河水中出现的漩涡使人相信有龙盘在水底，故而称作盘门。

接下来的传说与齐门有关——吴王阖闾征服齐国之后，齐国将公主嫁给吴国太子。年轻的齐国公主，很快就思念家乡，日夜以泪洗面，最终病倒。为了安慰她，阖闾在城北开了一道城门，并在城门上建了一座塔，这样年轻的公主就可以随时登上塔楼遥望故乡。因此，这座城门又被称为“望齐门”。

娄门因娄县街区而得名，娄江流经此门，不过街区的名称早已更改。葑门，通常又叫作“封门”，据说是因为封山而得名——最初的“封”字后来逐渐演变成“葑”字。还有其他关于此城门名字的说法，但都不确定。

公元 592 年，隋开皇十年十一月，也就是隋朝军队征服陈国之后的两年，吴地本土民众在沈玄桧和其他几人的带领下起兵反隋[3]，吴地属于当

[1] 即胥城。

[2] 此处潘慎文计算有误。

[3] 此处原文时间有误。公元 589 年正月，隋朝军队灭陈。隋开皇十年（590 年）十一月，沈玄侩又举兵反隋。

Shêng Yuen-hwai and others. Yang Soh, Duke of Yuih, was ordered to lead the imperial troops against the "robbers" (all rebels in China are "thieves and robbers" in the eyes of the government). It being impossible, in the opinion of Yang Soh, on account of the character of the ground, and perhaps for other reasons, to fortify and defend the city, he memorialized the Emperor to allow the people, governmental establishments, & c., to be removed to Hungshan, about four miles west of the city. Accordingly a new city or fortified town was built at the foot of Hungshan, and the old city was evacuated and left to the rebels. This state of things lasted nearly forty years. It is related that in the construction of the new fortifications, the mechanic was using chu (楮) timber—a kind of oak—with which to make the posts of the gates. Yang Soh on seeing it asked the workman how long that timber would last. "Forty years," was the reply. "That is sufficient," said Yang Soh, "for in less than forty years this city will be abandoned and the old city re-occupied." Sure enough, in the reign of Cheng Kwan, about thirty-eight years afterwards, the old city was retaken and the rebels driven out. But the city was the scene of many fierce conflicts in subsequent years between the imperial forces and the natives ("robbers") who attempted, time and again, to gain their independence. Hence in that part of the History relating to the wall, there are records of numerous breaches and demolitions of the wall and of the subsequent repairs. At one time in the reign of K'ai Hi of the Sung, A. D. 1205, the wall was almost totally destroyed, and the city moat was nearly filled with *débirs*, and was used for caltrop (菱) ponds and paddy fields.

There is a very minute and detailed account of the rebuilding of the wall about the end of the Yuen dynasty A. D. 1350, at the time of the insurrection of the Red Turbanned Thieves (红巾贼). But it was almost wholly destroyed again in the succeeding wars. The last time noted in the history of its repair, was that made in the reign of K'ang Hi, A. D. 1662, by the Governor of Suchow Han Shi-ki. He partially rebuilt and thoroughly repaired the wall.

"At present(1824)" writes the historian, "the wall is 15 miles long (i.e. the circumference of the city) 24 feet high and 15 feet thick. There are 57 bastions, 3,051 parapets, and 157 official establishments and barracks and arsenals."

Whatever breaches were made in the wall during the T'ai Ping rebellion have been long since repaired. The wall is officially inspected once a month and all needed repairs are promptly made. From all that I can learn, I believe the present wall stands on nearly the same foundation that was first laid by Wu Tz-sü

时陈国的一部分。隋朝越国公杨素奉命率军镇压叛乱（在中国统治者眼中，所有的造反者都是“小偷和强盗”）。考虑到苏州的地质特征，也许还有其他因素，杨素认为无法在苏州城内筑防御工事以加强防卫，因此，杨素奏请皇帝允许苏州民众、政府机构等搬迁至苏州城西约四英里处的横山。随后，一座新城在横山脚下建立起来，老城也被搬迁一空留给叛乱者。这一情况一直持续了近四十年。据说，在建造新的防御工事时，工匠们用楮木——一种橡木——做城门的支柱。杨素见后问工人这种木材可以维持多久。“四十年。”工人们回答道。“那足够了，”杨素说道，“要不了四十年，就会重新占领老城，新城也会因此而被遗弃。”事实的确如此，大约三十八年之后，在唐贞观年间，苏州老城被重新夺回，叛乱者也被驱逐出城。不过，在随后的几年中，政府军与试图独立的当地人（“强盗”）在苏州激战过多次。因此，在《苏州府志》中，有多处关于城墙断裂、拆毁以及修复的记录。公元 1205 年，宋朝开禧年间，苏州城墙几乎完全被毁，瓦屑碎片填满了护城河，护城河也一度被用来种植菱角和水稻。

公元 1350 年，元朝末年，在红巾军起义期间，苏州城墙得以重建，对此史书中亦有详细记载。不过，在随后的战争中，城墙又几乎全部被毁。历史上最后一次修复的记载是在公元 1662 年，康熙年间，由江苏巡抚韩世琦完成。韩世琦重建了部分城墙并对城墙进行了全面修复。

“目前（1824），”历史学家写道，“城墙长 15 英里（即苏州城的周长），高 24 英尺，厚 15 英尺。苏州共有 57 个堡垒，3 051 个防护矮墙，官方机构、军营和军火库共计 157 个。”

苏州城墙在太平天国运动期间屡遭破坏，不过这些破损早就修复完成。如今官府每月派人前来巡查一次，所有需要修复之处可以马上得到解决。就我所知，我认为目前城墙所在地基本就是 2 395 年前伍子胥最初建立城

2,395 years ago. There are considerable suburbs outside of each of the gates, containing in all perhaps 75,000 inhabitants. Probably one fifth of the area included in the walls is vacant ground, partly fields in cultivation, and partly covered with *débirs*. A large part of the destroyed district, however, has been built up during the last fifteen years.

The population of the city proper is about 225,000. These figures are based on a sort of census made this year by the Tithing Office (保甲局), which though not perfectly accurate, is still sufficiently so to afford a basis for a tolerably correct estimate of the population. It is an evidence of the curious notions of Chinese historians, as to what a topography or history of a city ought to set forth, that nowhere in the nearly 8,000 pages of this Topography and History of Suchow, is any mention made of the population of the city, from the time it was founded to the time the book was published. The census taken by the Tithing Office is not so much for the purpose of ascertaining the number of inhabitants, as to provide a means of accounting for every body that lives in the city, so that vagabonds and thieves may be more easily caught. The Tithing Office is charged with the duty of obtaining the name and occupation and residence of each head of a family, his wife's parents' name, the number of sons and daughters, and servants, and opium-smokers.

If the returns to the last item are correct it indicates that nearly half the adult population of the city take opium. It may be remarked, by the way, that the efforts of the former acting Governor and present Treasurer, Tan (谭) to suppress the opium dens have not been as permanently successful as was to be hoped. While he held the office of Fu T'ai, the dens were rigorously closed and violators of the law were promptly punished. But since the present Governor came into office much laxity has prevailed, and I notice that opium dens are being gradually opened again. But the efforts of acting Governor T'an were not wholly without good results, for I have been told by an intelligent native who is in a position to know, that the amount of opium smoking is very sensibly less than it was before Governor T'an began operations against it.

To return. The census, though having the appearance of giving great attention to detail, is really carelessly made, and cannot be depended on for perfect accuracy. The "census takers" do not in every case take pains to get exact answers to the questions—but either make an estimate from their own general knowledge of a given family, or ask a neighbor or acquaintance about the family in question.

墙之处。苏州各城门外都有相当多的郊区，共计有居民大约 75 000 人。苏州城内大约有五分之一的地方为空地，一部分是耕地，一部分则堆满了破砖碎瓦。在过去的十五年间，一大批被毁坏的街区得以重建。

苏州人口大约为 225 000 人。这一数字是根据今年保甲局所做的人口普查得来的，虽然这一数据并不十分准确，但却足以为苏州人口数量的大致测算提供依据。一直以来，中国史学家们对一个城市的地志或历史应该记录些什么都有不少奇特的想法，在这部近 8 000 页的关于苏州地志和历史的《苏州府志》中，竟然没有一处提到从苏州建成之日到《苏州府志》出版面世这段时间城市的人口状况。保甲局此次进行的人口普查，其主要目的并不是确认居民数量，而是提供一种方法来统计生活在城市中的每一个人，以便更容易抓住流浪汉和小偷。保甲局有责任获取每个家庭户主的姓名、职业和住址，以及他妻子父母的名字，还有他所有子女、仆人以及家庭内鸦片吸食者的数量。

如果最后一项统计数字正确,那么苏州城内有近一半的成人吸食鸦片。顺便提一句，前任代理巡抚、现任司库的谭均培曾大力整治烟馆，但效果似乎并没有预期那么理想。谭巡抚在任期间，烟馆严禁开张，违反者立刻受到严惩。但自从现任巡抚上任之后，禁烟防控日渐松懈，我注意到不少烟馆已经开始逐步恢复营业。尽管如此，谭巡抚的禁烟努力也并非完全没有效果，一位本地知情人士告诉我，目前鸦片吸食的数量要比谭巡抚开展禁烟活动之前少很多。

继续回到之前的话题。尽管人口普查看上去非常注重细节，但事实上做得非常粗糙，根本无法获得准确数字。“人口普查员”并不是尽心尽责地获取调查所需的数据——他们要么根据自己对普通家庭的了解做出推测，要么问一问调查的这户家庭的邻居或熟人以获取数据。尽管如此，根据此次普查数据，我们大致可以推算出包括郊区在内，苏州人口大约为

Still, taking this as a basis, we are not far wrong in estimating the population at 300,000 including the suburbs, and hence our former guesses of 500,000 to 700,000, are quite wide of the mark. In all probability, if a correct census of the whole of China could be taken, it would appear that the estimate of 400,000,000 population would be equally incorrect, and that there are in reality not more than 250,000,000 inhabitants in China. We frequently over-estimate the population of a Chinese city from seeing the crowds in the streets, while we do not make sufficient allowance for the narrowness of the streets, which cause a comparatively small number of people to have the appearance of a great crowd. If the streets were as wide as those of American and English cities, the crowd would be very much scattered and present the appearance of a much smaller population. The crowds that pass along the thoroughfares of many of the large cities of America could not be accommodated, even as foot passengers, in the narrow streets of the best of Chinese cities.

Another fact to be taken into account is, that there are no houses in Chinese cities built higher than two stories—at least none that I have seen. Hence the same amount of population cannot possibly exist on the same area as is the case in our home cities where houses are built from three to ten stories high.

I will conclude this paper with an account of a somewhat famous (among Suchow people) Taoist temple, known among foreigners as the city temple. This is perhaps the most noted and popular pleasure resort and place of worship in the city. It is situated near the centre of the city, and is called by the Chinese Yuen Miao Kwan (玄妙观). The grounds of the temples (there are two) embrace perhaps two acres, in the form of an oblong square. The two temples occupy one end of the enclosure. The one in front —" The Temple of the Three Pure Ones"—besides containing a very large idol, and the one hundred and twenty gods worshipped, each one by persons of a given age, has also very extensive picture galleries in the hall or outer room running around the central room which contains the idols. In these galleries may be obtained numerous specimens of Chinese fine art, pictures in water colors of flowers and pretty women, sages and genii, holy Buddhas and kitchens gods, temples, pagodas and landscapes innumerable, which though utterly devoid of perspective, and presenting many grotesque-looking combinations, still give a pretty correct idea of the object represented, and at all events have the merit of cheapness as compared to the works of Western masters.

Behind the temple of the Three Pure Ones, is the "Mi Lo" Precious Pavil-

300 000，因此，我们之前推测的 500 000 到 700 000 很显然偏离实际情况。如果在全中国进行一次准确的人口普查，那么之前推测的 400 000 000 人口也是不准确的，事实上，中国居民应该不超过 250 000 000 人。我们多次过高估算中国城市人口数量，是因为看到街上人群拥挤，而忽略了中国街道的狭窄，正是街道的狭窄才造成一小部分人看起来像一大群人。如果中国的街道都像美国和英国城市里的街道那么宽阔，那么一大群人就容易分散在各处，看上去人口数量会少很多。即便在中国最好的城市，其狭窄的街道也无法容纳美国许多大城市街道上的人群，哪怕是那些行走在街上的徒步旅行者。

另外一个需要考虑的因素是，在中国城市里，没有一座房子是超过两层楼高的——至少我没有见过。因此，在美国城市里，同样大小的地方，其容纳人口的数量和中国是不一样的，那里的房子都是 3 层到 10 层的高楼。

在本文的结尾处，我将介绍一个著名（在苏州人看来）的道观，外国人称之为“城市神坛”。这座道观也许是苏州城内最为著名和最受欢迎的休闲场所以及祭拜之处。它坐落于苏州城中心，中国人称之为玄妙观。道观的空地（有两处）大约占地两英亩[1]，是一个长方形广场。两座大殿占据了整个一圈建筑的一角。位于前方的大殿——“三清殿”——内有一尊巨大的雕像，还有一百二十尊供人朝拜的神像，每个神像都对应不同年纪的人，此外，在殿内大厅以及围绕主殿的屋子里都有长长的画廊。在这些画廊中，你可以欣赏到许多中国艺术的样本，这里有大量花卉、美女、圣人、神魔、佛陀、厨神、寺庙、宝塔以及风景的水彩图片，尽管这些图画完全没有透视效果，且呈现出许多奇形怪状的组合，但还是能够较好地表现出所绘事物之主要特征。这些画和西洋画师的作品相比，毫无疑问具有价格便宜的优势。

三清殿后面为弥罗宝阁。此处早已破损不堪，如今正在进行修复——

[1] 英亩，英美制地积单位，1 英亩合 4 046.86 平方米。

lion. This has long been in ruins, but is now being repaired — almost rebuilt — by Mr. Wu, the wealthy banker of Hangchow, at a cost of Tls.180,000. A large open space in front of the first temple is used as a kind of bazaar, and a large ground rent is derived from it by the Taoist. Here "all sorts and conditions" of peddlers and dealer in every kind of knick-knacks and toys "most do congregate." Many matsheds are built about in various places which are used for tea-drinking and story-telling and doctors' shops. Punch and Judy, peep shows—many of the pictures of the latter are foreign—mountebanks, monkey shows, comic singer, &c. &c., may always be seen there. It is the place where everybody goes that has nothing else to do. The haughty literateur, the clerk on the furlough, the artisan having a holiday, the devout woman leading her child and bringing her offering of incense and paper money, the loafer, the riff-raff, the scum and dregs of the city—all go there from time to time to drink tea and "talkee talkee," burn incense and seek their fortune, buy a curio, hear a story, or see a show. At times, when the crowd is not large, it is a good place to preach and distribute books, especially if one stands near the entrance on the street. But generally it is unpleasant, and sometimes unsafe for a foreigner to stop long in the place. Especially is this the case in the afternoons of fine days, and on the Chinese holidays. A fun-loving and impudent crowd will gather around a foreigner in an instant, and their boisterous language soon leads on to pulling and pushing, and sometimes to throwing brick-bats.

The History says that the temple was first built on this site in the reign of Hien Ning of the Tsin, A. D. 275. The Mi Lo Pavillion was built A. D. 1435. The temple of the Three Pure Ones was built A. D. 1177. These temples have undergone many vicissitudes since they were first built, having been at various times more or less injured or nearly destroyed by soldiers, fire or lighting, and again repaired, sometimes from Imperial donations, sometimes by the governor and other officials, and sometimes by the people. The emperor Kien Lung, during his southern progresses, visited the temple several times, and had three altars built there at which he worshiped. He also bestowed upon the temple Tls. 300 and three Imperial autographs. Wonderful stories are told in the History of the miracles that were wrought when these temples were being built or repaired.

When the Mi Lo Pavillion was to be repaired at one time, the contractor sent two men to Chinking to procure the necessary timbers. On their return to Suchow, a violent storm arose and their raft of timber was broken and scattered. In great

几乎是重建，由杭州一位富商胡先生出资 180 000 两银子。玄妙观正殿之前为一片开阔地，被租借出去作为集市场所，观中道士从中获得一大笔租金。在这里，有形形色色的商贩，各式各样的摆设和玩具聚集在一起。好多地方都搭起了凉棚供行人来此喝茶、听书和就诊。在这里还可以看到木偶戏、西洋镜（许多图片都是来自国外）江湖杂耍、耍猴、独角戏等众多表演。这里是整日无所事事之人消遣的去处。傲慢的文人、休假的职员、度假的工匠、带着孩子前来上香献祭的虔诚妇女、游手好闲者、地痞流氓以及城市最底层的人——都时不时去那里喝茶、聊天、烧香算命、买古玩、听书、看戏。当人群并不拥挤之时，这里非常适合宣教和分发书籍，尤其是在靠近入口处的地方。但一般来说，对于一个外国人而言，如果在这里停留时间太长，情况就会变得不愉快甚至很危险。特别是在天气晴朗的午后，或是在中国的节日里，一群好事的鲁莽之徒会马上围住外国人，他们粗鲁的语言很快便会引发拉拽推搡，有时他们甚至向外国人投掷砖块。

据《苏州府志》记载，玄妙观最初是在公元 275 年[1]，西晋咸宁年间建于此处。弥罗宝阁建于公元 1435 年。三清殿则建于公元 1177 年。这些殿自建立之后都历经沧桑，多次遭战争、火灾或雷电破坏甚至几乎全毁，同时也经过多次修复，有时靠皇家拨款，有时靠巡抚和官员，有时靠百姓。乾隆皇帝南巡期间曾多次到访玄妙观，并在观中修建了三处祭坛供其祭拜。他也给观中拨款三百两白银并留下三处亲笔题字。《苏州府志》中也记载了在修建或修复这些大殿时发生的奇妙故事。

有一次弥罗宝阁即将重修，承建商派了两个人前往镇江采购所需之木材。在他们返回苏州途中突遇暴风雨，所乘之木筏断裂，木材也随之四散。

[1] 玄妙观创建于西晋咸宁二年（公元 276 年），此处潘慎文误。

consternation they appealed to heaven, saying, "We have bought this timber to build a Pavillion with for the Gemmy Emperor, but now it is all scattered and lost, how can the Pavillion be built?" Immediately, it is said, the wind ceased and the waves became quiet, a Taoist divinity appeared in the sky and the men reverently worshipped him and went on their way. They had not gone far till they found their timbers all gathered together again, not one piece missing. They proceeded with the raft to its destination and the Pavillion was repaired with great reverence and amid great rejoicings.

When the Three-Pure Temple was to be repaired the last time in 1817, after it had been struck by lightning, a large pillar was needed but could not be obtained, and the work had to be abandoned in consequence. The next year, a fisherman of Chang Shuh, while fishing in the Yang-tz river, caught a heavy object in his net which he supposed to be a great fish. But on obtaining assistance and hauling it ashore at Fuh Shan, he found it to be a large log of timber, seventy feet long and perfectly round and straight. The contractor at Suchow was notified of this strange occurrence, and he immediately proceeded to have the wonderful timber brought to Suchow, and found it to be just what was wanted to repair the temple with. Hence it was called "The Divine Timber produced by the Efficiency of Mountain and Sea" (山海效灵神木).

The two buildings, as they now stand, were thoroughly repaired, the Pavillion in 1675, and the Temple in 1818. They were very much injured by the Tai P'ing rebels, who used many of the timbers with which to construct a look-out stand for use in watching the movements of the Imperial forces outside the city.

NOTES ON THE HISTORY OF SUCHOW III

By Rev. A. P. Parker

PAGODAS

The origin and the proposed benefit of pagodas is involved in considerable obscurity, though of course it must be understood that so far as the Chinese are concerned, these structures being built by believers in Buddhism and being generally under the control of Budhist priests, are of Buddhist origin. I have seen it stated by an English writer that "these towers originate in the Indian tradition

他们惊恐万分，向上天虔诚祷告，“我们运送木材是为了给玉帝修建亭子，如今木材却四散而去，叫我们如何修建呢？”据说，他们刚说完立刻风停雨歇，天空中出现了一位道教神仙，人们虔诚地跪拜神仙。之后，这两人继续赶路，未行多久便发现他们丢失的木材聚在一起，一根也不少。他们随后坐着木筏回到苏州，工匠们怀着虔诚和喜悦之心将弥罗宝阁修复一新。

三清殿最后一次修复是在1817年，之前因为遭受雷击，殿内需要更换一根大柱，但始终无法找到合适的木材，工程也被迫停工。第二年，一位常熟的渔夫在长江捕鱼时，用渔网捕到一个巨大的物体，他以为是一条大鱼。但在众人的帮助下将渔网拖至位于福山的岸边后，才发现原来是一根巨木，长达七十英尺，又圆又直。在苏州的承建商听闻这一怪事之后，立刻将这一巨木运回苏州，发现此木正是重修三清殿内所需之木材。因此，这一巨木又被称作“山海效灵神木”。

如今的弥罗宝阁和三清殿这两幢建筑，都已经过彻底修复。弥罗宝阁在1675年完成了修复，而三清殿则在1818年完成了修复。然而，在太平天国期间，这两座建筑遭受了极大破坏，殿内很多木头都被用来修造瞭望台，用来监视城外清政府军队的动向。

苏州历史摘录（3）

潘慎文

塔

关于塔的起源以及塔所带来之益处仍有许多不明之处，但对中国人而言，他们了解到塔源自佛教，由佛教信徒所建，并由寺庙僧侣负责管理。我曾见过一位英文作家这样写道：“塔源自印度传统，当佛祖去世之后，他

that when Buddha died his body was divided into eight parts which were enclosed in so many urns to be deposited in towers of eight floors. The number of these floors is however variable. Some are round, some are square, some are hexagonal or octagonal, and they are built of wood, of brick, and sometimes partly of earthenware,[porcelain] like that most celebrated tower at Nanking the facing of which being of porcelain has procured for it the name of 'The Porcelain Tower,' so familiar to us all from our childhood. It is now in ruins … Of these structures it should be premised that instead of indicating by their number any sort of deep religious feeling pervading the country, they are rather to be regarded as being the result of old customs, and as store houses for trumpery, Buddhist relics, &c." And he might have added, as one of the agencies used to bring good luck to the country.

Some pagodas were originally built as topes, or monuments, over the graves of noted Buddhist priests, as well as store houses for relics, as, for instance the Great Pagoda of Suchow. Some were built from motives of filial piety, like the "Auspicious Light Pagoda," which is situated just inside the south gate of this city, and which was built by Sun-kuen (孙权), the founder of the Wu dynasty, to requite his mother's favor. It was (and is still) believed that a pagoda helps a soul, for whom it is built, or even illuminated, out of purgatory (though how it does this, does not appear to be very clearly understood). Hence Sun-kuen's purpose was to help his mother out of purgatory by means of this pagoda.

Others are built (at least in recent times) to correct the fungshui, or luck of a region, as in the case of the black square pagoda, or Bell Tower, near the east gate of the city. But what a pagoda does to ward off evil, or what occult influence it exerts to induce good, the common people seem to know very little about. Everybody is familiar with the expression "correct the fungshui" (正风水), but as to how this is done very confused notions seem to prevail. Some say that, according to the principles of geomancy, on the left of a person or place is the Azure Dragon (青龙) and on the right is the White Tiger (白虎), and these two are in perpetual conflict. Therefore if the land or buildings are high on the left and low on the right, the luck of the place is good, and vice versa, hence the value of pagodas to give the advantage to the Azure Dragon. But it must be manifest that while a pagoda would bring good luck to the region of the left, it would be equally deleterious to the region on the right. But it must be confessed that there are depths of intricate nonsense in the science of geomancy that it is difficult to fathom.

的尸身被分成八份，装在许多骨灰盒中，这些骨灰盒又被存放在八层楼的塔中。不过，塔的层数会有变化。有的塔呈圆形，有的塔呈方形，还有的塔呈六边形或八边形。有的塔用木头搭建，有的塔则用砖块搭建，还有的塔，其一部分为陶瓷构造，就像南京最著名的大报恩寺琉璃塔一样，饰面均为陶瓷，故而又被称为‘瓷塔’，我们从小就对‘瓷塔’耳熟能详。如今该塔却已变成废墟……应该指出的是，这些塔并非通过数量来体现对宗教的深厚情感，而是被看作旧风俗的产物，作为储藏室用来存放杂物和佛教圣骨。”也许这位作家还会加上一句，塔还是带来好运的力量之一。

有些塔最初是作为佛塔或纪念碑，建在一些著名佛教僧侣的墓穴之上，同时又可当作存放圣骨的储物室，例如苏州的北寺塔。有些塔是出于孝敬之心而建的，就像位于苏州南门之内的“瑞光塔”，由三国时期吴国建立者孙权为回报母亲养育之恩而建。过去人们相信（如今还是相信），塔为谁而建，塔身为谁而亮，即可保佑谁的灵魂脱离炼狱（尽管我们对如何帮助灵魂脱离炼狱并不十分清楚）。因此，孙权的目的就是希望通过宝塔能够帮助其母之灵魂脱离炼狱。

有些塔的建造（至少在近代）是为了修正一个地区的风水，例如苏州东门附近的黑色方塔，又称作钟楼[1]。但是，宝塔如何驱邪避讳，又是如何在神秘力量影响下给人带来好运，普通民众知之甚少。每个人都很熟悉“正风水”这一词，但至于如何做到这一点，似乎存在各种说法。有人说，依据风水原理，一个人或一个地方的左边为青龙，右边为白虎，青龙和白虎始终处于争斗之中。因此，如果一块土地或一座建筑物左高右低，那么这个地方的运气就会好，反之亦然。因此，宝塔的功能就在于帮助青龙获得运势。必须说明的是，在宝塔给左边地区带来运势的同时，自然也会给右边地区带来损害。不过，必须承认，风水学中存在着错综复杂的说法，令人难以理解。

[1] 即文星阁。

Besides the superstitions connected with pagodas, there is also a feeling among some of the more intelligent of the Chinese that these high towers are an addition to the beauties of a landscape, and give a finer appearance to a city as seen from a distance, just as the high church steeples increase the beauty of, and give variety to, the appearance of a city in Christian lands.

Of the eight principal pagodas in Suchow and its immediate neighborhood, the largest and most famous, is the one situated near the north wall of the city, called Peh Sz T'ah—North Monastery Pagoda. This tower lifts its head above all the houses of the city, above the city wall and all the other pagodas in the neighborhood. It is the first building to be seen in the distance on approaching the city from any direction, and is said to be the largest pagoda in China. It is octagonal in shape and nine stories high. It is about 300 feet in circumference at the base and about 250 in height. It is built of brick, having a narrow verandah with banisters around each story. There is an outer and inner wall, between which is the passage way leading to the top by means of 18 flights of stairs. Numerous Buddhist idols occupy niches in the wall in the different stories. The size is gradually reduced as the top story is approached. A splendid view of the city and surrounding country is to be had from the upper stories. The vast array of black tiled roofs, intermitted here and there by an open space, the flag-staffs of the official residences scattered throughout the city, the other pagodas in and out of the city looming up in the distance, the long suburbs stretching away from the city-gates, the vast level plain dotted with villages and hamlets extending away to the north and east intersected with many a winding canal, while to the west the mountains lift their summits ornamented here and there with a pagoda or a temple, and on the south and south-east the silvery lakes sparkle in the sheen of the noonday sun—altogether present a view at once beautiful and unique. It is not to be wondered at that many of the poets of the "Beautiful Su" have been inspired to sing the natural and artistic beauties of the city and its surroundings. Many of these poetic descriptions of the scenery in and around Suchow, are collected in one of the volumes of the History ... This pagoda as it now stands nine stories high was built in the reign of Sao Hing of the Sung, about A. D. 1160. Anciently there was a tope (窣堵波) or Buddhist monument eleven stories high built on the same site. This was partially destroyed by fire and rebuilt in 1080. Su-she (苏轼) a celebrated statesman, poet and commentator, who flourished A. D. 1036-1101, at one time governor of Hangchow and Suchow, presented a bronze turtle to the temple of

除了与宝塔相关的迷信之外，一些中国知识分子还认为这些高塔为城市增加了亮丽的风景，从远处看，城市外观显得更加秀丽，就如同在基督教国度中，高耸的教堂尖塔令城市变得更加多姿多彩。

在苏州及周边地区的八座主要宝塔中，最大、最著名的，当数位于苏州北城墙附近的一座塔——北寺塔。该塔塔顶高出苏州城内所有房屋、城墙以及周边其他宝塔。无论从哪个方向进入苏州，在远处第一眼就能看见它，据说它也是中国最大的一座宝塔。北寺塔呈八边形，有九层高。塔基周长约为 300 英尺，高约 250 英尺。塔由砖块搭建而成，每层塔上均有狭窄的外廊和扶手环绕塔身。塔内分内外两层，外墙和内墙之间是通道，通道有 18 级台阶，沿着通道可直达塔顶。塔内各层墙上的壁龛内都摆放着各式各样的佛像，越往上壁龛的尺寸也随之越小。站在塔顶，整个城市和周边地区的美景一览无余。一眼望去，只见大片黑瓦覆盖的屋顶，屋顶之间间或相隔一片空间，官员府邸的旗杆分布在城内各处，苏州城内城外的其他几座宝塔在远处隐约可见，狭长的郊区从城门向外延伸出去，广袤的平原上村庄小镇星罗棋布。这些村庄小镇向北、向东延伸，许多蜿蜒的河流横穿其中；西面群山耸立，山顶上的宝塔或寺庙点缀着山峰；位于南面和东南方向的湖泊，在午后阳光照耀下波光粼粼——这一切都为人们呈现了美丽独特的风景。这也难怪这座美丽城市里的许多诗人都情不自禁地想要歌颂这座城市及其周边地区的自然风光和人文景观。这些描写景色的诗歌被收录在《苏州府志》的其中一卷之中……如今矗立于此的九层高塔大约建于公元 1160 年，南宋绍兴年间。在此之前，位于同一地点，曾建有一座窣堵波或是高十一层的佛教纪念碑，后来部分毁于大火，并在 1080 年进行重建。苏轼（公元 1036—1101）[1]，著名政治家、诗人和评论家，做过杭州和苏州太守，曾将一只青铜龟赠送给北寺塔所在的寺庙，寺庙将其作为舍利圣

[1] 苏轼生卒年应为 1037—1101，此处原作者误。

which the pagoda formed a part, to be preserved as relic (舍利). In the reign of Shao Hing the pagoda was again burned and was rebuilt nine stories high under the superintendence of a travelling priest (行者) named Ta-yuen (大圓) who seems to have collected the money necessary for the purpose.

A Buddhist monastery was build on a part of the same lot by the famous Sun-kuen, A. D. 245, in memory of his mother. Hence it is called "Recompensing Favor Monastery" (报恩寺). A remarkable manifestation of Buddhist divinity is related to have occurred in connection with this monastery. It is said that some fishermen on the seashore, somewhere in the region beyond Sung Kiang at a place called Hu-tuh (沪渎), saw a "divine light" (神光) shining upon the surface of the water at night. On viewing this strange phenomenon by daylight, they found that it was produced by two stone images floating on the water, and they immediately concluded that these were the Water Gods （水神）. They offered sacrificial worship and the images floated away. Not long after this some of the people of Wu (Suchow) hearing of this appearance, gathered a company of Buddhist priests and nuns, went to Hu-tuh, found the images, and brought and placed them in the above-named temple. Their light, it is said, shone brilliantly for seven successive days and nights! (Why it did not continue to shine for a longer period does not appear from the record). This event happened in the fourth year of Kien Hing of the Tsin, A. D. 317. Four years later, fishermen living at the same place, Hu-tuh, got a lapis lazuli alms bowl (帝青石钵). At first they took it to be a common mortar or bowl and used it to prepare their food in, meat, &c. But on the very first attempt at such desecration (preparing animal food in it) the image of Buddha appeared on the outside, whereby they knew that it was an auspicious omen left there by the two stone images that had appeared four years before. They therefore took it and dedicated it to Buddha in the temple in Suchow together with the stone images. Some time after the above-mentioned discoveries, certain Buddhist missionaries from a foreign country came to Suchow and said that the holy men of that country had recorded the fact that somewhere in the east were two stone images and a pagoda of Asoka, the great king who favored Buddhism, B. C. 319, and whoever could go and see them would thereby save himself from an incalculable amount of sin. It is believed that the two images found by the fishermen are the same as those referred to by the holy men of the foreign land. This pagoda has, like all the other ancient buildings in the city, suffered

物保存于寺中。绍兴年间，该塔再次被烧毁，后来在一位名叫大圆的行者监督下，重新修建了一座高九层的塔，而重修宝塔的费用也是大圆募集而来的。

公元245年，孙权为纪念其母，在北寺塔同一地段上修建了一座寺庙。因此，该寺又称作“报恩寺”。报恩寺还与一次佛光显灵事件有关。据说，住在淞江以外一个叫作沪渎地方的渔民们，夜间在海边看到水面上发出耀眼的“神光”。白天在日光下渔民们发现这一奇特的“神光”是由两座漂浮在水上的石像发出的，他们立刻认为这石像就是水神。于是，渔民们向石像祭拜，石像也随波漂走。不久之后，吴国（苏州）一些人听说此事，召集了一群僧人和尼姑前往沪渎，找到了石像，将它们带回并放置在报恩寺中。据说，石像发出的光一直持续了七天七夜！（为什么神像没有继续发光，记录中没有提及。）这件事发生在公元317年，晋建兴四年[1]。四年后，生活在沪渎同一地方的渔民们又得到了一个帝青石钵。起初，他们认为石钵只是一个普通的碗，用它做饭及盛肉。但这种亵渎佛祖（在钵中准备荤腥食物）的行为刚发生，佛祖的法相就显现在石钵外壁，由此渔民们才知道，这个钵是四年前出现的那两座石像所留下的吉祥之物。于是，他们将这个钵送到苏州报恩寺，和石像放在一起。上述事件发生后不久，一位外国云游僧来到苏州，他说公元前319年，他们国家的圣人曾记录下这样一件事，即在东方某处有两座石像和一座阿育王（阿育王是一位佛教的信徒）宝塔，谁能够去东方并看到石像和塔，就能够从罪孽中解脱出来，获得救赎。他相信，渔民们发现的两座石像就是圣人口中所提到的那两座石像。这座北

[1] 应为西晋建兴五年。

many vicissitudes during the more than one thousand years of its existence, but it still wears the crown as the largest and most famous pagoda in the land (尤为郡中塔寺之冠). But while it is the crown of pagodas, it is also distinguished as the tail of the dragon. The dragon's head is said to be near the south gate, where two wells are his eyes, his body extends north along the "Protecting Dragon Street" (护 龙 街), and the great pagoda situated at the north end of this street is his tail. It is therefore very necessary to the prosperity of the city that the "Dragon's Tail" be always kept in good repair. This pagoda was recently illuminated for three nights in succession. Lanterns were hung closely around each story, and a company of seven or eight Buddhist priests were employed on each floor of the nine stories in saying mass. The expenses, which are said to have amounted to some two hundred dollars for the three days and nights, were borne by three of the well-to-do families of the city, who had the illumination made and the masses said, to secure the release of deceased members of their families from purgatory.

The oldest pagoda in the city is the one situated just inside the south gate. It consists of seven stories and is about 180 feet high. It was first built by Sun-kuen, the founder of the Wu, A. D. 248, as a place for the preservation of [Buddhist] relics, and to recompense his mother's kindness (以报母恩), and was thirteen stories high. In the second year of T'ien Fuh of the T'ang, when it was repaired, the pagoda gave forth light of many colors, and a brass tablet was bestowed upon it by the emperor, which was placed in the top of the pagoda. In the second year of Yuen Fung of the Sung, A. D. 1080, the Grain Commissioner was ordered by the emperor to order a certain Buddhist priest to preach the law (说法) in the temple connected with this pagoda. While this was being done, the pagoda again gave forth its many-colored light, a white turtle appeared in the pond in front of the preaching hall, a withered bamboo tree budded again, and the drum of the law (法鼓) sounded of itself. From this time the name of the hall was called The Four Good Omen [Hall]. In the fourth year of Tsung Ning of the Sung, the temple was repaired at the emperor's expense and again gave forth its parti-colored light and the name was changed to "Heavenly Peace Myriad Years Precious Pagoda." In the reign of Sien Hwo, A.D. 1119, the pagoda was again repaired and changed to seven stories. It has been repeatedly repaired in the last 700 years. It is believed that this pagoda has a very great influence on the luck of the Fu T'ai's (Provincial Governor) official residence, from the front of which a full view of the pagoda is to be had. If it is allowed to fall into ruins, it is believed that some calamity is sure to overtake the governor or his family. Six or seven years ago the

寺塔，就和苏州城内其他古建筑一样，在其存在的一千多年中历经沧桑变化，尽管如此，尤为郡中塔寺之冠。不过，北寺塔的顶部又被看作龙尾。龙头据说是在南城门附近，而那里的两口井是龙眼，龙身则沿着“护龙街”[1]向北延伸，而北寺塔位于护龙街尾，因此就成了龙尾。为了确保整个城市的繁荣，“龙尾”必须要做好长期维护。最近，北寺塔连续三晚灯火通明。塔上每层灯笼环绕。每层都有七到八位佛教僧侣主持法事，据说三日三夜的费用达到两百美元，这些费用由城内三家富裕家庭共同承担，他们布置灯笼照明、举办法事，据说是为了确保他们家族死去的成员能够脱离炼狱。

苏州城内最古老的一座塔就位于南门之内。该塔现有 7 层，大约 180 英尺高。该塔最初由吴国缔造者孙权于公元 248 年所建，高 13 层，用来保存圣骨，以报母恩。唐天福二年[2]，该塔重修之时，塔身绽放五颜六色的光芒，后来皇帝赐一枚铜牌，置于塔顶。公元 1080 年，宋元丰年间，皇帝命大臣请一位佛教大师在塔旁的寺庙中讲经说法。大师开讲时，宝塔再次绽放出多彩的光芒，一只白色乌龟也出现在讲经大厅前的池塘里，一株已经枯萎的竹子再次发芽，法鼓自鸣。从那时起，讲经堂的名字就改为“四瑞堂”。宋熙宁四年，皇帝出资重修该塔，宝塔又一次绽放五彩的光芒，故而更名为“瑞光塔”。公元 1119 年，宋宣和年间，瑞光塔再次重修，改为七层。在随后的七百年的岁月中，瑞光塔历经多次重修。民间认为这座塔对府台（省长）官邸的运势有很大影响，因为在官邸门前可见宝塔全貌。如果任其沦为废墟，据说，就会有灾难发生在府台或其家人身上。六七年前，

[1] 即人民路。
[2] 应为后晋天福二年。

governor, who had just come into office and who had an old mother who might yield to any evil influence and give up the ghost at a very inconvenient season for his official prospects, set about repairing the pagoda as a means of prolonging the life of his mother. Several thousand dollars were raised by private subscriptions, and the work was commenced. But by the time the spire and roof of the top story were finished, it was found that there was not money enough to carry on the work, and so it had to be abandoned. Some say that the contractor failed, lost all his property in the undertaking. Sure enough, in a short time after work on the pagoda ceased, the governor's mother died, and he had to go to the expense of a costly funeral, vacate his official position for over two years, and lose all the gains of office for the length of time.

The History states that in 1624 a building called the "Seven Buddha Pavilion" was erected on the foundation of the Four Good Omen Hall. Just as the pillars of this building were being raised the eye of heaven gave forth light (天眼放光). On this account one of the high officials named the building "Heaven's Eye Pavilion" (天眼阁). In subsequent years the light was frequently seen. In the fourth year of K'ien Lung, A. D. 1740, the Provincial Governor of Kiangsu went to the temple connected with the pagoda to pray for rain. On obtaining answer to his prayers in the shape of refreshing showers on the thirsty earth, he gratefully gave the necessary means to have the temple and pagoda thoroughly repaired. The emperors K'ang Hi and K'ien Lung both visited the pagoda while on their southern progresses. The story is handed down that on the occasion of the visit of K'ien Lung, when the pagoda was illuminated with lanterns at night, the image of the pagoda was reflected in the waters of the Great Lake at a distance of ten miles, and the lake fishermen caught no fish that whole night!

A short distance outside of the north-west gate, on the Tiger Hill, is a pagoda that reminds one of the descriptions of the Leaning Tower of Pisa. It is several feet out of perpendicular. Whether it was originally built that way, or whether the foundation has settled to one side, is not stated. But it has stood in its present leaning position from the time immemorial, and bids fair to so stand for generations to come. Like the two pagodas already mentioned, it is built of large thick brick, having an outer and an inner wall, between which runs the stairway and passage for ascent. Around the outside of each story is (or was) a narrow verandah. All the wood work of this pagoda except three flights of rickety stairs leading to the first three stories, has been destroyed and only the brick work remains. Three or four Buddhist priests live in the lower story which they use as an idol

府台刚刚上任，其母年岁已大，随时可能去世，这势必对其子仕途造成不利影响，于是府台便着手修复瑞光塔，希望借此为其母续命。通过私人捐助，府台筹集到数千美金，随后便开始宝塔修复工程。然而，当塔顶和屋顶修复完成之后，却发现没有足够的资金继续工程，不得已唯有停工。有人说，承建商因此而破产。果然，停工后不久，府台母亲去世，府台花重金为其母举办丧礼，并且因此丁忧去职两年多，在很长一段时间内没有俸禄。

据《苏州府志》记载，1624年，一座名为“七佛亭”的建筑建在原来“四瑞堂”所在处。就在亭柱立起之时，天眼放光。由此，一位高官将该亭取名为“天眼阁”。在随后的几年中，人们经常看到神光。乾隆四年[1]，即公元1740年，江苏巡抚来到瑞光塔旁的寺庙求雨。他的祈求得到回应，雨水从天而降，落在干涸的土地上。巡抚满怀感激之情，竭尽所能对寺庙和宝塔进行了全面修复。康熙和乾隆两位皇帝南巡时均到访过瑞光塔。传说在乾隆造访期间，瑞光塔夜晚被灯笼照亮，宝塔的影子倒映在十里之外的太湖水中，以至于太湖的渔民整夜都捕不到一条鱼！

苏州西北城门外不远处的虎丘山上有一座塔，该塔令人不禁想起了比萨斜塔。这座塔偏离中垂线数英尺。究竟是最初建造就如此，还是地基逐渐偏向另一边而造成塔身倾斜，不得而知。但是，很久之前，虎丘塔就呈现出今日之倾斜态势，并且很有可能继续保持下去。和上文提及的两座宝塔一样，虎丘塔是由厚厚的砖块所建成的，塔内有外墙和内墙，可以通过两墙之间的楼梯通道登上塔顶。每层塔外均有（或者过去也有）环形游廊。除了三段摇摇欲坠的通往前三层的楼梯之外，塔内所有木制品均被毁坏，

[1] 应为乾隆五年。

temple in lieu of a fine temple that stood near the pagoda many years ago. This pagoda was built in the reign of Jên Show of the Sui, A. D. 603. A legend, given in the History, states that when the relics which were sent by the emperor Jên Show, to be placed in the pagoda, arrived near their destination, the waters (in the canal, presumably) gave forth a roaring sound for two days—in recognition, it would seem, of the holy character of the said relics, or it may be as a greeting to the imperial commissioner, a Buddhist priest, who escorted them thither. The same tradition relates that when the foundation for the pagoda was being dug, a small brick enclosure was found in which was a silver casket, and in the casket was a precious relic, which on being placed in a basin of water produced numerous gyratory motions which were regarded as of an auspicious character and therefore the relic was placed with the others in the pagoda. It would greatly assist our comprehension of this story to know the shape, size and general character of the aforesaid relic, but this information is not granted. The Buddhist temple near which the pagoda was built was first erected A. D. 328. It was one of the largest and most frequented of the Buddhist temples in and around the city. But many times has it been more or less injured or destroyed in various ways and as often repaired. Both of the emperors K'ang Hi and K'ien Lung honored it with their presence and the bestowed of imperial autographs and inscriptions. K'ien Lung's empress also visited it and made several gifts to it. The emperors Chêng T'ung and Wan Li of the Ming, both presented copies of the Buddhist scriptures to this temple, accompanied in each instance with an imperial decree stating the reason of the gift, and directing the manner of using it. In these edicts the emperors say, substantially, that having a heart in sympathy with heaven and earth, and a sincere disposition to care for the welfare of the people they have had printed complete copies of the Buddhist scriptures, and caused them to be placed in all the more important temples and monasteries throughout the empire, including this one on the Hu K'iu Hill in the department of Suchow. Let all the priests, both old and young in connection with this temple, with clean hands and reverential demeanor place these holy books in the place assigned to them, and let them reverently read them morning and evening, and expound them to the people, and pray [to Buddha] that the empire may be kept in peace, and that blessings and prosperity may be enjoyed by the people, and that all within the four seas may return to the paths of virtue and goodness. Let no visitors or idlers privily borrow these books or treat them with disrespect, and let care be taken that none of them be lost. If any disobey these instructions he will be rigorously dealt with.

只剩下砖制品。三四名僧人住在虎丘塔底层，并将这里作为大雄宝殿，代替多年前在虎丘塔边上的一座精美的寺庙。虎丘塔建于公元603年，隋文帝仁寿年间。《苏州府志》上曾记载过这样一段传说，据说隋文帝曾将佛舍利送至虎丘塔安放，舍利即将到达之际，河水（据推测应该是运河水）整整两天都发出轰鸣声——似乎是对舍利的圣洁表示认同，又像是在欢迎专门护送舍利前来的僧人。这个传说还提到，在挖塔基时，发现一小段用砖块建起的围栏，内有一个银质的精美小盒，盒内装有一块珍贵的舍利，当这块舍利被放入一盆水中，水里立刻生成许多漩涡，这被认为是吉祥之兆，因此，这块舍利和其他舍利一起被安放在塔内。如果知道上文所提及的舍利之形状、大小以及一般特征，将会有助于我们理解这个传说，然而，对于这些信息我们却一无所知。虎丘塔边上的寺庙最初建于公元328年。该寺是苏州周边最大，也是人们最常去的寺庙之一。不过，该寺曾多次遭到不同程度破坏，又被多次修复。康熙和乾隆两位皇帝都曾来过此地，并留下亲笔签名和题词。乾隆的皇后也曾到访过，并赐给寺庙一些礼物。明朝的正统和万历两位皇帝都曾将佛经副本送到该寺中，每次均附有诏书，阐明赠送原因及使用规定。在这些诏书中，皇帝主要想说他们对天地怀有怜悯之心，诚心关怀民众福祉，因此他们特令人将全套佛经印刷出版，并将佛经分发到全国各个重要的寺庙之中，包括位于苏州虎丘山上的寺庙。寺庙中所有僧侣，不论年纪大小，都要用干净的双手和虔诚的态度，将这些经书放到指定地点，每日清晨和夜晚虔诚诵读佛经，向民众宣讲佛经要义，并（向佛祖）祈求国家平安，人民丰衣足食，四海之内德行遍布。不允许访客和闲人私下借阅经书或对经书不敬，妥善保管好经书，不得遗失。任何违反这些规定的行为均要受到严厉惩罚。

It may be judged from the above what a foothold Buddhism has gained in China …

The hill on which this somewhat famous pagoda and temple are built was, before the civil war, a noted pleasure resort. And although its temples and pavilions, and teahouses, &c., were almost totally destroyed by the T'ai P'ings, it is again being built up, and will no doubt, in time, regain in a large measure its former position as a popular resort for idlers, pleasure seekers, &c.

Many interesting legends are connected with it. It holds the grave of Hoh Lü, King of Wu, and founder of the city of Suchow. When Hoh Lü died 600,000 men were employed to prepare his grave and attend his funeral. Three days after his burial a white tiger was seen crouching on his grave. A brass coffin containing three apartments (三重) and three thousand small swords of a peculiar make, and an immense amount of gold, silver, and precious stones, are said to have been buried in the king's grave. The name Tiger Hill (虎邱) is said to be derived from the appearance of the white tiger above-mentioned. When the first emperor of the Ts'in dynasty, Ts'in She Hwang Ti, returned from his visit to the seacoast and passed by Suchow, he attempted to open the grave of Hoh Lü and rob it of its treasures. But on this attempt being made to desecrate the grave of the distinguished king of Wu, a white tiger (Hoh Lü's guardian, possibly) appeared and attacked the emperor. The latter tried to plunge his sword into the tiger, but the tiger escaped and hid himself in the hill.

There is a pool on the hill known as the Sword Pool, where She Huang Ti is said to have whetted his sword—presumably on one of the rocks on the shore of the pool—hence the name. This pool is said to be about two hundred feet long and about twenty-five feet wide, and of unfathomable depth, and anciently contained a whirlpool. But no traces of a whirlpool are to be seen now, and the pool is only an insignificant basin fifty or sixty feet long by twenty or thirty feet wide, and supplied by a spring perhaps, or else by the gathered rain water from the hillsides.

There is a large flat rock near the Sword Pool on which it is said that a thousand men can sit at one time—though from its present size I should think they would be considerably crowded—and it is therefore call the "Thousand Men Rock" (千人石). Somewhere in the same neighborhood is the "Nodding Rock." It is related in the History that on one occasion when a noted Buddhist missionary was expounding the Law to the people in the temple there, so eloquently did

从上述内容可以断定佛教在中国已经深深扎根……

正因为山上建有如此著名的宝塔和寺庙，虎丘，在内战之前，已成为著名的旅游胜地。尽管寺庙、凉亭以及茶室等地都被太平军毁坏殆尽，但目前正在重新修建之中，毫无疑问，用不了多久，这里又将恢复之前的盛况，成为闲人、游玩者喜爱的中意场所。

许多有趣的传说与这座小山丘有关。这里埋葬着吴国国王、苏州城的创建者阖闾。阖闾去世之后，600 000 人被征集过来修建墓地并参加了他的葬礼。葬礼后三天，有人看见一只白色的老虎蹲在阖闾的墓前。阖闾墓中有铜椁三重，还有三千柄特制的宝剑、大量金银珠宝陪葬。虎丘之名，据说就是源自上文所提及的白虎。秦朝第一位皇帝，秦始皇，从海边巡视归来路过苏州，曾试图打开阖闾的坟墓以掠夺墓中珍宝。但就在准备挖掘这位吴国著名君主的墓穴之时，一只白虎（有可能是阖闾墓的守护者）出现，袭击了秦始皇。后者持剑刺向老虎，但老虎逃脱并隐藏在山中。

虎丘有一个叫剑池的池子，据说始皇帝曾在那里磨过剑——有可能就是在剑池边上的某一块岩石上——剑池也因此得名。剑池据说长约 200 英尺，宽 25 英尺，深不可测，古时池内还有漩涡。但如今已看不见漩涡的痕迹，剑池也变成了只有五六十英尺长，二三十英尺宽的小池子，池水也许来自山泉，抑或是从山坡上流下的雨水。

剑池附近有一块巨大的扁平大石，据说石头上一次可以坐满 1 000 人——但从目前石头的尺寸看，我认为他们应该坐得非常拥挤——因此该石头被称为“千人石”。附近还有一块石头叫作“点头石”。据《苏州府志》记载，一次一位著名的僧人来到这里的寺庙向民众讲经说法，他讲得非常

he preach, that a stone in front of the temple nodded to the priest in recognition of the power of his oratory and perhaps of the force of his teaching!

The Twin Pagodas (双塔) which are situated a short distance inside of the east wall of the city were built by Wang Wen-han in the reign of Yung Hi of the Sung, A. D. 985. They are seven stories high and are much smaller than either of the pagodas above described. They have been repaired at various times in the past thousand years—the last time in 1822. They stand side by side a few feet apart, and are supposed to exert a most excellent influence, on the Provincial Examination Hall situated near them on the west.

Not far from these Twin Pagodas and close to the east city wall is a five storied black square pagoda, or more properly a temple to the God of Literature (文星阁). This pagoda, or Bell Tower as it is generally called, was built in 1598 to correct the fungshui of this region. Certain geomancers found that the twin pagodas on the right of the Changcheu District College being higher than any building on the left, gave the advantage to the White Tiger over the Azure Dragon, in consequence of which the scholars of that district did not succeed very well in the examinations. It was resolved, therefore, to build a high temple or Bell Tower, to the god of literature, whereby it was hoped to correct this bad state of affairs. Accordingly a number of the gentry of the district, led by Sü Hien K'ing raised several hundred dollars, and being assisted by a government subsidy were enabled to build the proposed tower. Their generosity was rewarded within a few years by seeing a large increase in the number of graduates from the district! This tower was repaired by P'ing Ting-k'ien in the 42nd year of K'ang Hi, 1774, at an expense of over "two thousand ounces"—about $3,000—of silver. A temple called Kwé Hiang Tien was built at the same time. The whole property is now under the control of the Pêng (彭) family, who contribute rice and cash to the amount of some $2 a month to keep a man there to look after it. The third day of the second moon is the birthday of the god of literature, and on that day the temple and pagoda are thrown open and hundreds of people go there to worship and to enjoy a holiday. Sometimes on other days, a mother will lead her little boy to this temple to worship, preparatory to his entering school.

生动，以至于寺庙前的一块石头都点头，认同他的宣讲能力以及教义产生的力量。

位于苏州东城墙内不远处的双塔为王文罕所建，建于宋雍熙年间，公元985年。双塔高七层，比上文所提及的所有的塔都要小很多。在过去的一千年中，双塔历经多次修复——最后一次是在1822年。双塔并排矗立，两塔之间仅数英尺之隔，据说对位于其西面的贡院产生了极大影响。

离双塔不远，靠近东城墙处有一座五层楼高的黑色方塔，确切地说叫作文星阁。这座塔，通常又被称为钟楼，建于1598年，为修正当地风水而建。一些风水师发现，位于长洲县学右侧的双塔要比其左侧任何一座建筑物都高，在风水上就是白虎压过青龙，从而导致县学的学子们在科举考试中无法取得好成绩。因此，为了解决这一问题，当地人就决定为文曲星修建一座高塔或钟楼，希望借此修正不好的运势。于是，以徐显卿为首的当地乡绅们筹集了数百美元，并在政府补贴的资助下，修建了这座塔。他们的慷慨在随后的数年中得到了回报，县学学子中举的数字大幅增长！康熙四十二年，1774年[1]，彭定求花费了两千多盎司的银子——大约3 000美金——修复了文星阁。与此同时，又修建了桂香殿。如今，文星阁归彭氏家族管理。彭氏家族每月捐献折合2美金的米和现钱让人专门打理文星阁。每年农历二月三日是文曲星诞辰之日。当天文星阁对外开放，数百人会聚集于此祈祷与过节。有时，在其他日子里，也会有母亲领着她的孩子前来朝拜，希望保佑孩子能顺利入学。

[1] 应为1703年。

NOTES ON THE HISTORY OF SUCHOW IV

By Rev. A. P. Parker

The Hills

The hills in the neighborhood of Suchow are invested with considerable interest in connection with the History of Suchow. The region west of the city, on the shores of the Great Lake is quite mountainous. The mountains, or, more properly speaking, the hills vary from 200 feet to 1100 feet in height, according to barometrical measurement of a number of them that I have made. Many of them seem to be composed mostly of granite, covered in many instances with a thin layer of clayey soil which supports a scant growth of vegetation. In others limestone abounds. Groves of small pine trees cover the sides of some of them, but there are no extensive tracts of large trees. Forests would doubtless grow on many of the hills in the course of time were it not that the trees are always cut down for fuel after having attained a few years' growth. Even the grass and weeds are taken off for the same purpose, so that the hills generally present a barren appearance. On many of them huge boulders of solid granite jut out above the surface, weather beaten and bare. From many of them, stone of a superior quality for building purposes is obtained.

Many of these hills are named for various animals. One is call "Tiger Hill," another is called "Sheep Mountain," and a kind of white porcelain clay is obtained there (白磰) is said to be the brains of the sheep! A third, having a striking resemblance to a crouching lion, is called "Lion Hill."Two others are said to be the "Dragon Mountain" and the "Elephant Mountain," though not commonly called by these names; but they represent, or are, the bodies of these animals. On this account stone quarrying in most of the hills is strictly prohibited—that is in name. It is commonly believed by everybody, officials and people, that quarrying in the hills is the same as digging into the bodies of the animals, which would, in some incomprehensible manner, bring great calamity on the country. But I have heard that the fears of the officials on the fungshui question are very materially allayed by a douceur from those who wish to quarry stone. As a matter of fact, vast quantities of limestone and granite are quarried there every year.

One of the most famous of these hills in the annals of the country Wu, is

苏州历史摘录（4）

潘慎文

山

《苏州府志》中有关于苏州周边群山的记载，内容十分有趣。苏州城西，太湖之滨，群山绵延。这些山，或者确切地说，这些小山丘，根据我所采用的气压测量法，高度在 200 英尺到 1 100 英尺之间不等。很多小山丘主要由花岗岩构成，岩石外覆盖着一层薄薄的黏土，供少量植被生长。还有一些小山丘以石灰岩为主。虽然山上一些地方被小松树林覆盖，却看不到成片大树。要不是长了几年就总是被砍掉充当燃料，随着时间推移，山上的树木一定会长成一片森林。有时，甚至连山上的野草也被拔光作为燃料，以至于这些小山丘外表常年呈现贫瘠之状。许多小山丘上巨大的花岗岩突出地表，经受风吹日晒，表面光秃。这些花岗岩也成了优质建筑石材的来源。

许多小山丘都是用不同动物的名字来命名的。一座叫“虎丘”，另一座叫“羊山”，据说是因为这座山产一种叫白礶的白色瓷土，像羊脑。第三座山叫“狮山”，其外形与蹲着的狮子极其相似。还有其他两座据说叫“龙山”和“象山”，尽管不常用这些名字，但这两座山分别代表了龙和象的身体。有鉴于此，大多数山上严禁采石——这只是名义上的。因为每个人，不论是官员还是平民，都认为，在山上采石就如同在动物的身体内挖掘，这一举动，会通过某种难以理解的方式，给周边地区带来极大灾难。但我听说，官员不再担心由于改变风水而造成不良后果，这是因为他们接受了那些希望开采石矿的人所送的巨额贿赂。事实上，每年有大量的石灰岩和花岗岩从这里被开采出去。

在吴国史书所记载的这些著名的小山丘中，有一座灵岩山（灵峰）。

called Ling Yien ("Spirit Peak") Hill. It is situated near the town of Muh-tuh, about 10 miles south-west of Suchow. There are many ancient remains and historical associations (古迹) connected with it. On its summit Hoh-lü, the king, built his summer palace and divided his time between it and his palace in the city. The following is a translation of what the History says about it: — " It is situated 30 *li* south-west of the city. It is 3,600 feet high. Formerly it produced a kind of stone that was used for making inkstones [a kind of argillite or shale] hence it was called Inkstone Mountain. According to the History of Yüe there was a stone wall or fortification on this hill, hence it was also called Stone-wall Mountain. It was on this hill that the king of Yüe presented Si-she [the famous female beauty] to the king of Wu. There is a stone image of a horse on this hill that has the appearance, at a distance, of carrying a rider. Near by is a stone target. The highest peak is called the Harp Stand. Fan Ch'ing-ta says: Looking down from this summit and viewing the Great Lake and the two F'ung F'eng Islands in the lake, the appearance is as if showers of green jadite were falling upon forests of jadestone growing in a world of white silver. Going on east from the Harp Stand you pass the Horse Road. Still east of this are three pools called the Inkstone Pool, the Palyflower Pool, and the Moon Pool. According to the History of Wu there is a pool on this hill that never goes dry, and in it is a kind of vegetable which if eaten in summer will counteract the heat. Near by this pool are two wells, one of which is circular and the other octagonal. The former is named the Well of the King of Wu, and the other the Well of the Abbot Chi-tsih. South of these is the Han K'ung Pavilion (涵空阁) ... South-east of this is the Ling Yen monastery, near which is a brick pagoda of the same name ... A little south of this is the Resounding Sandal Piazza (响屧廊). On the east of this is the Hundred Step Street, near which is to be seen the Stone Tortoise and the Stone Lohan [disciple of Budda]. There are tracks of a man and woman in the solid rock there, which are said to be the tracks of Fu-ch'ai (king of Wu) and Si-she. On the south of the street is the Cave of Si-she, where the King of Wu imprisoned Fanli (the ambassador from Yüe). On the right of the cave is a stone image of sleeping cow. On the right and left were the two oar-boat harbors, where the king of Wu is said to have amused himself with the dragon boat. Below these is the Subtle Serene Fountain, which was opened (得) by a scholar of T'ai T'sang during the Ming dynasty. This fountain may be seen at a distance of several *li* from the hill. Kao K'i said — The Spiritual Mount [referring to the hill under consideration] excels in wonders and abounds in beauties, and stands forth as if it were not willing to be

灵岩山位于苏州西南约10英里之外的木渎镇附近。有很多历史古迹与此山有关。吴王阖闾在山顶建了一处避暑行宫，此后阖闾轮流住在行宫和苏州城内宫殿之中。接下来一段译自《苏州府志》中关于灵岩山的一段描述：“灵岩山坐落在苏州西南30里处，山高3 600英尺。山中产石可制作砚台（一种泥板岩或页岩），因此又叫作砚石山。据《越绝书》记载，灵岩山上有座石城，因此又被称作石城山。也正是在灵岩山上，越王向吴王献上西施（著名的美女）。山上有匹马的石像，从远处看像是有人骑在上面。石像附近还有石头做的靶子。灵岩山最高处叫作琴台。范成大曾说，从山顶俯视可见太湖以及湖中的洞庭两山，此景就如同一串串翡翠掉落到生长在白银世界中的玉石森林之中。琴台往东走为走马街。再往东有三座池塘，分别叫作砚池、玩花池和月池。据《吴志》记载，山上有池，从未干涸，池内长有蔬菜，夏天食之可去暑。该池边上有两口井，一口呈圆形，另一口呈八角形。圆形井叫吴王井，另一井称智积禅师井。井的南面为涵空阁……东南面为灵岩寺，附近有一座砖塔，与灵岩寺同名……南面为响屧廊。响屧廊东面为百步街，附近可见石龟和石罗汉（佛祖徒弟）。岩石上有男女足印，据说是夫差（吴王）和西施所留。百步街南为西施洞，这里也是吴王囚禁范蠡（越国大使）之所在。西施洞右侧有牛眠石，其左右两侧为双桨划船码头，据说吴王在此坐龙舟以自娱。下面为妙湛泉，为明朝一太仓学者所开凿。山数里之外都能见该泉，高启说：灵山（即指我们所讨论的灵岩山）美景奇观众多，远超其他山峰，仿佛不愿和周围其他山峰

placed on an equality with its numerous neighboring peaks."

"There are also many strange stones on it. But since the time of Kia Tsing of the Ming, many quarries have been opened in this hill, and three-tenths of these curious formations have been taken away. In the 41st year of Wan Li a certain official named Ma Chi-tsung took possession of the rocks in this hill, in the name of the government, and forbade further quarrying or private trade in them forever. The emperor K'ang-hi and K'ien-lung both visited this mountain and established temporary palaces on its summit."

According to the above account, this hill is 3,600 feet high. I measured it with an aneroid and found it to be 557 feet high above the level of the plain. Quite a difference! The Chinese must have measured, or more likely guessed at, the distance up the side of the hill. One of the priests in the temple on the hill was very much interested in my barometer, and thought it very strange that I could measure the height of the mountain with it. He immediately jumped to the conclusion that there must be some occult science connected with it, and thought that I could also, by means of it, penetrate into the secrets of the future, for he asked me if I could also tell him when that place would again revive as a resort for worshippers and pleasure-seekers—when the temples and pavilions, &c., would again be built up and take the place of the present ruins. He seemed a little dubious as to my sincerity when I confessed my inability to tell him the date of the "good time coming."

It is said that the emperor K'ien-lung occupied the Harp Stand—a flat rock some 8 or 10 feet square—and played the harp while looking out over the Great Lake. Hence the name. The mortices in the rock are still there where stood the posts of the pavilion under which the travelling emperor played the harp 98 years ago. The brick pagoda, above referred to, was built by Sên Ch'ên-yin in 978, in memory of his sisters, queens of Wu and Yüeh. The same priest, already mentioned, told me, evidently with the utmost faith in the truth of his story, that this pagoda was built by a fairy all in one night, and that afterward a fairy cut out the inside rounding it into the shape of a cylinder, and that this also had been done in one night! The knavery and credulity of heathenism are astonishing.

The shape of the inside of the pagoda, evidently corresponded originally to that of the outside, that is octagonal, and it seems to have had some woodwork about it, banisters on the outside and stairways on the inside for each storey, but it has all been burnt or taken away, and the projecting corners on the inside have been cut out, so that it now has the form of a hollow cylinder. This may have

并列平齐。”

“灵岩山上还有不少其他奇石。但自明朝嘉靖年间，山上开了很多采石场，故而这些奇石中的十分之三都被运走了。万历四十一年，一位名叫马之骏的官员买下了整座山的石头，并以官府的名义禁止开采石矿或进行私下石头买卖。康熙和乾隆两位皇帝都到访过灵岩山，并在山顶建造临时行宫。”

根据上面的描述，灵岩山高 3 600 英尺。但我用无液气压计测量之后，却发现灵岩山只高出地平线 557 英尺。这是多么大的差距啊！中国人一定是测量了，或者更有可能是估计，从地面到山坡上的距离。山上寺庙里的一位和尚对我的气压计非常感兴趣，见我能用它测量山的高度，他感觉很不可思议。他随即得出了结论，这个气压计一定与超自然的神秘力量有关联。他认为，我能通过它，洞察未来，因为他问我是否可以告诉他这地方何时能够再次成为香客和游客们的胜地——什么时候能够重建寺庙和亭子等建筑，改变当前一片废墟的状况。当我坦承我无法告诉他“好日子来临”的具体日期时，他似乎有些怀疑我的诚意。

据说，乾隆皇帝曾在琴台（一块 8 到 10 平方英尺的扁平大石）上一面眺望太湖一面抚琴。琴台由此得名。岩石上支撑凉亭柱子的榫眼还在那，98 年前，南巡的乾隆皇帝就是在这个亭子里弹琴。上文提及的砖塔，由孙承祐于公元 978 年所建，用来纪念他的妹妹，吴越国的皇后。上文提到的那位僧人，很显然完全相信自己所讲的故事，他告诉我，这座塔是由一位仙女在一夜之间建成的，之后，一位仙女又将宝塔内部切成圆柱形，同样也是在一夜之间完成的！异教文化的欺骗和轻信真是令人震惊。

塔的内部形状与外部显然完全一样，呈八角形，似乎之前塔内有木构部分，外面有栏杆，内部每层都有楼梯，但都被烧毁或移走，而且内部突出的角落均被去除，以至于形成了目前塔内的空心状态。这也许是寺内僧

been done by the priest for their especial purpose of imposing this fairy story on the credulity of the people, and thus gain notoriety and make money, or it may have been done as a military measure during the civil war, so as to prevent the pagoda being used for a lookout station. The pagoda has 8 stories and is about 150 feet high.

Near the pagoda are extensive ruins where stood the palaces of the king of Wu and Yüeh, and the "travelling palaces" (行宫) of the emperors K'ang-hi and K'ien-lung. A wide paved walk leads up the side of the hill which was prepared expressly for K'ien-lung's use. On the south slope are pieces of broken-down walls, around what was some 400 years ago, an extensive pleasure garden. The cave of Si Shi is a very small affair—being evidently an artificial excavation in the solid rock, and only some 12 or 15 feet deep and about the same height and width. The stone Lohan is a very striking representation of a Buddist priest in full canonical dress, and the belief is general that it is a natural formation. But it is more probable that art has assisted nature in the production of this wonder. The same may be said of the stone tortoises. Not far from the latter is a level place called the Earth Drum, because a stamp with the foot there produces a considerable resonance, as if there were a hollow space underneath. The Resounding Sandal Piazza was made by preparing an extensive platform of cedar timber on the side of the hill, and covering it with earth, so as to make it appear to be a natural formation. Si Shi and other inmates of the harem were made to walk on it for the amusement of the king, and it resounded to the steps of their feet.

In front of the hill is a canal running straight out south towards the Great Lake. The common name is Arrow Creek, —because of its straightness. But its original name was the Plucking Fragrance Way, and was opened by order of Hoh Lü. This king had flower-gardens on the Fragrant Mountain (香山) on the shore of the Great Lake, and was wont to send beautiful women in boats along the Fragrant Way to bring him flowers from the gardens.

About seven miles S. W. of the city is a range of hills some three or four miles long, bearing various names. The highest is called Yao Peak in the History, though it is commonly called the Seven Son's Hill (七子山) by the people. It is said that in the time of the emperor Yao, when the floods prevailed, the people of Wu fled to the top of this hill for safety, hence it has also been named the Flood-escape Hill. North-east of the Yao Peak is the famous Hung Shan (横山), to the east slope of which the city of Suchow was removed by Yang Soh, leader

人为了让人相信他们所编神话故事而有意为之，从而可以获取名声和钱财，也有可能是为了避免在战争期间被当作军事观察哨。这座塔共有 8 层，高约 150 英尺。

塔的附近有一大片废墟，吴越国国王的宫殿以及康熙与乾隆的行宫曾建在此处。一条宽阔的大道向上直达山坡，这是专为乾隆皇帝准备的御道。山坡南面是一堆残垣断壁，大约 400 年前，这里曾是大型游乐园。西施洞是一个非常小的地方——很明显是由人工挖掘而成的，大约只有 12 到 15 英尺深，高度和宽度也是如此。石罗汉是一个穿着佛教袈裟、引人注目的雕像，人们普遍认为这个雕像浑然天成。但更有可能的是，自然形态加上艺术加工方能产生这样的奇迹。石龟也是如此。离石龟不远处有一处平地叫作地鼓，因为用脚踩在上面会产生很大的回声，就仿佛地下是空的一样。响屧廊则是在山坡上用雪松木搭建一处平台，然后用泥土覆盖其上，令其看似浑然天成。西施和后宫其他宫女为取悦吴王走在上面，廊上回响着她们的脚步声。

灵岩山前有一条河，一直向南直达太湖。这条河的名字叫作箭泾河——因为该河笔直如箭，但它最初叫采香泾，是奉阖闾之命而开凿的。阖闾在太湖之滨的香山建有花园，常命美女坐船沿此泾将鲜花从香山花园带回。

苏州西南方向大约 7 英里处有一处山脉，长 3 到 4 英里，山峰名称各异。尽管民众称其最高处为七子山，但据《苏州府志》所载，此处为尧峰山。据说在尧统治期间，洪水泛滥，吴国民众逃至山顶以避洪水，故又称为免水山。尧峰山东北处是著名的横山，公元 585 年，当苏州老城被叛军占据

of the Imperial forces, about A. D. 585, when the old city was captured and held by the rebels.

The most easterly peak of this range of hills is called Lêng-ka Hill or Shang-fang Hill (上方山). It is about 250 feet high. On its summit is the Lêng-ka or Shang-fang pagoda, a brick structure seven stories high, which was built in the 4th year of Ta Yih of the Sui, A. D. 609. The wood work on it has been long since burned or taken away. There were a Buddhist Monastery and a temple to the Wu T'ung Shên (五通神) or Five Communicating Gods there, but these have been destroyed, and only ruins remain.

The Wu T'ung are classed with evil spirits (邪神) and the worship of them is regarded by the generality of the Chinese as heterodox or superstitious（淫祀）. It seems a little odd to find the heathen Chinese talking about false gods and superstitious worship. One would think that where such credulity exists as is capable of accepting as true the mass of absurdities and fantastic nonsense connected with what are regarded as true and proper object of worship, that nothing in the shape of a god could be too foolish or extravagant to command belief and worship. But it is a fact that there is a distinction even in China between the true and the false gods, the true, in general, being only those recognized or appointed by imperial authority, while all others are false.

The origin of the worship of the Wu T'ung dates from the time of Hung Wu of the Ming, some 500 years ago. The emperor Hung Wu, had a dream, it is said, in which, five spirits appeared to him demanding a gift or benefit of some kind, and he told them to go to Kiang-nan, of which Suchow is the capital, and get whatever they wanted. They were spirits of soldiers, and the story has it, that their appearance to Hung Wu in a dream was something very much in the nature of highway robbery, and Hung Wu, being afraid of them, sent them to Kiang-nan to get rid of them. On this dream of the emperor becoming known, certain Buddhist priests, together with a number of sorcerers of Suchow, took advantage of it and started the report of the Wu T'ung had come, according to the decree of Hung Wu, the Son of Heaven. They (the priests and sorcerers) proceeded accordingly to build a temple for the worship of the Wu T'ung on the Shang-fang Hill, and gave out that the Wu T'ung could cast spells over people, and could also bring riches and honor to all who worshipped them and hence must be conciliated by worship and offerings of money, &c. It was also stated that the Wu T'ung principally wanted beautiful women for wives in the infernal regions. Hence when they

之后，隋朝军队统帅杨素将苏州城迁至横山东坡。

山脉最东处叫楞伽山或上方山。山高约 250 英尺，山顶有一座高 7 层的砖塔，建于公元 609 年，隋大业四年[1]。塔上木制品早已被烧毁或搬走。山上有一座佛寺和一座五通神庙，但均已毁坏，仅剩废墟。

五通神被归为邪神，祭拜五通神则被认为是淫祀，即非其所祭而祭之。听到作为异教徒的中国人谈论假神和迷信崇拜感觉似乎有些古怪。有人会认为，如果存在这种轻信，存在着将大量荒谬和假想的无稽之谈当成真正的信仰去崇拜的现象，那么，只要是与神相关的任何事务，都是可以相信和崇拜的。但事实上，中国还存在着真神和假神之分，所谓真神就是官方认可的神，而其他的均为假神。

祭拜五通神可以追溯到五百多年前的明朝洪武年间。洪武皇帝做了一个梦，据说，在梦中有五位神灵要求他给予礼物或其他好处，洪武皇帝告诉他们去江南可以得到他们所想要的，而苏州则是江南省会。这五位是士兵的亡灵，据传闻，他们出现在洪武皇帝梦中，就如同拦路打劫一般，皇帝非常害怕，就打发他们去江南，好除掉他们。皇帝的这个梦后来被人得知，于是苏州的一些僧人以及术士利用这个梦，开始到处宣扬，五通神是依据天子洪武皇帝命令来苏州的。他们（僧人和术士）在上方山上建立起一座庙来祭拜五通神，并宣扬五通神可以对民众念咒施法，给祭拜他们的人带来财富和荣誉，因此必须供奉五通神并进贡钱财等。他们还说，五通神主要想在阴间娶美女为妻，因此，在他们选中美女之后，他们会给美女施咒，

[1] 应为隋大业五年。

had selected a pretty woman, they would throw a spell over her and she would sicken and die, and her spirit went to be a wife of the Wu T'ung. According to the History this form of superstition was very rife during the reign of K'ang-hi 200 years ago, and really serious consequences resulted from it. It came to such a pass that whenever a pretty woman in the region around the Shang-fang Hill fell ill from any cause, usual or whimsical, the people immediately said that the Wu T'ung wanted her for a wife, and had cast a spell over her, and if she died, the parents and relatives, instead of mourning her loss, rejoiced that they had been so distinguished as to be called on to furnish a wife for Wu T'ung, and believed that great prosperity would result to the family. The people seem to have been completely infatuated with this absurd delusion, while the priests and the sorcerers reaped a rich harvest. So serious had matters become, that in the 24th year of K'ang-hi, the Provincial Governor T'ang Ping (汤斌), determined to put a stop to it. He accordingly had the images pulled down, the wooden ones burned, and the mud and stone ones thrown into Stone Lake at the foot of the hill. He also had the temple torn down, and the timbers used to repair one of the government school buildings in the city. There is a long memorial from governor T'ang to the emperor, printed in the History, in which he relates with great disgust, the miserable superstitions of the people, and how that wicked and designing men had imposed on the ignorance of stupid men and women (愚夫愚妇) to both get gain for themselves and corrupt the morals of the people. He states that in obedience to imperial command he had, at stated intervals, instructed the people in the precepts of the *Sacred Edict* [a book containing moral precepts prepared by the emperor K'ang-hi] and had also done his utmost in various ways to reform the morals and manners of the people, having among other things to this end, forbidden women going into the temples to worship. As a result of his efforts for more than a year, he had noticed a very decided improvement in the general conduct of the people, —women had entirely ceased their visits to the temples, and the sounds of bachanalian revelry in the public pleasure resorts were seldom heard. He tells of his destruction of the temple of the Wu T'ung, and begs the emperor to issue an edict forever prohibiting the revival of this wicked superstition.

Whether the edict was issued or not, does not appear, but after the righteous T'ang left, the superstition again became rife, and in subsequent years was again repressed in a somewhat similar manner. But it seems impossible to root it out entirely, as there is a temple to the Wu T'ung still standing at the foot of the

美女就会生病死去，而她的灵魂就成为五通神的妻子。据《苏州府志》记载，两百年前，康熙年间，祭拜五通神这种迷信活动非常猖獗，并由此造成了严重后果。甚至无论何时，只要上方山附近的美女生病，不论什么病因，人们立刻就会说五通神想娶她为妻，所以给她施咒，如果她去世，她的父母和亲戚们，不但不会哀悼她的离去，反而会感到高兴，认为他们家与众不同，能被选中为五通神提供妻子，并认为此后家族将会因此而兴旺发达。人们似乎完全迷失在这种荒谬的骗局中，而那些僧人和术士则大赚一笔。事态发展到非常严重之地步，康熙二十四年，江苏巡抚汤斌决定禁止民众祭拜五通神。他命人推倒五通神神像，将木质神像烧掉，将泥石雕像投入上方山山脚下的石湖之中。他同时还将山上的寺庙拆掉，将庙里的木材用来修建苏州城内的一所官办学堂。汤斌曾向皇帝上过一篇很长的奏折，《苏州府志》上亦有记载。在奏折中，汤斌描述了民众可悲的迷信，以及这些邪恶和别有用心之人如何欺骗愚夫愚妇，在为自己谋取利益的同时败坏民众道德，汤斌对此深恶痛绝。汤斌还说，为遵照皇命，他每隔一段时间，就用《圣谕十六条》（康熙皇帝颁布的包含道德戒律的一本书）中的戒律教导民众，同时他也通过各种方式尽最大努力来改善民众的道德和礼仪，此外，还禁止妇女前往寺庙举行祭拜。经过一年多的努力，汤斌发现民众的行为有了根本性的改变——妇女们不再去五通神庙，而且在公众场合里也很少再听到狂欢的声音。汤斌向皇帝讲述了他拆封五通神庙的经过，并请求皇帝颁布命令永久禁止祭拜五通神，防止这种邪恶的迷信卷土重来。

皇帝是否颁布法令，书中并未提及，但是正直的汤巡抚离任之后，祭拜五通神的迷信活动再次猖獗，在接下来的数年中，又再次受到打压。然而祭拜五通神的陋习似乎不可能完全去除，因为如今上方山山脚下仍旧还

Shang-fang Hill; although the people of the present generation do not seem to be so carried away by this miserable delusion as their fathers were.

The Cha Nogh Hill is 15 *li* south-west of the city. Its shape very much resembles a lion lying down, and hence it is commonly called "Lion Hill."Wang Liao, king of Wu, immediate predecessor of Hoh Lü, and who was slain by him (Hoh Lü), was buried on this hill. On the side of the hill is a large stone that is said to be of meteoric origin, and to the east is a canal called the "Fallen Star Creek." There is a curious tradition given in the History, and said to have been handed down from ancient times, to the effect that this hill once stood in the Great Lake, and that when Yü the Great was regulating the waters of the empire, he dragged this hill eastward out of the lake, and placed it in its present position. On the south and west of the hill, there are said to be two smaller hills containing stones of the shape of coils of rope, and it is averred that Yü used these to drag the hill with Petrified ropes! There is a shallow place in the lake which is said to be the former base of the hill, and a long deep place leading from this in the direction of the present position of the hill, is the ditch or sluice along which the hill was dragged! Many years ago there were two rocky prominences on the hill which were said to be the "lion's ears," but they have been long since quarried away.

Besides those already mentioned, there are 80 or 90 more principal hills and mountains described in the History, included in the three districts in which the city of Suchow is situated. These, besides a great number of smaller hills and peaks all have names derived from some natural peculiarity, or from some temple built on them, or from some historical or legendary association. The Hill of the Goddess of Mercy (观音山) takes its name from the fact that a temple to that goddess is built on it. It is also called Whetstone Hill because stone for whetstones is obtained there.

The Balance Hill (天平山) holds the grave of the Fan (范) family of which Fan Wên Chên Kung (范文正公) was the most illustrious member, and hence it is now commonly known as Fan Fen Hill (范坟山). There are many natural curiosities on this hill, such as the Lotus Cave, the White Cloud Cave (a partly natural and partly artificial excavation in the side of the hill some 20 feet deep), the Pencil Peak, the Rock Gulch, the Sleeping Dragon Peak, the Lake View Stand, the Turban Peak, Lake Mirror, &c., —all of them curious natural formations, which have been thus named for some peculiarity in their shape, position, &c.

有一座供奉五通神的寺庙；不过，如今的民众不像他们的祖先一样完全被这一悲惨的幻觉所迷惑。

岝崿山在苏州城西 15 里处。该山形似一只卧躺的狮子，因此，通常又被称作“狮山”。吴国君主王僚，就葬在这座山上，王僚是阖闾未登基之前的吴国国王，后被阖闾谋害致死。山边有一块大石，据说是陨石，山东边有一条溪叫作“落星泾”。《苏州府志》上记载了一个据说是从上古时代流传下来的关于此山的奇闻传说。该山最初曾立于太湖之中，大禹治水之时，将此山向东拖出太湖，最后安放在当前的位置上。在此山的南面和西面，据说有两座更小的山，山上有石如绳索状，据说大禹就是用这些已经石化的绳子来拖动狮山的。太湖中有一处浅地，据说就是当年狮山的山基之所在，湖中还有一条沟，又长又深，一直延伸到狮山当前位置，据说山就是沿着这条沟被拖走的。很多年前，山上还有两块突出的岩石，据说是“狮子的耳朵”，但早就被开采挖走了。

除上述提到的小山之外，《苏州府志》中还记载了包括苏州所在的三个地区的 80—90 座主要的小山丘和高山。这些山，除了许多小山丘和山峰之外，其他山的名称要么源自其自然特征，要么源自山上所建之寺庙，要么源自相关历史和传说。观音山就是因山上所建观音庙而得名的。观音山也叫“支硎山”，因为山上多平石。[1]

范氏家族祖坟位于天平山，因此现如今天平山又被称为“范坟山”，而范文正公正是其家族中最为著名的一位。天平山上有许多自然奇观，例如莲花洞、白云洞（半自然、半人工挖掘，洞深约 20 英尺）、卓笔峰、岩石峡谷、卧龙峰、望湖台、巾子峰、照湖镜等——所有景观都是自然形成的，因此按照各自形状、位置特征而命名。

[1] 据《苏州府志》记载，“平石为硎，山多平石，故因支遁，以支硎为号”，故得此名。

The Sü Hill (胥山) is situated west of the town of Muh-tuh, on the shore of the Great Lake , and near it is the temple of Wu Tzi-sü, who was executed by Fu-ch'ai, king of Wu, and his body thrown into the canal at that place. Years after his death the people of Wu, sorrowing over his untimely end, and the calamities which had befallen the country through the king's refusal to follow the advice of the faithful Tz-sü, built a temple there in honor of him and the hill takes its name from the temple.

Some 30 *li* west of the city is the Flowery Hill (华山), which takes its name from the story that in the 2nd year of T'ai K'ang of the Tsin, A. D. 282, a thousand-leaved lotus flower grew on it. Near the Fan Fên Hill is the Gold Hill, where it is asserted that gold was obtained during the Tsin and Sung dynasties. No gold is to be found there at present, however. Anciently there were many natural curiosities on this hill, but they have been all destroyed. A large part of the hill, which seems to have been one solid mass of granite rock, has been quarried away. Granite of a very superior quality is obtained there for building, street-paving, millstones, &c. Hundreds of men are constantly at work quarrying the stone. The work is all done with hammers and iron wedges. A row of mortices, about a foot apart and one to three inches deep, is made where a block of stone is to be split out, steel wedges are placed in the mortices, and the workman strikes them alternately heavy overhanded blows with an iron hammer having a limber wooden handle to prevent jarring the hand. After many vigorous blows have been dealt, the stone begins to split along the line of the mortices and soon comes loose. They are able to split this stone in pieces of any length or thickness almost like splitting timber.

About fifteen miles south-west of the city is the K'iung-lung Mountain (穹窿山) , which is perhaps the highest hill—1,100 feet high—and also the most noted place of worship in all this region. Great crowds of people from far and near go there during the third and eighth moons to worship at the Taoist temples on the hill. It is said that Ch'ih Sung-tz (赤松子), a rain-priest in the time of the emperor Shen Nung, B. C. 2700, (cf. Mayer's *Manual*), lived on this Mountain. On the summit are supposed ruins of the Ascending-fairy Stand, and of the Sublimating Elixir Stand (炼丹台) where Ch'ih Sung-tz is said to have practiced his magical arts. There are several springs in this mountain whose waters are said to be unfailing. Formerly there was a Buddist temple on the mountain, but for some reason the Taoists have obtained possession of the place and have built extensive

胥山位于木渎镇西、太湖之滨，该山附近有伍子胥祠堂一座。吴王夫差处死伍子胥后，将其尸身投入该山附近的河中。伍子胥死后数年，吴国人感怀其悲惨结局，同时也感伤吴国因吴王拒绝听从忠心耿耿的伍子胥所提之建议而承受的灾难，因此建造了一座祠堂以纪念伍子胥，而该山也因此祠堂而得名。

苏州城西约30里处有一座华山[1]，其名来自一个故事。据说在公元282年，晋太康二年[2]，山上长出了一株千叶莲花。靠近范坟山还有一座金山，在晋朝和宋朝年间曾有人凿石得金。但如今，却未曾在山上发现金子。在古时，山上有许多自然奇观，但都已遭毁坏。山体大部分看上去就如同一块巨大的花岗岩，已经被开采一空。山上的花岗岩质地非常好，适合建房、铺路、磨石等。数以百计的人在这里开采石矿。采石工作靠锤子和铁楔来完成。工人们会在要被劈开的石块上钉一排榫眼，彼此间隔一英尺，三英寸深，然后在榫眼中放置钢楔，接下来工人们用铁锤交替重击钢楔，锤柄是由较柔软的木质材料所制作的，以防震伤手臂。经过多次用力敲击之后，石头开始沿着榫眼线裂开，很快就松动了。这样工人们几乎就可以像劈木材一样将石头劈成任何长度或厚度。

苏州西南约15英里处有一座穹窿山，大概是苏州地区最高的山——1 100英尺——也是最著名的朝拜之地。每年三月和八月，周边地区的大量人群都前往山上的道观进香。据说，赤松子，公元前2700年神农氏统治时期的雨师，就居住在此山之中。山顶之上还有升仙台和炼丹台遗迹，据说赤松子就在那里修炼仙法。山上有多处泉水，据说永不干涸。之前曾有一座佛教寺庙，但由于种种原因，道士占据此地并在此修建了一排道观。铜

[1] 即花山。
[2] 应为太康三年。

temples there. On the shore of the Great Lake not far from K'iung-lung Mountain is the Copper Well Hill, where copper is said to have been mined during the Tsin and Sung dynasties.

But the time would fail me to tell of all the noted hills in the neighborhood of this city—of their natural and artificial curiosities, their ancient remains (古迹), their legendary and historical associations, &c. There are many of them, and the history connected with them is interesting. There they stand—the everlasting hills—silent but mighty witnesses of the littleness and the transitory character of all things human. Magnificent palaces, grand towers, holy temples and strong fortifications have been built on many of these hills during the 3,000 years that this country has been inhabited by civilized man. But time has destroyed them all, and only heaps of ruins remain where once shone the splendor of kingly courts. The buildings that now occupy some of the ancient sites are mostly but the work of yesterday. A hundred generations of kings and courtiers, nobles and peasants, have come, played their little parts, and passed away, but the hills, the handiwork of God, endure, outlasting the mightiest works of man.

NOTES ON THE HISTORY OF SUCHOW V

By Rev. A. P. Parker

The Kingdom of Wu

The "Kingdom of Wu" was the name of the state of which Suchow was the capital, when the city was founded. It embraced all of that part of the present province of Kiangsu, south of the Yang Tz river, and a part of Chehkiang and Anhwei provinces. And while it has not for many centuries been an independent state, the name of Wu still clings to the country, and Suchow and the region around is quite commonly called "the Country of Wu," (吴地 or 吴)[1]. Its history embraces the period from about B. C. 1260 to 475. But little, however, of importance is recorded of its history during the greater part of these 800 years. From the time of Yü the Great to B. C. 1260, the country of Wu was included in the district of Yangchow, and was inhabited by barbarians. These barbarians were

[1] 本篇原文采用了英文夹用中文注释的形式，收入本书时统一改为中文括注。

井山也位于太湖之滨，离穹窿山不远，据说在晋朝和宋朝年间曾出土过铜矿。

可惜时间不允许我一一讲述苏州周边的名山——讲述它们自然和人工奇观、它们留存的古迹、与之相关的历史传说等。有很多这样的故事，和历史相结合就变得非常有趣。它们虽然静静地矗立在那里——这些永恒的山峦——却见证了人类社会的渺小和短暂。这个国家有三千年文明发展史，在此期间，许多山上都建起了气势恢宏的宫殿、雄伟高大的宝塔、神圣的寺庙以及坚固的要塞。然后，岁月摧毁了一切，只留下一堆堆废墟，而这些废墟中有些曾是王宫所在地。如今还在历史遗址上的建筑物大多数都是以往留下的。上百代的帝王将相、贵族农夫，先后来到世间，扮演着自己的角色，最后离开人世，但这些山峦，神的杰作，却依旧矗立在那里，比人类最伟大的作品还要长久。

苏州历史摘录（5）

潘慎文

吴国

“吴国”是国名，苏州建成之后便成为吴国首都。吴国地界包括目前江苏省部分地区、长江以南以及浙江、安徽两省的部分地区。尽管早已不再是一个独立国家，但“吴”这个名字，几百年来，一直保留了下来，苏州周边地区因此通常也被称为吴地。吴国历史大约从公元前 1260 年起到公元前 475 年止。但在这约 800 年的大部分时间里，几乎没有什么重要的历史记录。从大禹时代起到公元前 1260 年，吴国就划分在扬州地区，当时住

wholly uncivilized—living on the natural products of the land, tattooing their bodies, and knowing nothing of letters. Where they originally came from there are no means of knowing.

The kingdom of Wu was founded by the descendants of Tan Fu（亶父）, the progentor of Wu Wang（武王） the founder of the Cheu dynasty. Tan Fu had three sons, the youngest of whom Ki Lih（季历）, was regarded by his father as the most worthy to be made his successor to the government of the principality of Cheu.

The two oldest sons, T'ai Peh and Ch'ung Yung, on learning their father's purpose concerning the succession, determined to avoid any possibility of trouble, by leaving the country so as to allow the youngest brother to succeed to the dominion without opposition. Hence, on one occasion, when the "Old Duck"(古公) was sick and the two brothers went to the hills to hunt some medicinal herbs for their father, they availed themselves of the opportunity to steal away unawares, and taking their journey to the southward, they travelled a distance of several hundred *li* to a region, south of the Yang Tz river, called King Man(荆蛮) and there settled, somewhere in the region of the present city of Chang Cheu.

The influence of their example on the natives seems to have been very salutary. In a few years many of them learned of the two brothers some of the arts of civilized life, —agriculture, house-building, making clothes, &c. &c. — and subsequently the inhabitants of quite a large region of country, including more than 1,000 families, agreed to make T'ai Peh their ruler, and the kingdom or principality thus founded was called Ken Wu（句吴）, a name which was probably derived from sounds in the aboriginal tongue. T'ai Peh made his capital at a place called Mei Li（梅里）, which, though it was never a walled city, was strongly fortified. The ruins of this fortification were still to be seen, it is said, at the time the History was written, 60 years ago. T'ai Peh ruled with such justice and probity that his sway over his adopted country soon became firmly established.

When Tan Fu came to die, he expressed a wish that T'ai Peh might still become his successor, notwithstanding his former purpose to leave the kingdom to Ki Lih. He had long mourned over the loss of his two sons, and promised the kingdom to T'ai Peh if he would return to his father's house. Accordingly when T'ai Peh learned of his father's death, and returned home to assist in the performance of the funeral rites, Ki Lih offered him the kingdom, but he would not accept it. The offer was twice repeated, and as often rejected. Hence it is said that

着一批原始居民。这些原始居民完全没有文化——过着茹毛饮血的生活，遍体文身，不识文字。至于他们从何而来，我们无从得知。

吴国由亶父的后裔、周朝创建者武王的祖先所建立。亶父有三个儿子，最小的名叫季历，他被其父认为最有资格成为封邑的继承人。

亶父的长子和次子，即泰伯[1]与仲雍，了解到他们父亲关于王位继承的考虑后，为避免可能出现的麻烦，决定离开自己的国家，这样就可以让最小的弟弟顺利继承王位。因此，有一次，趁“古公”[2]生病之时，兄弟俩去山中采药，乘机偷偷溜走，他们向南走了数百里，来到了长江以南一个叫作荆蛮的地方，并在那里定居了下来，也就是现在常州的某处。

泰伯和仲雍为当地人树立了榜样，并产生了积极的影响。在随后的几年中，他们中很多人向这两位兄弟学习文明生活的技艺——耕种、造房、制衣等——后来，当地大部分居民，包括一千多户的家庭，都同意让泰伯成为他们的统治者，而他们成立的国家就叫作句吴，句吴这个名字大概来自当地居民方言的发音。泰伯以梅里为首都，尽管梅里没有建造城墙，但防御性很好。据说，60 年前《苏州府志》编纂之时，当时防御工事的废墟在梅里依旧可见。泰伯的统治公平公正，因此他很快便在收留他的这个地方建立了稳固的统治。

亶父弥留之际，希望泰伯仍然能够成为他的继承者，尽管此前他曾打算将王位传给季历。亶父因失去两个儿子而哀伤很久，他承诺只要泰伯归来，他就将王位传给泰伯。泰伯听闻他父亲去世，便返回家中协助办理丧事，季历将王位拱手让出，但泰伯并未接受。此后季历又两次将王位让给泰伯，但泰伯还是不肯接受，因此便有了“泰伯以天下三让”的说法。泰伯

[1] 本篇原文在发表时，作者使用了“泰伯”这一名称，而非前面几篇原文中的“太伯”，故译文使用“泰伯”。

[2] 即亶父。

"T'ai Peh thrice declined the kingdom"（泰伯以天下三让）. His magnanimity in thus relinquishing his rights in favor of his youngest brother, is regarded by the Chinese as worthy of very high praise.

He ruled the kingdom of Wu some 49 years and at his death was succeeded by his brother Ch'ung Yung. The son of the latter succeeded him at his death. Thus the government was handed down from father to son for 19 successive generations till it reached Sheu Mung（寿梦）. He had four sons, of whom he regarded the youngest, Ki Chah（季札）, as the best qualified to succeed to the rule of the state. But Ki Chah refused to acquiesce in his father's plans, and the succession therefore devolved on the oldest son, who, on his death, was succeeded by the second son. He ruled only a short time, and dying, was succeeded by his third son. Strange to say the third son only lived a few years after his accession to the kingdom, and on his death, it was the general desire that Ki Chah should succeed him. Ki Chah had by this time reached a good age having outlived his three elder brothers, and by his faithfulness in the official positions that he had held during the three successive reigns, had confirmed the good judgment of his father as to his fitness to rule the kingdom. But he cared not for kingly power and glory, and to avoid further importunity, he left the court and, retiring to a secluded spot, spent his time in the quiet of agricultural pursuits. On this account he has a place in the History among the noted sages（名贤）, that the country of Wu has produced.

On Ki Chah's positive refusal to be king, Wang Liao（王僚）, the son of Yü Chai（馀祭）, Shen Mung's third son was made king, about B. C. 535. Up to this date very little is recorded of the progress of the country of Wu in the arts of civilized life. T'ai Peh seems to have built up a considerable town called Mei Li, and to have fortified it with a mud wall. Shen Mung is also said to have founded the city of Kwên-shan（昆山）, although there was no brick wall built around it till the time of the Sung dynasty. There is no record of the productions and manufactures of the country, nor of the number of its inhabitants. The absence of such records is attributed to the "Burning of the Books" by T'sin Sz Hwang Ti, the first emperor of the T'sin, by whose order all the books in the empire of every description were destroyed. Only the "Book of Changes" was spared and a few other books including some of the Classics were successfully hidden and escaped destruction. This calamity fell upon the literature of the country A. D. 212. Hence it is said that the records of the Kingdom of Wu were destroyed at that time, and

这种为了成全弟弟而放弃自己王位的高尚品德，在中国人看来，值得高度赞扬。

泰伯统治吴国达 49 年，他去世之后，其弟仲雍继承王位。仲雍死后，仲雍之子继承王位。就这样王位从父到子传承下来，传到寿梦时已经是第 19 代了。寿梦有四个儿子，他认为最小的儿子季札最有资格继承王位。但是季札并不认同其父，因此王位最终由寿梦的长子继承。寿梦长子去世之后，王位由寿梦的二儿子馀祭继承，但馀祭在位时间很短，他死后，王位由寿梦的三儿子馀眛继承。奇怪的是，馀眛继承王位没多久便去世了，民众普遍希望季札能够继承王位。此时，季札年事已高，比他三个哥哥活得都要长久，在这三朝统治期间，季札在其所担任的职位上兢兢业业，证实了其父认为他适合管理国家的看法是正确的。但季札对权力和荣誉不感兴趣，为避免卷入其中，季札离开了宫廷，寻到了一处隐居之所，过起了平静的农耕生活。也正因为如此，季札，作为吴国的名贤，被记载在《苏州府志》中。

季札拒绝担任国王之后，约公元前 535 年，寿梦的第三子馀祭[1]之子王僚，成为吴国国王[2]。此时吴国在文明生活方面取得进步的记载几乎没有。泰伯建造了一座叫梅里的大城，并用泥墙加固了城市的防御。寿梦据说也在昆山建了一座城市，但直到宋朝，昆山周围才建起砖墙。此时，还没有关于吴国生产和手工制作的记录，也没有居住人口数量的记载。这些记录的缺少是由秦朝第一位皇帝秦始皇“焚书”造成的。秦始皇下令烧毁其帝国内所有书籍，只有《周易》幸免于难，还有一些其他经典著作因被成功隐藏起来而逃过一劫。这场落在中国文学上的灾难发生于公元 212 年[3]。据说吴国的记录就是毁于此，因此，吴国的早期历史被掩埋在黑暗

[1] 馀祭应为寿梦第二子，此处潘慎文有误。
[2] 此处潘慎文有误，王僚公元前 526 年成为吴国国王。
[3] 应为公元前 212 年。

its early history is therefore enveloped in some obscurity.

To return from this digression. Wang Liao had a dangerous and resolute rival in the person of Kung Tz Kwang（公子光）, his cousin. This cousin was the son of his uncle Sheu Mung's first son, Chu Fan（诸樊）, and considered that as his uncle Ki Chah had refused the throne, the succession rightly belonged to him as the eldest son. Hence, when Wang Liao was made king, Kung Tz Kwang resolved on his destruction. He was enabled to accomplish his purpose thirteen years after Wang Liao's accession, by the assistance of Wu Tz-sü（伍子胥）, son of Wu Shieh（伍奢）, prime minister of the state of T'su. Wu Shieh together with his elder son Wu Shang（伍尚）, were put to death at the instigation of a rival statesman, and Tz-sü, took to flight to save his life. The eldest son of the king of T'su also fled with him, and the two found refuge at the court of Ch'en（陈）. Subsequently the son of the king of T'su was found engaged in a plot to seize the government of Ch'en, and had to flee again for his life. Tz-sü, though having no part in this plot, was suspected by the king of Ch'en, and had to flee also. This time he came to the court of Wu and offered his services to Wang Liao. The latter was at first inclined to accept him, but was dissuaded from doing so by Kung Tz Kuang, who represented to him that as Tz-sü had been twice accused of treachery and had fled for his life, he could not be a trustworthy servant of the king of Wu. Kung Tz Kuang's real purpose was to secure the services of Wu Tz-sü for himself. He saw in Tz-sü a man of unusual ability, and he determined, if possible, to secure his assistance in carrying out his plan of wresting the throne from Wang Liao. Wang Liao listened to the advice of his treacherous cousin, and thus unwittingly hastened his own downfall. On Liao's refusal to employ Tz-sü, the latter was secretly taken into the service of Kung Tz Kuang who, by reason of his near relationship to the king, occupied a commanding position at the court of Wu. In order to cover up his schemes, Kung Tz Kuang caused Tz-sü to retire from the court to some secluded place where he could better assist in perfecting a plan to put down Wang Liao and secure the throne to Kung Tz Kuang. Tz-sü was not long in devising a plan and securing a man to execute it. Wang Liao was very fond of broiled fish, and Wu Tz-sü's plan was to take advantage of this fact to compass his destruction. In his rambles through the country he found a man of great strength and courage named Chan Chu（专诸）, whom he took into his employ, and sent him to the shores of the Great Lake to study the art of broiling fish according to Wang Liao's favorite method. After three year's practice he was introduced to Wang Liao and employed by him, and the latter soon became so pleased with him that

之中。

言归正传。吴王僚有一个性格坚毅的危险对手，那就是他的堂兄公子光。公子光是吴王僚的大伯诸樊之子，而诸樊则是寿梦长子。公子光认为，由于他的叔叔季札已经拒绝接受王位，那么作为长子，王位应该由他来继承。因此，当吴王僚登上王位之后，公子光决定杀死他。在吴王僚继位 13 年后，在伍子胥的帮助下，公子光终于完成这一目标。伍子胥是楚国大夫伍奢之子。伍奢及他的大儿子伍尚，受政敌陷害而被处死，伍子胥则逃了出来。楚国太子也随着伍子胥一同流亡，他们二人逃往陈国避难。后来，楚国太子被发现参与了试图推翻陈国统治的政变，不得已再次逃亡。尽管伍子胥并未参与其中，但也遭到陈王的怀疑，无奈之下也只好逃亡。这一次，伍子胥来到吴国，并主动向吴王僚表示愿意为其效力。吴王僚最初很想接纳伍子胥，但被公子光劝住，公子光对他说，伍子胥两次被指控背信弃义而亡命天涯，因此，对吴国而言，他不是一个值得信任之人。公子光真正的目的是为自己争取伍子胥的辅佐。他见伍子胥才华出众，因此决定，如有可能，将其揽入门下，协助自己完成从吴王僚手中抢过王位的计划。吴王僚听从了其奸诈表兄的建议，因此在无意之中加速了自己的灭亡。在得知吴王僚拒绝招募自己之后，伍子胥悄悄地加入了公子光的阵营，而公子光则凭借其与吴王的亲密关系，在吴国宫廷内占据了主导地位。为了隐藏他的计划，公子光让伍子胥从宫廷隐退到一个隐蔽之处，以更好地帮助其完成推倒吴王僚夺取王位的计划。不久之后，伍子胥设计了一个方案，并安排专人执行。吴王僚非常喜欢吃烤鱼，而伍子胥的计划就是利用这一点来杀死他。在一次闲逛中，伍子胥发现一个名叫专诸的人，此人力大无穷且非常勇敢，伍子胥将他招致麾下，并将他送往太湖之滨学艺，学习如何按照吴王僚最喜欢的方式来烤鱼。经过三年实践，专诸被推荐给吴王僚并被雇用，吴王

he would eat no fish except such as had been prepared by Chan Chu.

Having succeeded so far in his plot, Kung Tz Kuang determined to bring matters to a crisis. He accordingly invited Wang Liao to a feast, the principal article of which was to be broiled fish prepared by Chan Chu. Liao came to the house of Kung Tz Kuang on the day appointed, well protected by his own trusty body-guard, having had his suspicious aroused as to the sincerity of his cousin in inviting him to this feast. Meantime Kung Tz Kuang had placed a company of his minions in ambush in an adjoining room, and ordered Chan Chu to hide a short sword of a peculiar make in one of the broiled fish that he was to bring in for the king's feast. On arriving, Liao took his place at the feast, with his body-guard drawn up in order on either side. Chan Chu, while in the act of setting the dish of broiled fish before the king, opened it and seizing the knife concealed therein, stabbed the king. Wang Liao's bodyguard immediately fell upon Chan Chu and struck him down. But rising with one tremendous effort, he again struck his sword into the body of Wang Liao who immediately fell dead. Liao's soldiers made short work with Chan Chu, but they were soon overpowered and nearly massacred by Kung Tz Kuang's followers who had been placed in ambush for the occasion.

On the death of Wang Liao, Kung Tz Kuang proclaimed himself king of Wu with the title of Hoh Lü（阖闾）. This is the famous Hoh Lü that founded the city of Suchow.

NOTES ON THE HISTORY OF SUCHOW VI

By Rev. A. P. Parker

The Kingdom of Wu

HOH LÜ on getting possession of the kingdom immediately set about strengthening the defences of the country and preparing for a vigorous prosecution of the war with Yuen on the South and Ts'i on the North. These petty principalities into which China was divided at that time were constantly quarrelling with each other and war seems to have been almost their normal condition. At the time that Hoh Lü overthrew Wang Liao his capital appears to have been at Wu Sieh, though this is not clearly stated. But wherever it was, Hoh Lü was not satis-

僚很快对专诸的厨艺感到满意，以至于非专诸烹饪之鱼不食。

公子光的计划已经成功了一大半，于是他决定孤注一掷。他随即宴请吴王僚，而主菜就是专诸做的烤鱼。由于吴王僚对公子光宴请他的诚意有所怀疑，因此在宴请当日，他带上自己信任的护卫来到公子光的住所赴宴。与此同时，公子光让他的手下埋伏在隔壁的房间里，并且令专诸将一把特制的短剑，即鱼肠剑藏在端给吴王僚享用的烤鱼肚中。来到宴会地点之后，吴王僚在宴席上就座，他的护卫则分列两旁。专诸将烤鱼端至吴王僚面前，剖开鱼肚，拿起藏在里面的宝剑刺向吴王僚。吴王僚的护卫立刻扑向专诸，并将他击倒，但专诸奋力站起，再次将剑刺入吴王僚的身体，吴王僚随即倒地身亡。吴王僚的护卫和专诸进行了短暂搏斗，但很快就被公子光事先埋伏的手下制服，几乎全军覆没。

吴王僚一死，公子光便称吴王，号阖闾，这就是那个建造了苏州城的著名的阖闾。

苏州历史摘录（6）

潘慎文

吴国

阖闾登上王位之后，立刻着手加强国土防御，并积极准备与南面的越国以及北面的齐国的战争。当时中国的各诸侯国之间争执不断，战争已成为常态。当阖闾推翻吴王僚之时，虽然没有明确记载，但吴国首都似乎是在无锡。姑且不论吴国首都到底在何处，阖闾对都城的地理位置、城池大

fied with it, either as regards location, size or strength. He felt the need of a large walled city where his people could dwell safely in time of danger, and where his government stores could be protected from the enemies that constantly menaced his kingdom. The city of Suchow was founded, as stated in a former article, to supply this want.

Owing principally to the good judgment of Wu Tz-sü, to whom Hoh Lü largely committed the affairs of his kingdom, the country was soon brought to a great state of strength and prosperity, so that Hoh Lü asserted his independence and threw off even the semblance of allegiance to the House of Cheu which his predecessors had acknowledged as due to the central or Proper Government（正统）. He succeeded in subjugating Ts'i and Yueh, capturing the king of the latter, who together with his principal minister were held in close captivity for many years, and made to perform services to the king of Wu of the most degrading character. The cause of the quarrel between Wu and Yueh is not stated, but it was probably rival ambition to be possessed of larger territory and mutual jealousy of encroachments on each other's dominions.

After having built and fortified his new capital, Hoh Lü selected Ling Yen Hill as a place for a summer palace. Here he spent much of his time in the summer, and evidently made of it a most beautiful and pleasant summer resort. He spent a good deal of the means and labor of the people in providing various pleasure resorts for himself, and his court, and several of the mountains in and around the shores of the Great Lake afforded him places for game parks, hunting grounds, pleasure gardens, &c. But while spending large amounts for his own gratification, he also did much to improve the general condition of the country, especially in opening up the water communications, and draining the swampy lands that abounded. By his wise and just government he gained the confidence of the people and succeeded ere long in firmly establishing himself on the throne. He brought his army into a great state of efficiency, and none of the neighboring principalities could cope with him, so that he was able to dictate his own terms on the conclusion of every one of the four or five wars in which he engaged.

But notwithstanding his power and prosperity, there was one man still alive that Hoh Lü feared. This was Wang Liao's son, and the rightful successor to the throne of Wu which Hoh Lü had usurped. This son, whose name was K'ing K'i, had gone with the army of Wu to invade Yueh, and it was during his absence, and while nearly all the available forces of the country were called off on this expedi-

小以及防御能力均不满意。他感到有必要建立一座带城墙的大城，这样便可以在危急时刻保护他的臣民，也可以使国库免受来自敌国的长期侵扰。正如前文所述，苏州城的建立满足了这一需求。

基于对伍子胥的信任和欣赏，阖闾将国家大事委托给他，吴国很快便繁荣富强起来，阖闾进而宣布吴国独立，甚至抛弃了吴国前几位君主对周朝正统统治地位的认同和效忠。他成功征服了齐国和越国，俘虏了越国国王，并将越王和他的大臣们囚禁多年，令他们为吴王提供各种服务，极尽羞辱之能事。虽然书中没有提及吴、越之间的纷争起源，但很可能是两国都有侵占更大领土的野心以及对各自所占领土的觊觎。

在建造和加固了新都城之后，阖闾选择了灵岩山作为他的夏季行宫。在夏季的大部分时间里，阖闾都是在这里度过的，很显然这是一个风景最为优美的避暑度假胜地。阖闾花费和动用了大量人力和物力为他自己及王室修建各种娱乐场所，太湖之滨周边的几座山成为他的猎苑、狩猎场和游乐园。在花费大量金钱满足个人需求的同时，阖闾还采取很多措施来提升国家整体实力，尤其是开放水上交通，排干大量沼泽湿地。正是阖闾睿智、公正的领导令他获得了民众的支持，统治日趋稳固。他精兵强军，邻近诸国皆不能敌，因此在他参加的四到五次战争中，他均能打败对手并按照自己意愿与对方签订条约。

尽管阖闾夺得王位，吴国发展欣欣向荣，但有一个人仍然活着，这令阖闾非常害怕。这个人就是吴王僚的儿子，也是被阖闾篡夺的吴国王位的合法继承人。他叫庆忌，早前随吴国军队入侵越国，为了此次出征，吴国

tion, that Hoh Lü had, by Wu Tz-sü's advice, taken advantage of the occasion to execute his purpose to destroy Liao and seize the throne. K'ing K'i on hearing of his father's death fled to a neighboring court for safety, and Hoh Lü feared that he might finally succeed in inducing that country to assist him to avenge his father's death, and obtain his rightful possession of the kingdom. So great was Hoh Lü's dread that he told Tz-sü that he could neither eat with relish nor sleep in peace. Tz-sü came to his rescue as usual, and provided him with a plan to rid him of K'ing K'i, and a man to execute that plan. This tool of Tz-sü, named Yao Li was a former acquaintance, a desperate man and ready for any work of blood. He agreed to put K'ing K'i out of the way, but in order to gain his confidence, preparatory to his destruction, Yao Li pretended to flee for his life and came to the court where K'ing K'i had taken refuge, while Hoh Lü, according to the previous agreement, put Yao Li's wife and children to death, —Yao Li thus sacrificing his family from devotion to his king. Yao Li pretended to complain bitterly to K'ing K'i of the injustice and oppression he had suffered from Hoh Lü and urged him to join him in a plot to avenge themselves on the tyrant for the wrongs that they both had suffered. K'ing K'i believed his story, and three months later they started for the court of Wu with the purpose of assassinating Hoh Lü. On crossing a certain stream in a boat and while K'ing K'i was entirely off his guard, Yao Li ran his sword through him and threw his body into the water.

But although he had succeeded so well in his plot, Yao Li was filled with remorse for the murder he had committed, and would not return to Hoh Lü to report his success and receive his reward, but died by his own hand lamenting with his dying breath the perfidy and ambition that had caused the sacrifice of so many innocent lives. Hoh Lü reigned twenty years, during which time he succeeded in extending the borders of his kingdom and improving the condition of the people to such a degree that the country of Wu came to be one of the strongest and most famous of the principalities into which the country of China was practically divided at that time, B. C. 500. On his death he was succeeded by his son Fu Ch'ai.

This son had none of the energy or ambition of his illustrious father. He soon gave evidence of an entire want of qualification for his high position—preferring his own ease and comfort to the strength and prosperity of his kingdom. He wasted the revenues of the country in building and adorning palaces and towers, in laying out and maintaining game parks and pleasure gardens, and in

几乎出动了所有能调动的兵力，而正是在他离开吴国期间，阖闾在伍子胥的建议之下，趁机实现了杀死吴王僚夺取王位的计划。当听闻其父被杀的消息之后，庆忌逃往邻国避难。阖闾担心庆忌最终会说服邻国助其为父报仇，进而夺回原本属于他的王位。阖闾告诉伍子胥，他为此整日吃不香睡不好。伍子胥像以往一样替阖闾分忧解难，提供了一个除去庆忌的计划以及一个执行该计划的人。伍子胥提到的这个人，名叫要离，是伍子胥的老熟人，一个亡命之徒，随时准备从事任何血腥工作。要离同意去刺杀庆忌，但为了获得庆忌的信任为刺杀做准备，要离假装逃命来到庆忌所避难的国家，而阖闾，根据之前约定，将要离的妻子和孩子处死——要离为了向他的国王尽忠，牺牲了自己的家庭。要离假装痛苦地向庆忌抱怨，阖闾让他遭受了不公待遇和压迫，并且鼓动庆忌加入他的计划，为他们两人所受之冤屈向暴君复仇。庆忌相信了要离的话，三个月后，他们前往吴国王宫试图刺杀阖闾。当他们乘坐的小船横渡小溪之时，要离趁庆忌没有防备，用剑刺穿庆忌，并将他的尸体扔入水中。

尽管刺杀计划执行得非常完美，但要离因为谋杀庆忌而感到悔恨，不愿回到阖闾那里汇报并领取奖赏。要离最后自杀，临终前他为自己的背叛以及为达目的而牺牲这么多无辜的性命感到哀伤。阖闾一共统治了20年，在此期间，他成功地开拓了疆土，提高了人民生活水平，吴国也成为当时（公元前500年）中国各大诸侯国之中最为强大、最著名的国家。阖闾死后，其子夫差继承王位。

与其名声显赫的父亲相比，夫差没有阖闾那样的精力和雄心。很快事实便证明他完全没有资格继承王位——相比国家的繁荣和强大，夫差更追求个人的安逸和舒适。他将国家收入浪费在宫殿和宝塔的修建与装修上，

supporting a gorgeous and dissolute court.

Entirely engrossed in present pleasure, he had no policy to pursue in government affairs. He therefore most foolishly released Keu Tsien, King of Yueh, and his minister, Fan Li, whom Hoh Lü had left in captivity. Not only so but he appointed the ex-king of Yueh as feudal lord of a large portion of his former dominions embracing the principal part of the modern Chehkiang province, with Hangchow as his capital. The far seeing Wu Tz-sü, knowing the folly of such a procedure, earnestly remonstrated with Fu Ch'ai against such a suicidal movement, taking occasion at the same time to warn him as to the results that were to be apprehended from his dissolute life and useless extravagance. Fu Ch'ai became exasperated at such presumptuous reproof, and instead of regarding the counsel of his faithful servant, he sent him a sword and ordered him to commit suicide. Tz-sü died accordingly by his own hand mourning the ingratitude of the dissolute king, who owed his throne and the strength of his kingdom principally to the wise counsel and faithful administration of Tz-sü. But Fu Ch'ai was glad to be rid of such a troublesome counselor whose frequent remonstrances were as thorns in his side, and who had nothing but words of reproach and warning for him amid all the pleasures and revelries in which he desired to be left unmolested.

He had the body of Tz-sü thrown into the canal near Sü K'eu on the shore of the Great Lake, where in subsequent years a temple was erected to his memory.

Keu Tsieu on being restored to his dominions, immediately began preparations for fulfilling the vow that he had made while a captive and a menial of the king of Wu to be avenged on Wu for his long and bitter captivity. But the execution of this purpose was an arduous and apparently hopeless undertaking. He found his country prostrate at the feet of Wu without an army and without resources, while Wu was in the full career of victory and prosperity. But notwithstanding the difficulties in the way, his purpose was fixed and he pursued it unflinchingly for more than ten long years, and whenever he found himself disposed to become contented with his surroundings while his wrongs remained unavenged, he would eat bitter herbs with his food, and make his bed on leaves and limbs of trees, that he might not forget the bitterness of his sufferings in Wu, or his purpose to be avenged.

His first aim was to secure the confidence and esteem of the people. This he did by lightening their burdens of taxation; by constant regard for their lives and

浪费在猎苑和游乐场的规划与维护上，浪费在维持宫中豪华奢靡的生活上。

夫差完全沉溺于当前的享乐之中，无心处理国家事务。夫差做得最为愚蠢的一件事就是释放了被阖闾囚禁的越王勾践和他的大臣范蠡。不仅如此，夫差还将之前属于越国的一大块土地分封给勾践，这块土地包括了现在浙江省的大部分地区，而现今杭州则是浙江省省会。目光长远的伍子胥，得知夫差这一愚蠢的做法之后，严肃地向夫差提出了抗议，反对这一自杀式的决定，并趁此机会告诫夫差，无谓的奢侈和放荡的生活将会带来严重后果。夫差被伍子胥的冒犯和批评激怒，他不但不重视这位忠臣提出的建议，反而派人送了一把剑给伍子胥，并令伍子胥自杀。伍子胥在哀伤这位放荡君主忘恩负义的同时，只好遵命自杀。事实上，夫差能够坐稳王位以及吴国能够不断壮大，主要都归功于伍子胥的建议和管理。但夫差很高兴除掉这样一位麻烦的谋士，伍子胥的抗议常常令他如芒刺在背，而且每当夫差沉浸在狂欢中不想被打扰之时，伍子胥往往对其进行批评和劝告。

夫差将伍子胥的尸体扔进靠近太湖之滨的胥口镇的运河之中，几年之后民众在那里建起了一座祠堂以纪念伍子胥。

一回到自己的领土，勾践便立刻着手准备为自己所长期遭受的囚禁之苦复仇，以兑现自己在成为吴王囚犯和仆人时立下的誓言。但实现这一目标是一项极其艰难而且看似毫无希望的任务。勾践发现自己的国家既无军队又无资源，屈服在吴国脚下，而吴国则处于鼎盛时期，繁荣昌盛。尽管前路充满困难，但勾践的目标不变，他坚持不懈地努力了10年，每次当他发现自己对周围环境感到满意之时，只要一想到大仇未报，他便会在吃饭时尝苦菜，在睡床上铺上树叶和树枝，以提醒自己不忘在吴国所遭受的痛苦和屈辱，不忘复仇。

勾践的第一个目标就是重拾民众对他的信心和尊重。通过减轻民众税

property; by his just government and by the simplicity of his own life. It was not long ere the people were united as one man in his support, and ready to follow wherever he should lead. But Wu was too strong to be successfully invaded. Strategy must first be employed to weaken the country and throw its king off his guard. Kue Tsien's minister Fan Li, knowing the dissolute character of Fu Ch'ai and his love of pleasure and display, devised ten different plans that were to be pursued by his master in order to accomplish the overthrow of Wu, each of the plans depending for its success upon the dissipated habits of Fu Ch'ai. Among these plans the first was to send heavy tribute and costly presents to the king of Wu. These presents were always willingly received by Fu Ch'ai, who believed them to be evidences of the good will of Keu Tsien. Another plan was to send the most skilled workmen that Yueh could produce to Fu Ch'ai to assist in building his palaces, pleasure houses &c. This plan succeeded admirably. For Fu Ch'ai, on obtaining skilled mechanics of a superior kind, was incited to greater extravagance in building, and his waste of money, and the enforced labor of many thousands of his subjects on his extravagant building operations, caused widespread murmuring and dissatisfaction among the people. The "Beautiful Su Tower" was built at this time, and the waste of money and the oppression of the people that occurred in connection with its erection were almost enough of themselves to cause Fu Ch'ai the loss of his kingdom. Another of Fan Li's plans was to send to Fu Ch'ai presents of the most beautiful women that could be found in Yueh. Several such were sent, and Fu Ch'ai gladly accepted them as he did former presents from the same source, blind to the object of the donor, and oblivious of the fact that for several years his kingdom had been growing weaker, his army scattered and his defences falling into ruin. Among the last of the women sent by Keu Tsien was Si She, whom he had found and trained in all the female accomplishments of the time. She has been regarded in all subsequent time as the *ne plus ultra* of feminine beauty. Fu Ch'ai was delighted with her, and went to still greater lengths of extravagance in fitting up his palace and pleasure resorts for her, and wholly abandoned himself to dissipation and revelry.

The time was now ripe for executing the tenth and last plan of Fan Li, which was to invade Wu. Keu Tsien accordingly led his army, which he had to brought to a state of great strength, to the attack of Wu, Fu Ch'ai was wholly unprepared for this invasion. He had all along flattered himself that Keu Tsien was his faithful vassal and firm friend. But he was undeceived when it was too late. His sol-

收负担，关心民众生活和财产，给予公正领导以及要求自己过艰苦朴素的生活，勾践达成了这一目标。不久之后，越国民众再次团结起来支持勾践，并且随时准备追随勾践。但是吴国过于强大，很难入侵。因此，首先必须采取策略来削弱吴国实力，让吴王放松警惕。勾践的大夫范蠡非常了解夫差放荡的性格以及对享乐的追求，他提出了10条不同的方案，由勾践执行，为了达到推翻吴国的目的，每一条方案都是针对夫差铺张浪费的习惯。在这些方案中，第一条就是向夫差进献大量贡品以及贵重礼物。对此，夫差总是非常乐意笑纳，在他看来，这就是勾践示好的证明。另一条方案是派送越国的能工巧匠到吴国，帮助夫差修建宫殿、游乐场所等。这一方案很快便收到成效。在得到了这些能工巧匠之后，夫差大兴土木，花费大量金钱、动用成千上万劳力修建奢华建筑，从而引起了国内民众的普遍不满和抱怨。著名的"姑苏台"就修建于此时。建造"姑苏台"所花费的金钱以及对人民的压迫，足以让夫差失去他的国家。范蠡另一条方案就是将越国最漂亮的女子进献给夫差。很多这样的美女先后被献给夫差，夫差愉快地接受下来，就如同接受之前的礼物一样，对进献者的目的不闻不问，同时也忘记了吴国的现实状况，经过这些年，吴国国力越来越弱，军队四散而去，防御工事也沦为废墟。在勾践进献的最后一批美女中，有一位叫西施，她是由勾践发现的，勾践对其进行了女性才艺全方位的培训。西施被后世公认为女性美貌的完美典范。夫差非常喜欢西施，不遗余力地为西施修建宫殿和游乐场，自己完全沉溺于寻欢作乐之中。

范蠡的第10条方案也是最后一条方案，即攻占吴国，如今时机已经成熟。勾践率领着他的军队进攻吴国，越国军队整体实力很强。夫差对于越国入侵完全没有准备。长期以来，夫差自认为勾践是他忠实的臣子和坚定的朋友。但当他醒悟过来时，一切已经太晚了。他的军队在纪律严明的越

diers fled before the disciplined forces of Keu Tsien, and his dilapidated fortifications fell an easy prey to his now powerful enemy. In a very short time Keu Tsien made a complete conquest of the country. Fu Ch'ai fled and vainly sought a place of safety, but finding that he could not escape, he committed suicide, lamenting his foolishness and rashness in refusing to listen to the advice of the faithful Tz-sü. But his lamentations were useless. He paid the penalty of his folly by the loss of his throne and his life, and the principality of Wu that had continued intact for nearly 800 years became extinct.

The Kingdom of Wu never regained its independence. Yueh held it as a tributary for a number of years, when both were subjugated by Ts'u. About B. C. 300, Ts'u was in turn conquered and annexed to the dominions of She Hwang Ti, the first emperor of the T'sin. He divided the whole empire into districts or provinces（郡）, and the former kingdom of Wu was a part of the province of Kew Ki of which Hangchow was the capital.

During the time of the Three Kingdoms, about A. D. 250, the old kingdom of Wu formed a part of the new kingdom of Wu founded by Sun Kuen（孙权）whose capital was at Nanking.

国军队面前四散逃亡，年久失修的防御工事很轻易地落入了强劲的敌方之手。在很短时间内，勾践征服了整个吴国。夫差仓皇出逃并找到了一处藏身之所，但他发现已无路可逃。夫差哀叹自己的愚蠢和鲁莽，后悔没有听取忠诚的伍子胥所提出的建议，但是，哀叹并没有用处，他最终选择了自杀。夫差为自己的愚蠢付出了代价，不但失去了王位也失去了生命，而延续了近 800 年的吴国也因此而灭亡。

此后，吴国再也没有恢复独立，而是作为越国的附属国存在了很多年，直到越国和吴国一起被楚国所征服。公元前 300 年前后，楚国接连战败，后来又被秦朝的第一位皇帝秦始皇所征服，并成为秦国的附属国。秦始皇后将整个天下划分成不同的郡县，而之前的吴国则成了会稽郡的一部分，杭州则是会稽郡的治所。

三国期间，大约在公元 250 年，旧的吴国成为由孙权建立的新吴国的一部分，而新吴国的国都设在南京。

My Chinese Days

我的在华岁月

（古列尔玛 · F. 阿尔索普著　徐冰、徐舟涟译）

古列尔玛·F.阿尔索普(Gulielma F. Alsop, 1881—1978),美国内科医生，20 世纪初曾作为传教士医生来到中国工作，在上海生活多年并在广仁医院（St. Elizabeth's Hospital for Women and Children）担任住院医生。1917 年回到美国，同年任职于伯纳德学院（Barnard's College），创建该校的医学系并担任系主任达 35 年。古列尔玛著书颇多，其中《我的在华岁月》（*My Chinese Days*）(利特尔 & 布朗出版社, 1918)共 20 章，主要讲述主人公——年轻的威廉敏娜医生——到上海圣玛格丽特医院（St. Margaret's Hospital）当传教士医生的所见所闻及其在此背景之下的个人恋情发展。

节选部分为该书第十一至十三章内容，主要讲述威廉敏娜医生应友人格瑞斯医生之邀来苏州的实习、休闲之旅。她以西方女性的视角分别描绘了苏城内外的风光、传统工艺、传说，以及陆上与水上居民不同的生活方式等。第十一章主要讲述威廉敏娜医生乘坐轿子从火车站初进苏州城的一路见闻；第十二章主要介绍格瑞斯医生带她坐船出城，观赏鱼鹰捕鱼并讲述相关传说；第十三章则是威廉敏娜医生在深夜跟随格瑞斯医生去李宅出诊辅助接生，骑着毛驴穿梭于苏州街巷时的历险故事。三个章节环环相扣，勾勒出 20 世纪初苏城内外的景致风貌。

XI THE WALLED CITY

EDWARD insisted that I accept an invitation that came for me from Soochow a few days later. Doctor Donnellon also wanted me to go, and it was my regular vacation time. Around Shanghai the government troops were victorious, and the panic was subsiding. One by one the refugee families returned to the Native City, and the hospital began to take on its usual appearance of order and quiet. In the afternoons after tea it became a fad to ride out to the Arsenal and pick up spent bullets for souvenirs. Miss Chase at Jessfield had two tall conical shells on the mantelpiece which she had picked up after a riot. Always when I visited her my eyes returned to those unexploded shells on the mantelpiece among the vases of blue and white plum blossoms. One of the men said they might explode some day. They were to me symbolic of life in China, so smooth and shiny and symmetrical, yet with a deadly power hidden within. Here and there through the settlement, broken windows and tiny round holes through the solid wood doorways testified to the excitement of the past weeks. But otherwise it seemed all over. Up the river however the rebels were drawing near Nankin.

I hated to admit it, but I found myself rather shaky after the episode at Kaung Wan, and I was glad enough to accept my Soochow invitation. So far I had not been out of Shanghai; I had been too busy. As the wide pathless fields of the country around Shanghai had caught my imagination, so my first sight of a walled city rising on the plain was to take my breath away.

Edward came to the station to see me off. " I wish you were coming with me," I said. " I suddenly feel that I am going to be homesick."

"For me?" asked Edward. "That is the first real sign of devotion on your part that I have seen."

"I know you pine for the clinging vine," I said to tease him a little.

第十一章　有城墙的城市

几天后我收到一份来自苏州的邀请函，爱德华竭力怂恿我受邀前行。多娜伦医生也表达了同样的意见，而且邀约的时间恰好是我通常的休假时段。在上海，国民军取得了决定性胜利，城里的恐慌气氛逐渐消退。逃难家庭纷纷回到老城厢，医院也开始恢复以往的秩序和安静。下午喝完茶，大家会坐车到江南制造局捡拾弹壳当纪念品，此举风靡一时。蔡斯小姐住在杰斯菲尔德附近[1]，她家壁炉架上就放着两颗圆锥形的长长的子弹，都是她在一次暴乱后捡到的。每次去她那儿，我的眼睛就不由自主地被她壁炉架上那些尚未爆炸的子弹头吸引，它们陈列在印有蓝白梅花的花瓶中间。有个男性访客曾经说，这些子弹没准哪一天就会爆炸。于我而言，它们象征着中国式生活，表面平静、闪亮而对称，内里却隐藏着致命的力量。我们的租界区到处都是破碎的窗户，坚实的木制门框上布满弹孔，它们表明过去几周里战争激烈到何等程度。不过除此之外，一切似乎已然归于平静。然而，国民军沿黄浦江北上，正向南京逼近。

不得不承认，江湾战役后我发现自己变得相当脆弱，所以非常乐意接受苏州之邀。至今为止，这还是我第一次离开上海，之前一直很忙。上海周边有大片旷野，人迹罕至，一度令我沉醉不已，即将看到平原上升起一座带城墙的城市，我想当它映入我眼帘的那一刻，我必定会激动得难以言表。

爱德华来车站为我送行。“我希望你能和我一起去，”我说，“突然感觉我会想念上海的。”

“因为我的缘故吗？”爱德华问，“这可是你第一次流露出对我们的感情很投入的样子。”

“我知道你思慕小鸟依人型的姑娘。”我稍微揶揄了他一下。

[1]　今上海中山公园。

"No, I don't," he said. "I only pine for you. Set a date and set it soon, and we'll go off and take a lovely honeymoon all over China, and you shall see all the world."

"It sounds like a famous temptation," I said.

"Well?" he questioned.

" I can't decide right here, all in a moment," I said.

" But I thought you had been deciding at your leisure all these last weeks. You said you were deciding. I want you."

The guard came along, clanging to the carriage doors. The vendors of food, of eggs boiled in tea, of soggy dough balls, of bottled TanSan water, moved away reluctantly from the carriage windows and lost their interest in this particular trainload of people.

"Good-by," said Edward, holding my hand through the open window. "Don't forget I will want an answer when you come back."

Off we went. It took only a few moments to leave Shanghai behind and to run out into those limitless plains that had so allured me all winter. It was unbelievable! Like some dinosaur, huge and crushing, the train streaked through those fields of the past. On each side they stretched, quiet, waving with groves of fresh green bamboo grasses and the lush green of the new rice. The planting season was over, but here and there a few farmers were thigh deep in mud, transplanting. Lazy buffaloes browsed between the cultivated patches, guarded each by an urchin. The little boys lolled side-saddle on the wide backs of the huge animals and switched at the flies with a leaf-tipped branch. No fences, no walls, no dividing partitions of any kind were in sight. Around the clan-like family dwellings grew groves of bamboo and camphor and an occasional sycamore. Through the leaves I caught glimpses of the pointed, thatched roofs of the houses. The walls were of plaited bamboo branches. Of course there was no paint anywhere, and the houses seemed as much an integral part of the fields as the trees. Between the fields meandered little rills of muddy water. Across the fields I suddenly saw the slow, stately sails of junks. The hulls of the boats were invisible; only the billowing brown sails moved along over the fields like cloud shadows. It

“不，不是这样的，”他说，“我只思慕你一人。只要你定个日子，越快越好，我们就立即出发去度蜜月，走遍中国，畅游世界。”

“这话听起来像一个极好的诱惑。”我说。

“那么你会如何作答？”他问道。

“现在还没法儿决定，太仓促了。”我说。

“可是我以为过去几个礼拜你一直在闲暇时考虑这件事呢。你说过你在认真考虑的。我需要你。”

列车员来了，哐当一声关上了车厢门。那些兜售食物的小贩，卖茶叶蛋的、卖汤团的、卖瓶装碳酸水的，都极不情愿地纷纷从车窗跟前走开了，对于这一车即将出发的乘客，他们迅速失去了兴趣。

“再见。”爱德华说道，穿过敞开的车窗，他还紧握着我的手不放，“别忘记，等你回来，我想得到你的答复。”

出发！不消片刻，列车便将上海抛在身后，驶入了那片整个冬季都令我着迷的广袤无垠的平原。坐火车简直太不可思议了！列车如同一只碾压一切的大恐龙，在历史底蕴浓厚的田野上疾驰而过。车窗外，田野向两侧铺展开去，静谧沉稳，嫩绿的竹林和新种下的长势茂盛的禾苗在向我们招手。播种季节虽已结束，田里三三两两还有农民踩着及膝的泥土在轮种。水牛懒洋洋地吃着草，闲步于秩序井然的稻田间，每头牛都由一个小屁孩看着。牧童们悠闲地侧骑在水牛宽大的背脊上，用一根带叶子的树枝驱赶着苍蝇。目力所及之处，没有篱笆，没有墙垣，没有任何形式的隔断。类似家族群落的住家附近，长着成片翠竹、樟树，间或还有一棵美国梧桐。透过繁茂的枝叶，我瞥见一座座尖顶的、覆有茅草的房子，墙面由竹子编成。整栋房子没有一处刷过油漆，因此看上去和周围的树木一样与田野浑然一体。浑浊的细沟迂回在稻田之间。越过田野，我猛然看到了庄严而缓慢移动的船帆。船体不见踪影，唯见棕色的船帆随风摇摆，在田野上缓缓移动，如

was Soochow Creek off there, below its banks, winding down from the interior to the shore. "The Interior", "Up River", are magic words to the dweller in Shanghai. They represent the unknown and its magic. I took a little quick breath of delight. Here was I too going to "the Interior", voyaging back fathoms deep into the unconscious past of the race.

My friend, Doctor Grace, had been a college mate in Old Philadelphia. I had met her at the wharf when she came out, but I had not seen her since. She had said in her letter that she would meet me at the station if she could get through with clinic in time. If not, she would send the hospital boy. I had only a suit case for my short visit.

The two hours passed like two minutes. With startling suddenness I saw the walled city rise on the horizon quite distinct and clear. It must have been visible several minutes before I saw it, because when I first turned, there it was, battlemented and hoary and romantic, like any Maxfield Parrish picture but a thousand times more real. Around it swept the wide brown moat, a real moat full of water and busy with rowboats and junks. The walls were great, high, massive structures. I saw people walking on them. Turrets marked the octagonal corners. Ramparts of green sod ran up to the edge of the walls, and tangled masses of vines with delicate white blossoms cascaded from the top. I couldn't take my eyes from the sight.

At the station a crowd of coolies, sedan-chair carriers, and donkey men clustered around the exit, crying their fare to the city of Beautiful Soo, for the railroad station is outside the city and across the moat. I looked in vain for Doctor Grace. Not a familiar face is in sight. I picked up my suit case and followed the rest of the passengers out of the exit gate. A tall coolie waved a piece of paper at every foreigner who passed him. I saw them looking at the paper and shaking their heads and passing on. I was curious about the paper. I walked in line so that I too should have a chance to look at the strange writing on the paper. The

同云彩的影子一般。远处就是苏州河，顺着堤岸蜿蜒曲折地自内地流向黄浦江。“内地”和“上游”对于居住在上海的人而言是富有魔力的词语，它们代表了未知地域及其神奇魅力。我愉悦地快速吸了一口气，现在我也将去往“内地”，穿越回这个民族潜意识里的记忆深处。

我的朋友格瑞斯医生和我是老费城的大学校友。我与她曾在码头邂逅，当时她正巧从船上出来，不过自那之后却未曾和她谋过面。她在信中表示，如果诊所工作能及时完成，她就会去车站接我。否则，会派医院的帮工去接站。因为此次拜访很短暂，我只带了一只箱子。

两小时的车程犹如两分钟飞逝而过。蓦然抬头，但见那座被城墙环绕的城市矗立在地平线上，真切而醒目。当我尚未在意之时，它一定早已出现，因为我第一次转头时，苏州便赫然在目了。城墙上垛口分明，显得古老悠远，传奇而浪漫，仿佛马科斯菲尔德·帕里斯[1]笔下的每一幅绘画都变成了现实，但是眼前的景致比那些画作更真实千百倍。城外有条宽阔的护城河，呈棕褐色，那是一条真正河水充盈的护城河，手划船和帆船往来其上，好不繁忙。城墙结构高耸、巨大、厚实。我看到上面人来人往。八角形的城墙角上设有碉楼。满墙的青草蔓延到城墙边缘，大片相互缠绕的藤蔓从墙顶悬垂而下，上面盛开着细小的白花，如瀑布般倾泻。此番美景把我看呆了。

一群苦力、抬轿人以及赶驴人拥堵在火车站的出口处，为带游客去游览姑苏，争相吆喝着车价，这是因为火车站建在城外护城河对岸的缘故。人群中我没有找到格瑞斯医生。四周也看不见任何熟悉的面孔。我提起行李箱，跟着其他乘客来到出口处大门外。一个高个子苦力在向每一个经过的外国人挥舞一张纸。只见那些外国人看看纸上的内容，摇摇头就继续往前走了。我颇感好奇，很想知道那上面写着什么。我排在那些人后面，这

[1] 马科斯菲尔德·帕里斯：美国画家、插画家（1870—1966），出生于宾夕法尼亚州的费城，作品里常出现黑白色、蓝色和几何图案等，因这些饱满的色调和理想化的新古典主义意象而闻名。

man before me had passed on. The coolie thrust the paper in my face. I gasped in sheer surprise, for on that mysterious paper that had been presented to each passenger who had descended from the train was my name.

"For Doctor Wilhelmina," it said in Doctor Grace's familiar handwriting. What a primitive method, yet how simple and effective! At my smile of recognition, the coolie nodded as if relieved, grabbed my suit case, and led me out of the station towards the stand of sedan chairs. Like waiting palanquins, they were ranged along the path with their groups of bearers, sometimes two by the poorer chairs, more usually three, and occasionally four, if the chair was meant for a fat man. Some were ancient affairs with closely drawn curtains; some more modern, of wicker, with their gay curtains looped back. All around me was the bustle of people making bargains and stowing away their belongings. Just before me a portly Chinaman with several bundles done up in silk handkerchiefs got into a sedan chair. The little bearers stooped into position under the shafts. One gave a guttural grunt as signal to the man behind. With a sideways lurch they rose to their feet and swung off down the path at a brisk walk. Fascinated, I was standing watching them.

"Take care," shouted the hospital coolie at my elbow. I jumped aside to let a string of donkeys pass. Astride each little fellow dangled a Chinaman, their long legs quite able to help along by giving the ground a kick.

Then I got into my first sedan chair. The hospital coolie tucked my suit case under my feet and then disappeared. I supposed he had given ample instructions to the bearers. With a simultaneous swoop, they crawled into the shafts which are closed with a crossbar before and behind. This bar rests on the back of their shoulders across the neck. They have rags that they roll into a bundle and stick under the crossbar, much as a violinist sticks a handkerchief under his chin. The shafts, that stick out before and behind the chair, are about four feet long. Swung

样便也有机会瞄一眼那纸上的奇怪内容。排在我前面的乘客经过那位苦力后，后者猛地将纸张挥到我面前。我惊讶地张大了嘴巴，因为那张让每位下车旅客驻足辨认的神秘纸张上写着的正是我的名字。

“致威廉敏娜医生。”纸上写着。那是格瑞斯医生熟悉的笔迹。多么原始的接站方法，却又那么简单奏效！看到我微笑着示意自己便是纸上的接站对象，那位苦力连连点头，仿佛如释重负，他一把接过我的箱子，带我走出车站，来到接客的轿子停歇处。如同东方古代的肩舆，这些轿子沿小径一字排开，旁边就是三五成群的轿夫们，蹩脚点的轿子边有两位轿夫，多数轿子边通常是三位轿夫，偶尔如果接到的客人是个胖子，轿子要四人才能抬得动。有些轿子造型古旧，挂着密不透风的帘子；另一些则款式现代，由柳条编织而成，上面艳丽的帘子被打成结向后卷了起来。我的周围一片嘈杂，人们不是忙于讨价还价，就是在搬运行李。排在我之前的是一位发福的中国人，他拿着好几个用丝巾扎好的包裹，爬进了一乘轿子。矮小的轿夫们弯腰走到杠子下面各就各位。一人发出低沉的哼声，作为示意后面的轿夫起轿的信号。轿子稍微前倾之际，轿夫们便同时起身，将之晃晃悠悠从地面抬起，跑了起来，步履轻盈。我站在那儿端详着他们的动作，十分着迷。

“小心！”那位从医院来的苦力在一旁喊道。我赶忙跳到一边，给一队驴子让道。每头驴子上都坐着一个晃荡着腿的中国人，他们的长腿足以蹬地，助力毛驴一路前行。

平生第一次，我坐进了轿子。医院派来的苦力将行李箱塞到我脚下后就不见了踪影，想来他必定已向轿夫们交代清楚要把我送去何地。轿夫们同时俯下身子，钻进抬杆构成的轿框中，抬杆前后各装有一根可以开合的横杆。横杆越过轿夫的脖子，落在他们的肩背上。轿夫们把破布卷成一团垫在横杆下，这与小提琴手演奏时将一方手帕垫在下巴上的做法如出一辙。抬杆自轿座前后伸出，各有约 4 英尺长。晃晃荡荡地，我如同一位被高抬

aloft in the air like a veritable queen we started down the rough path. I had three bearers. They walked with a rhythmic jerky movement, and at every twenty paces or so one of the bearers gave a different grunt. The third man, who had been walking alongside mopping himself, eyes and chest and abdomen, would spring into place. There would be an infinitesimal halt while the exchange was made from shoulder to shoulder, and on we would go. Over it all streamed the yellow sunshine, and on my left rose the green ramparts and lichen gray walls of the ancient city.

At the edge of the moat I was put down, and we all boarded a ferry. On the opposite side I got in again. With a whoop they caught me up and off we went, up and up, through the side gate in the walls, and into the city itself. Never will I forget that first ride through Soochow. Perhaps the fact that I was alone, with no one to talk to, and that I was a stranger, going I knew not where, lent me a sense of adventure. However it came about, I felt transported into the land of Aladdin and the forty thieves. All the sights that met my eyes were fantastic and bizarre, out of shape and proportion with modern life. Great jars of tea stood at the corners of the streets, out of which any one who thirsted dipped a cup of brown tea in a pale, sand-colored, wooden dipper. I watched the carry-coolies set down their burdens, wipe the sweat from out their eyes, and lift up a dripping dipperful of tea to their mouths. Each jar stood in a wooden stand under a bent roof, like the shelter one sometimes sees over old-fashioned gates. Each one was big enough to hide a man.

The curtains of my chair were looped back, for was I not a bold, foreign woman who looked at the passers-by! I saw hardly any women on the streets, — now and then a coolie woman carrying a kettle of boiling water which she had bought at the nearest cook-shop for a few cash, or an old hag sitting in a doorway. The streets were like the alleyways of Venice. At any moment I could put out my two hands and touch the houses on either side. The Soochow Creek entered the city and ran through the town in a network of canals. The beautiful arched bridges

在空中的、真正的女王，我们顺着高低不平的小路出发了。我的轿子有三位轿夫。他们行走时轿子一颤一颤的，富有节奏，每走 20 步左右，其中一人便会发出不同于另外两人的哼声。第三位轿夫原本一直跟在旁边，不时抹着额头、胸膛和肚子上的汗水，这时他会根据节奏，迅速就位，换下一位轿夫。每当他们换肩膀抬时大家就稍做休息，再继续赶路。金色的阳光倾洒在轿子上，成片覆盖着绿色植被的壁垒和青灰色的古城墙开始在我左手边出现了。

到了护城河边，他们让我下轿，大家一起登上一条摆渡船。渡到对岸，我又坐回轿子里。随着一声吆喝，他们抬起我坐的轿子出发了，走啊走，穿过城墙边门，我们进到古城中。我永远不会忘记这头一回坐轿子穿越苏城的经历。论其缘由，或许因为我当时孤身一人，连个说话的伴儿也没有，而且作为外来者，又不知即将去向何处，这些都赋予我以某种冒险感。闯荡的情绪如何形成，且不去探究，反正我感到自己似乎一下置身于阿拉丁和四十大盗的神奇国度。目力所及，皆乃光怪陆离，奇妙无比，现代生活在此变得面目全非、支离破碎。巨大的茶缸安放在各个街角，任何一位口渴的路人，只需用一个沙色、发了白的木勺，就能从中舀上一杯棕色茶水饮用。我看到拉货的苦力会将货物卸下，把它放在茶缸旁，擦擦额头的汗水，从茶缸里舀上一勺，勺子还滴滴答答的，他就径直将茶水倒进嘴里了。每只茶缸都放在一个木架上，上面搭有倾斜的顶棚，就像人们时常在旧式大门上方见到的顶棚一样。每个顶棚的面积足以容下一人站立。

轿子上的帘子打成结卷了起来，这不就是为我这个胆大的外国女子看往来行人准备的嘛！街上几乎看不到什么女性，时不时只有提着一壶沸水的苦力女子走过，水是她花几个铜板从最近的灶头买的，或者偶尔能看到门口坐着位老婆婆。苏州的街道和威尼斯的巷子差不多。我随时都能从轿子里伸手触摸到两边的房子。苏州河流入城中，形成密集的河道网络，贯

of China spanned the crossings at every turn. Without warning, up we would go, over high flights of irregular steps. At the summit of the bridge I would look up and down the canal and see the houses built like a solid wall along its edge. Some of the streets were empty and deserted, and again we traversed the thoroughfares of the town. We went along the Street of the Weavers. In each low, open room I saw the looms on which were stretched wondrous fabrics of flowered brocade, palest pink and baby blue and bridal crimson. I wondered how they were kept so clean in such darkened houses. From the Street of the Weavers we turned into the Street of the Jade Cutters. Here the whirring sound of the wheels filled the air, and the cutters stood stooping over their ancient revolving grindstones. We came out on the market square before a huge temple. The air smelt faintly of incense and the sound of temple bells hung over the place.

On and on we went. A sense of unreality stole over me. We weren't going anywhere in particular, we were just going on and on, as I had always wanted to, seeing all the wonder of the whole world. I felt that this ancient, walled city contained everything in the world.

After an hour and a half of this wild, silent carrying into the unknown, I began to feel that I was being carried off in earnest. I wasn't really scared, but I felt pleasantly thrilled. Should I presently have to call out to a chance passer-by to rescue me? Did these silent, jogging men know where they were going, or had they become hypnotized by the regular motion? We were passing along an empty street. A wide stream of water ran at one side, and beyond it rose the walls of a house more pretentious than most. It was two stories high. Small grilled windows as big as a napkin overlooked the stream. A heavy wooden door studded with brass nails opened on to a steep flight of steps that led to the water's edge. The fringes of two black cypresses tipped the walls that ran down the side of the stream from the house. The water itself was sluggish, and a faint, iridescent green scum floated on its surface. Two or three helpless brown leaves were caught in this green mesh and lay listless and motionless. We were the only people in sight. A queer, dank smell pervaded the place. In the ooze between the house and the water, a large green toad with purple spots blinked his protruding eyes.

穿整座古城。每一次转弯，都能在路口看到横跨在那里的中式拱桥，线条优美。每次上桥前，我们都毫无防备，却不想台阶又高又陡、很不规则。到了桥顶，我仔细打量河道周边，发现成排的房子如墙体般傍河而建，坚不可摧。有些街道空寂无人，我们又一次穿过城里的主干大街。沿着织工街行进，我看到每一间低矮、敞开的房子里都放着织机，机子上绷着团花图案的织锦，浅粉、淡蓝、喜气的大红色跃然其上，精美绝伦。在光线如此黑黢黢的屋内，这些织品何以保存得如此干净，令人讶异。从织工街我们转进玉工街。此地到处是机轮的嗡嗡声，匠人们弯腰站在飞速转动的古老的切割机旁作业。出了巷子，我们来到一个市集广场，后面有座很大的殿阁。空气中隐约有香烛的味道，从殿里传来的钟声笼罩大地。

我们继续赶路。一种不真实感袭上心头，仿佛大家并非正前往任何特定之处，而只是一味地走呀走，好似我一直渴望去旅行，饱览世上所有美景一样。我感觉这座围在城墙里的古城装着整个世界。

这段旅程深入未知的街巷，悄然而疯狂，一个半小时后，我开始意识到轿夫们其实行色匆匆。这并没有令我害怕，反倒使我感到一种莫名的激动。我现在应该朝任何一个迎面走来的路人呼叫求救吗？这些沉默不语、步履匆匆的轿夫们知道该去哪里吗？还是他们已经被有规律的抬轿节奏给催了眠？我们正走在一条空荡荡的街上。一侧是条宽宽的河道，再远处便是一个深宅大院的外墙。房子有两层高，威风凛凛，傲然突兀。带栅栏的小窗犹如餐巾般大小，俯视着那条小河。木门沉重，上面嵌有铜钉，门前一段陡直的石阶通向河边。两棵深色柏树斜伸出墙外，高墙自房子展开，沿着小河一侧延伸开去。流水缓缓，水面隐隐漂着一层绿色浮沫。三两片落叶掉在这绿渊里，无精打采，动弹不得。街上只有我们一行人。一种怪异而潮湿的气味弥漫在此地。深宅与河道中间有一片泥地，一只背上长着紫色斑点的大蛤蟆趴在上面，它突出的眼睛忽闪忽闪。

"What man live this side?" I asked in Chinese.

At the sound of my voice, the front bearer turned around in surprise. This threw the back bearer out of step, and they both stopped. They sat my chair down and began mopping their brows. The third bearer joined the one in front.

"Ah! Teacher knows to speak Middle Kingdom speech," the man exclaimed in surprise.

"A little, little," I said. "Who lives in that big house?"

"A very rich man, oh Teacher, born before. But very sad. He has no sons. He is now old in years, already sixty and very venerable. He has four wives, but they all bear daughters. Only one year ago he married a young and beautiful wife. There was great rejoicing in the whole house. She will soon bear a child. All year he and all his wives have prayed daily at the temple that the child may be a son. The Small Wife was carried out herself daily, so devout was she, but now she goes out no longer. They are all awaiting the great day."

I looked at the silent, barred house with added interest. In what frame of mind was the young girl waiting within? A boy would mean the road to happiness. She would be the old man's favorite, the darling of his eyes. The Great First wife would no longer look down on her and lord it over her. But a girl meant despair. And as I looked at the house, a face appeared at one of the small, barred upper windows in the second story, at one of those windows no larger than a napkin. It was the face of a girl, and her eyes looked across at me, riding so brazenly, so jauntily through the streets of the strange city, in my outlandish clothes, with big feet. I wondered did she envy my freedom, or did she shrink from it? Did she think I was a "foreign devil" with bold, forward manners, or did she think I was the forerunner of a like liberty for the girls of China? I couldn't tell what she thought, but I felt her eyes calling to me. She held the bars that spanned the window in her fingers and pressed her face closer and closer against them. Her hands looked very slim and transparent, and her eyes held a look of appeal.

“什么人住这边？”我用中文问道。

听到我说话，前面的轿夫惊讶地回过头来。这一动作让后面的轿夫乱了方寸，于是两人都停了下来，把我的轿子放下，开始擦汗。第三位轿夫加入前面一起抬轿。

“啊！老师会说中国话！”他惊讶地喊道。

“一点点。”我说，“那座大房子里住着什么人？”

“哦，老师，住着一个非常有钱的人，早就养过小孩，可是十分不幸，他没有儿子。现在年纪大了，已经六十岁了，身体很虚弱。他有四个老婆，四个老婆都给他生了女儿。就在一年前，他又讨了一房年轻貌美的老婆。一大家子现在高兴得不得了，因为这个老婆马上就要生了。一年以来，这位老爷和他的四个老婆每天都去庙里拜菩萨，乞求生男孩。那个小老婆每天也被抬去许愿，真是虔诚，现在她是不能出门了。他们都在等待光宗耀祖那天早日到来。”

怀着愈加浓厚的兴趣，我看着这座寂静深锁的宅子。里面那位年轻姑娘究竟带着怎样的心情在待产呢？生男孩就意味着平步青云，她将成为老爷最得宠的妻子，他的心肝宝贝，再也不会被家中的大老婆瞧不起，被她欺负。但如果生的是女孩，那将是灭顶之灾。我正注视着房子，这时二楼一扇用栅栏防护的小窗后——那些还不如餐巾大小的窗户中的一扇后面——出现了一张人脸，一张女孩的脸，她的目光落在我身上，落在我这个穿着奇装异服，露着一双大脚，如此不知羞耻，如此洋洋自得，坐着轿子在陌生城市招摇过市的女子身上。不知道她是羡慕我所拥有的自由呢，还是在回避这种自由？她是把我视为举止勇敢前卫的“洋鬼子”呢，还是将我视为，对于中国姑娘而言，类似于追求自由的先行者？我不清楚她究竟怎么想，但感觉她的眼神在跟我说话。窗前的栅栏被她紧紧攥着，她把脸越发紧密地贴到横栅上。她的双手显得修长而苍白，眼中流露出求助的神情。

I smiled at her and waved my hand. She looked at me a moment, then she too smiled. Some one appeared over her shoulder and drew her away.

"Good to look upon," said the bearers with a sly smile. "The first wife is fierce come death."

They picked me up again and started off at the never-tiring dogtrot down the street.

"This house, call itself how?" I asked.

"The House of Li," they answered.

In about fifteen minutes we reached the compound. The mission had bought land on both sides of the street long years ago and had planted rows of trees. Frame cottages that reminded me of New England stood on both sides. More pretentious brick buildings, the girls' school and the boys' college, stood in their own campuses. Sweet peas look at me over the low fence, and a mass of petunias covered the posts of the porch. A wonderful sense of peace and cleanliness and busy activity pervaded the place. I heard the clear voices of children at play and the thud of a falling ball.

In the round stone gateway, the entrance to the hospital, which was built in Chinese style, stood Doctor Grace to receive me.

XII THE FISHING BIRDS

I NEVER got over my feeling of enchantment in Soochow. It has always remained for me a place of marvels, yet the people who lived there took it all as a matter of course. The contrast between the community of missionaries and the Chinese was sharper than in Shanghai. Each was more individual, more remote from the other. And to me the strangest thing about the situation was that the ultimate point of contact was not material but spiritual. Each separate race held fast to its own customs of eating and sleeping and dressing. The Chinese women saw our unbound feet, and, though some daring ones followed suit, the great mass of the women were satisfied with small feet, were still even proud of them.

我朝她微微一笑，挥了挥手，她看了我片刻，也笑了起来。有个人在她身后出现，把她拉走了。

“最好不要去管她，”轿夫们说时会心地一笑，“这家的大老婆凶来西。”

他们抬起我的轿子，不知疲倦地一路小跑，又出发了。

“这座房子，叫什么？”我问道。

“李宅。”他们答道。

15 分钟后我们抵达了大院。教会许多年前就已在这条街的两边购置了土地，并已种上了成排的树木。道路两旁一幢幢框架结构的小屋，使我想到了新英格兰。此地还建有许多气派的砖楼建筑，分别是女子学校和男子大学，它们各自坐落在独立的校园里。低矮的栅栏上，甜美的豌豆花探出头，一大丛矮牵牛把门廊的柱子给爬满了。这里洋溢着一种美妙的平静和整洁感，上下好一派繁忙的景象。我听到了孩子们做游戏时发出的清脆的声音，还有皮球落地的扑通声。

就在圆形石拱门下，就是这座中式风格医院的入口处，格瑞斯医生正站在那里迎接我的到来。

第十二章　鱼鹰

苏州魅力无穷，永远给我新鲜感。于我而言，这座城市不断上演着不可思议的故事，而苏州人却视之为稀松平常，不为所动。这里传教士群体与当地居民的矛盾比上海的情况更加尖锐。在苏州，这两个群体都更加独立，彼此也更加疏离。据我观察，双方关系中最奇怪之处在于，最终促成他们沟通的东西并不在物质层面，而在精神层面。每一边都是独立主体，会固守各自在饮食起居、着装打扮方面的习俗。见到我们不用缠足，虽然有些勇敢的中国女子也会刻意效仿，但是大多数妇女依然会满足于裹小脚，甚

And we saw the freedom of the daintily trousered Chinese women, yet none of us adopted their custom, much as some of us wanted to. No, it was not on the plane of material things that the two races touched, it was on that utterly essential plane of things spiritual. The whole human race is forever groping with out-stretched hands towards the light, and these groping, unseeing hands touch in the darkness. That common need and common desire was welding the two communities, the ancient Chinese of the Walled City and the Modern American missionaries, into one community.

The mission had made itself a beautiful home at the extreme end of the town up against the inner moat. A lane paved with bricks, wider than the city streets, ran through the center of the compound. On one side was the university with a campus of its own for the boys, and on the other side was the girls' school and the woman's hospital and the nurses' training school. The trees in the lane had been planted long ago by those heroic, pioneer missionaries who came into the unknown when a voyage to China was like a voyage to another planet, and China seemed as far away from home as Mars. When I think of them, they seem a different race from us. They were heroes and martyrs, while nowadays it's only a joy to be a missionary.

That evening after supper Doctor Grace and I walked up and down the shady lane with our arms wrapped around each other's waists in the fashion of long ago. We talked of everything under the sun, of Philadelphia and all the girls we had known there. One had gone to Persia and had married a minister and had a daughter. Another had gone to Mexico, had married, and had had to leave the country during the revolutions. Still another was in India. I had recently met a nurse from the old hospital who had gone to Syria. Her surgery over-looked the deep blue waters of the Mediterranean. We talked them all over, marveling at the strange destinies of people once so near together in daily work, now scattered to the end of the world.

The city was very still. The water gates are closed at sundown, and the cumbrous, iron-toothed portcullis lowered into the water. We walked to the end of the lane and stood at the top of a flight of stone steps that led to a landing

至以此为傲。尽管我们看到有些中国女子穿着裤子在街上行走，步态轻盈优雅，充分享受这般着装的自由，但是我们中并没有人敢于接受她们的习惯，虽然许多人非常想这么做。不，中美两国人真正能触动彼此的，不在物质层面的东西，而在绝对关键的精神层面的东西。人类永远伸出双手，渴望摸索到那束光芒，一双双不断探寻的、看不见的双手在黑暗中触碰到彼此。这一共同的需要和渴求将两大群体紧密联系起来，把城墙内古老的中国人与现代美国传教士们融为一体。

教会在苏城最东端、紧靠内城河的位置建起一个美丽家园。穿过这一大院的中心，有一条砖石铺就的小路，比城里的马路还宽。它的一侧是男子大学，里面有一个围起来的校园，另一侧则是女子学校、妇孺医院以及护士学校。那些英雄的传教士先人们不远万里，敢于探索未知，来到这里，小路周边的树木就是他们栽下的，当时来中国的航行犹如去往外星球那么艰难，对于普通美国人而言，去往中国的路途和去火星一样遥远。每当想起这些先行者们，我感觉他们是与我们完全不同的一群人。他们曾是英雄和殉道者，而如今，当传教士只是出于一种乐趣。

那天晚上用罢晚餐，我和格瑞斯医生徘徊在绿树成荫的小路上，像过去那样，互相揽着对方的腰。我们谈天说地，谈到费城以及许多在费城我们所共同认识的姑娘。一个姑娘去了波斯，嫁给了一位外交使节，有了一个女儿。另一个去了墨西哥，也已结婚，在革命时期又被迫离开那里。还有一个在印度。我最近遇到一位来自以前医院的护士，她刚从叙利亚回来。她说曾在能眺望深蓝色地中海的地方给病人开过刀。我们把每个人都说了一遍，那些曾经在日常工作中与我们关系那么亲密的人，现在却各奔东西，去了世界各地，命运迥异，真是令人唏嘘。

城里一片静寂。太阳落山，水门就关了，笨重累赘的钉耙式铁闸门沉入河中。我们走到小路的尽头，站在一段石阶最上面的一级，石阶通向内

along the inner moat. A few wakeful boatmen were poling themselves lazily past. At the landing two boats were anchored, and a couple of coolies were loading them with bulky bales of silk. Lanterns, striped in rings of red and white, hung on the boats. Behind us the lane was unlit and shadowy. Before us the sluggish water looked solid and stationary. Above us rose the wall, silhouetted like a battlemented shadow against the starry sky. We could hardly see it, but we saw a space in the sky where there should have been stars, and where instead there was a regular turreted blackness. We were shut in for the night! The water gates were doubly closed, and all the little postern gates in the walls were barred and guarded by sentries.

Like the little woman who lost her petticoat, I hugged myself and said, "This is none of I!"

From beyond the wall came the faint, distant sound of frogs. It was not really a sound; rather it made the air vibrate as a shell vibrates when pressed against the ear.

"It's time to go to bed," said Doctor Grace. "We all go to bed with the Chinese."

"I hate to go in," I said, "and lose any of this enchantment."

Doctor Grace laughed. "It won't evaporate overnight," she said. "It has been here for thousands and thousands of years. If ever anything in the history of mankind can be called permanent, this can."

"But you can't tell!" I cried. "It has never before met western civilization. It's a solvent. All the old things crumble at its touch."

"You are inconsistent," said Doctor Grace. "If you regret the past, why be a missionary?"

"No, I am not," I answered. "I don't think China is perfect, nor do I think we are perfect. I have come to bring the love of Jesus Christ, not our habits. But don't let's argue. I'd rather just walk up and down under these old trees and feel myself a part of the antiquity."

城河边的一个平台。几个船夫还未就寝，懒散地撑着船经过。平台边停靠着两条小船，三五个苦力正将厚重的大捆丝绸抬进船。船上挂着灯笼，灯笼上有一圈圈红白相间的条纹。我们身后有一条巷子，黑暗而朦胧。在我们面前，河水缓缓流淌，显得纯粹而凝滞。城墙高耸过我们头顶，在星空的映衬下，勾勒出城垛的剪影。我们几乎看不到墙体本身，但能看见一方天空，那里本应有星光，现在却出现了一个角楼方正的黑影。夜晚降临，我们被关在城里了！两道水门都已关闭，城墙上所有的小边门也被闩上，由哨兵把守。

我像那个丢失了衬裙的小女人[1]，紧紧抱住自己说:“我不再是我了！”

城墙外隐约传来微弱、遥远的蛙鸣声。那声音并不真切，倒像是空气震动，如同一枚贝壳被贴到耳边时发出的震颤声。

“该去睡了，”格瑞斯医生说，“我们都遵从中国人的作息时间。”

“我不想进屋，”我说，“而弃此刻的美景于不顾。”

格瑞斯医生笑了。“美景不会在一夜之间消失，”她说，“它已存在于此地千百年了。倘若人类历史上有什么东西可以用‘永恒’来形容，那么这些美景于此便恰如其分。”

“但你还不能下论断！”我大声答道，“它以前从未遭遇西方文明。后者是一副溶剂，所有的旧事物一触及它就会坍塌。”

“你的话自相矛盾，”格瑞斯医生说，“如果你痛惜过去，何必来当传教者？”

“不，我没有自相矛盾，”我答道，“我认为中国并不完美，我们美国也不完美。我之所以来，是想播撒耶稣基督的大爱，而不是传播美国人的生活习俗。不过我俩不要再争辩了。我宁愿在这些古树下多走几回，让自己融入这座古城之中。”

[1] 指一首美国童谣中的人物，同句中“This is none of I！”也出自该童谣。

"You foolish child! We'll go to bed."

So we did. I hadn't slept outside my own room since coming to China. Once shut in alone, within four walls, I felt suddenly homesick. I wanted to be back at St. Margaret's; I wanted to see Edward. At least, I wanted a letter from him to put under my pillow when I went to sleep. I crawled in under the canopy of the mosquito netting. Close outside my window grew some willows. It was so still that I heard their tiny leaves slithering against each other. And this desert-like quietness was in the midst of a city, of a walled city of teeming millions. If a baby cried, I felt the whole city would hear it. You feel that such profound quiet is the preparation for a stupendous event.

Before I knew it, it was morning. I made rounds with Doctor Grace and helped with clinic. In the afternoon she had prepared a treat for me. One of the men in the mission had a rowboat which he loaned to us. That again caught my breath away. Here I was in a rowboat, floating along on the inner moat of Soochow! We went down the watersteps, Mr. Jackson held the boat for us, and we pushed off. Doctor Grace insisted upon rowing, for, she said, I was to sit in the stern and see the sights. We rowed down to the nearest watergate. It was as thick as a house and the old blocks of stone were green with moss. Overhead I saw the black teeth of the raised portcullis hanging suspended above me. The air under the wide, thick gate was damp and cool as in a cellar. Near the gate, the inner moat was crowded with boats. As each long house-boat approached the entrance, the oarsman, standing at the stern, gave a guttural call, and the prow, seeming to move of itself, swung sharply into sight. Once through it and on the outer moat, we were plunged into another sphere of life. House boats drifted slowly by, a man at the stern oar, and children sprawling all over the narrow space. Litter tots, dressed in red rags, climbed around the edges of the boat precariously. The next moment I saw one fall overboard. Before I had time to scream out, its mother jerked it up again by a rope which was tied around its middle.

"Don't they mind it at all?" I asked.

“傻孩子！我们去睡吧。”

于是我们就寝了。自从来中国后，我还没有在上海那间自己的卧室以外过过夜。房门一关，我孑然一人，面对四面墙壁，我突然感到思乡心切。我想回圣玛格丽特医院，渴望见到爱德华。至少我盼望能收到一封他的来信，这样我就可以枕着它入睡了。我爬进蚊帐。窗外种着几棵柳树。夜晚寂静之极，我听见细小的柳叶相互纠缠时发出的声音。而这沙漠般的静谧竟然出现在一座古城之中，一座人口千百万、熙熙攘攘带城墙的古城中。如果哪里有婴孩啼哭，我估计整座城市都能听见。你会觉得如此深沉的静寂正酝酿着惊心动魄的大事件。

迷迷糊糊，不觉已是清晨。我先跟格瑞斯医生去查房，后又在诊所做了些帮衬活。她已提前做好准备，下午要款待我一番。教会里有人有一条手划船，并将之借给了我们。这又一次使我惊讶不已。我居然能够坐船在苏州内城河上游览！我们走下河滩石阶，杰克逊先生为我们稳住船，然后我们驶将开去。格瑞斯医生主张由她划桨，她说因为要让我坐在船尾看风景。我们划向最近的水门。它如同房子一样厚实，古城砖因布满青苔而呈青绿色。我抬头看见升起的闸门露出黑色锯齿，高悬在空中。宽大、沉重的水门周遭，空气如地窖般湿冷。城门附近的内城河上挤满了船只。每条长长的住家船靠近水门入口时，桨手会站在船尾，只需粗声粗气地喊一声，船头仿佛能自己移动似的，很快就荡进来，清晰可见了。一旦穿过城门进入外城河，我们便蓦然置身于另一个世界。一条条住家船慢悠悠地来来往往，只见一人坐在船尾的桨边，边上狭窄的地方被他几个孩子占满了。那些小毛孩穿着红肚兜，在船的边缘爬来爬去，危险得很。下一秒我就看见其中一个从船沿掉了下去。我还来不及大声呼救，他母亲便再次用拴在他腰间的那条绳子把他给提溜上来了。

“他们难道一点也不担心？”我问道。

"Oh, no," said Doctor Grace. "They must fall in a dozen times a day. Whenever I come out, I see mothers pulling up their dangling infants."

Away to the horizon stretched the fields, those limitless, pathless fields I had grown to love so well. To my utter delight we followed the streams right into them. I had never seen them from the winding waterways, and at once I knew this was the proper way to approach them. The little huts faced the water. Flights of crooked stone steps led down the banks to the edge of the water. Women stooped on the last step, washing the evening rice. We passed two lengths of the river which had been fenced off with anchored buoys and twisted lines of straw rope. The stretch of water inside had been sewn with grain. On and on we went.

"Are we going anywhere in particular?" I asked. "Or don't you know where you are going?

"Of course I do," said Doctor Grace. "We are going to see the fishing birds."

"The what?" I asked.

"The fishing birds," said Doctor Grace. "Wait till you see them. They belong to the husband of one of our patients. The women and children of the family come to the hospital. Only a month ago the last baby was born there."

It was about five o'clock. The shadows were long and level. Wafts of the sweet fragrance of blossoming beans blew to us from the banks. I recognized the smell; I knew the look of the plants—low, grey-green, with the blossoms close against the stems as if a host of purple and gray butterflies had cuddled against the bushes for the night. Birds were flying across the sky, swift crows, jet black, against the sunset, and the plumper "Sau Sau Man Hau"(the Cook Cook Rice Well bird) that cries as it flies.

We turned a bend in the stream and came upon the queerest sight I have ever seen in my life.

The point of land where the streams divide rose steeply from the water. A house of wicker and bamboo, larger than most of the farmers' houses, stood in a grove of fresh green bamboo trees. The evening wind, rustling through their papery leaves, made a clear, soft, calling sound. Buffaloes and chickens roamed along the shore. On the lowest step of the water stairs stood a group of women

“噢，不用担心，”格瑞斯医生说，“这些孩子想必一天之中从船上掉下去，要有十几次之多。每次我坐船出来，总能看到很多母亲用绳子正捞着落水的孩子呢，晃来晃去的。”

开阔的田野一望无垠，它广袤而人迹罕至，长久以来我特别喜爱它这些样子。令我无比愉快的是，我们顺着河流径直划到了田野之间。我从未在蜿蜒的水道里观赏过它们，现在发现坐船才是走进田野的最佳方式。岸边坐落着一间间小棚屋。不时有一段段弯曲的石阶伸向河边的堤岸。妇女们弯着腰在最低的台阶上淘米，准备晚饭。我们划过两段河道，它们都被定点浮标和稻草绳拧成的分界线与周边水域分隔开来。人们已在围栏内的水域里播撒了粮食作物。我们继续向前划去。

“我们有明确的目的地吗？”我问道，“还是你也不知道要去哪儿？”

“我当然知道，”格瑞斯医生说，“我们要去看鱼鹰。”

“什么？”我问。

“鱼鹰。”格瑞斯医生说，“坐好，一会儿你就见到了。这些鸟是我们一个病人的丈夫养的。这家的妇女和孩子都来我们医院看过病。就在一个月前，他家最小的孩子就是在我们那儿生的。”

大约5点了。太阳拖着长长的、水平的影子。岸上传来阵阵蚕豆花的甜香。我闻得出这种花的味道，因为知道蚕豆苗的模样——植株低矮，呈灰绿色，花紧贴在茎梗上，就像傍晚时分落在豆苗中的一群灰紫色的蝴蝶。空中时有飞鸟掠过，身姿敏捷的乌鸦，在落日的衬托下漆黑一团，还有一种胖胖的“烧烧蛮好/烧烧饭好”鸟，一边飞一边大声鸣叫着。

我们转了个弯，映入我眼帘的竟是一幅从未见过的奇特画面。

河道分流的地方，地势陡然高出水面许多。在一片翠绿的竹林间，有一间由柳条和竹篾搭建而成的房子，它比周围其他农民的房子都大。晚风吹来，拂过薄翼般的竹叶，发出清脆、低柔的声响。水牛和小鸡漫步河岸。

and children watching a boat in the river.

A long narrow boat swung mid-stream. At first glance it looked as if the boat were not floating on the water, but as if it were being held just over its surface by a flock of black, strong birds as large as eagles, which hovered on both sides of it and flapped their great black wings, screaming harshly. Two men stood in the boat, which was shaped liked a long scooped-out canoe. The men were motionless and silent. The little group on the shore was also motionless and silent. Doctor Grace stopped rowing. We caught the branch of an overhanging tree and moored ourselves at the bank, and we too were motionless and silent.

Fascinated, I watched the birds. They screamed and fluttered their wings. Suddenly one swooped into the water, more plunged after it. I saw them struggling and flapping their sooty black wings over the brown water as does a white sea gull when it snatches a fish. The men sprang into sudden activity. They pulled the birds up by stout strings tied around their legs. They caught the struggling birds under their arms and jerked the fishes from their mouths. I saw a gleam of silver as they tossed the fish into a wicker fishing basket. The commotion among the birds subsided. They settled down into quietness on the rows of horizontal perches, making a soft blackness on the water beneath by the shadow of their wings.

"How many?" called a voice from the shore.

"Three," answered one of the men. "Later, more," he said. "The sun not yet falls down the Hill of Heaven. Wait till the fish see not the shadow of the black birds."

Doctor Grace explained the custom of cormorant fishing to me. It is an ancient Soochow industry. The birds, tied by a stout rope, three or four deep on the perches which stick out in parallel rows from each side of the boat, are kept very hungry. They fish, and the men steal the fish from their beaks. Along the outer moat they can often be seen fishing by daylight.

"Suppose all the birds flew up in the air at once?" I said. "Wouldn't they carry the boat right out of the water?"

"There is an ancient legend about a fisherman who was cruel to his birds," said Doctor Grace. "He took all the fish from them, not even giving them their just and due reward at the end of an evening's fishing. The birds were fierce and

一群妇女和儿童站在近水最低的台阶上，看着河上的一条船。

一条窄而长的小船漂在河中央，船身酷似一条中间挖空的独木舟。乍一看，仿佛这船不是自己浮在水面上，而是由一群壮如老鹰的大黑鸟托在水面上似的。这些水鸟栖息在船两边，扑打着巨大的黑色翅膀，尖声地叫唤着。船上有两个男人，一动不动，静默无声。岸上的围观者也一动不动，静默无声。格瑞斯医生不再划桨。有棵树斜伸到眼前，我们抓住上面的树枝，将船停靠到岸边，随后也变得一动不动，静默无声。

我看着这些水鸟入了迷。它们尖叫着，扑棱着翅膀。突然，有一只扎进水里，随后更多黑鸟潜入水中。我看到它们在棕褐色的水面上奋力拍打漆黑的翅膀，如同抓到鱼的白色海鸥一样。船上的渔夫顿时变得活跃起来。他们抓住水鸟腿上系好的那些粗绳，将它们提出水面，把不断扑腾的水鸟夹到胳肢窝下，从它们嘴里挤出鱼来。当他们将鱼扔进柳条鱼篓时，只见银光一闪。黑鸟之间的骚动逐渐平息，它们趋于平静，停落在船上成排的栖息处，其翅膀所投下的影子在水面形成一道柔和的暗色。

“捉到几条了？”岸上有人问道。

“三条。”男子之一答道。“待会儿，能捉更多，”他说，“太阳还没落到天平山后头去。要等到鱼在水里看不见黑鸟的影子才行。”

格瑞斯医生给我介绍此地用鸬鹚捕鱼的习俗。这一行当在苏州历史悠久。这些水鸟或三只或四只地栖息在船沿两边几排平行突出的横杆上，并用粗绳系住。渔夫让水鸟处于非常饥饿的状态。鸬鹚会潜入水中捕鱼，随后渔民就把鱼从其喙里偷走。白天在外城河边，人们经常能看到鸬鹚捕鱼。

“假如一下子所有的水鸟都飞到天上去，该怎么办？”我问，“难道它们不会把船一起从水面带走吗？”

“此地有个古老的传说，故事关于一个渔夫，他对自己的鸬鹚很残忍，”格瑞斯医生说，“他将它们捕到的所有鱼都占为己有，每天傍晚捕完鱼后，

lean and hungry, and caught fish well. At night, the oldest son of the fisherman crept out to the tied birds and fed them stolen morsels of rice and left-over bits of fish. This kept the birds strong. The friends of the fisherman warned him that he must give his birds more to eat. Day by day the birds became fiercer and leaner. They flapped their black pinions angrily over their perches and screamed harshly whenever the fisherman pulled open their beaks and robbed them of their fish. Once the fisherman was ill, and a neighbor took the birds out fishing. That day the birds gorged themselves, and the neighbor came home with his hand scratched and bleeding.

"' Your birds are not cormorants but evil spirits,' he said to his friend. ' If I were you, I would set them loose and let them fly away in a great black cloud over the sky.'

"But the fisherman only laughed and continued to treat the birds as before. He grew rich from his daily catch. And at night his little son crept out, in the shivery darkness, to feed the birds. He loved the birds. Sometimes in the early dawn he played to them on his little, hollow bamboo flute. As his father grew richer, he seemed to think all the world was his, and he treated everybody just as he treated his fishing birds. Everybody in the house grew afraid of him. The children hid away when they saw him coming home at night, and the women retired into their own quarters. At night when the birds were tied in safety, he sat under the cypresses at the little table in the front yard, and counted his fish. His little son would crouch behind the shutters and watch the long, lithe bodies of the fish slip through his father's hands like shining pieces of silver.

"One day the little boy was sick. He had smallpox and lay moaning on a mattress on the floor in his mother's room. When evening came he remembered the hungry birds, but he was afraid to tell his mother lest she feed them clumsily and his father catch her at it and beat her. He tried to get up, but he fell back fainting on his mattress. So that night the birds had no food.

"The next day when the fisherman tied them in orderly rows on the side perches of the boat, the birds were very still and lifeless. Like black, wooden images they sat motionless and without sound. The sun hung low over the fields,

他连水鸟们应得的、作为犒赏的鱼都不给它们吃。他的鸬鹚凶猛、瘦弱、饥肠辘辘，却都是捕鱼好手。晚上，渔夫的大儿子会蹑手蹑脚地出去，给拴住的鸬鹚们喂一些偷出来的米饭和主人吃剩的鱼，水鸟们这才勉强得以保持强壮。渔夫的朋友们纷纷警告他，必须给他的水鸟们再多喂些食物。日复一日，它们变得越发凶狠和瘦弱。每当渔夫掰开它们的喙，抢走它们的鱼时，它们总是站在停落处，愤怒地拍打翅膀，凄厉地尖叫着。一次，渔夫病了，让一个邻居带他的黑鸟外出捕鱼。那天这些水鸟们拼命吞鱼，塞饱自己，邻居回来时，他的双手已被水鸟们抓得伤痕累累、血流不止。

“‘你的这些鸟不是鸬鹚，是恶鬼，’邻居跟渔夫说，‘我要是你，就会给它们松绑，让它们飞走，飞进天上一朵大乌云里去。’

“可这位渔夫只是笑了笑，仍然像以前一样对待他的鸬鹚。每天的收获令他发了财。而每到夜晚，他的小儿子会偷偷溜出去，给水鸟们喂食，在黑夜里冻得瑟瑟发抖。他爱它们。有时，他会在清晨给它们吹那根短小而中空的竹笛。他的父亲日渐富有，大有视全世界为己所有的趋势，就连待人接物也变得如同对待他的鱼鹰一般吝啬。家人都开始怕他。孩子们晚上看到他回家就躲起来，女人们则回到各自的房间回避他。夜里把所有的水鸟都在船上绑妥后，他就会坐到前院那棵柏树底下的小桌前数他的鱼。那时他的小儿子会蹲在护窗板后，看从父亲手指缝里滑出的一条条长而柔软的死鱼，它们像银条一样闪闪发光。

“有一天，小男孩病了。他得了天花，只能躺在母亲房间地板上的一张草席上苦苦呻吟。夜色降临，他想起那些饥饿的水鸟，却不敢告诉母亲，生怕她会因粗手粗脚地去投喂它们而被父亲当场发现并挨一顿打。他试图爬起来，又昏倒在席子上。因此，那天晚上，鸬鹚们没有吃到食物。

“次日，渔夫把它们拴到船舷两边成排的停落处时，水鸟们一动不动，毫无生气。如同黑色的木雕，它们木然而无声地坐在那里。太阳在田野上

making the shadows ebony-black, and the light places like patches of gold. On the farther side of the boat, where its shadow lay over the water, the cormorants saw the swift shadows of the gliding fishes. They saw the instantaneous flash of silver as the fish darted out of the shadow into the sunlit water before disappearing from their sight. Usually this was the signal for diving, but the birds waited. Not one moved, or fluttered a pinion. The fisherman stood waiting, too, wondering what had come over the birds. He also saw the fish shadows in the water like immaterial phantoms.

"The sun slipped slowly down the vault of the sky. A Minne bird called from the rice fields, a star hung in the west. Still the birds waited; and the fisherman waited, too. It grew night. The fisherman could barely see the mass of birds on his right and on his left. Finally a strip of the rising moon showed scarlet over the rice fields. It was the signal. With harsh cries the birds flapped their wings in unison. The boat swayed and rocked on the water. A wind swept along the water from the rice fields and the moon. The birds lifted the boat free of the water, and it hung like a cradle between their soaring black wings.

"The people in the house heard the screaming of the cormorants and the rush of their wings, and they ran to the front door. Above the rice fields they saw the boat carried away. Like a black feather, it floated across the moon, which rose up scarlet and still over the water. The man was never seen or heard of again.

"And so," said Doctor Grace, "every cormorant fisher is careful to feed his birds well after the catch."

I wanted to wait for the sunset, but it was not allowed.

"That's one of the penalties of living in a walled city," said Doctor Grace. "You can never see the sun set or rise out in the fields. You can only see it from the walls of the city. If you don't pass through the water gates before sunset, you have to stay out all night, for at sunset the portcullis is lowered."

落得很低，投下乌木色的暗影，光亮的地方则如同金片一般。远处，在船的另一边，即阴影落在水面的位置，停在那里的鸬鹚们看到了鱼群泛着银光迅速游过的身影。它们看到鱼群冲出船的阴影，游进漾着阳光的水域，又迅速从其视线中消失，那一瞬间的银光闪烁。通常，这是提醒它们潜入水里的信号，可是今天这些水鸟却不为所动。它们一动不动，没有扇动翅膀。渔夫也站在一旁等待，他不知道这些水鸟今天怎么了。他也看到了水中鱼群像鬼魅幻影一般。

“太阳慢慢从天穹落下。稻田里传来一只玄鸟的鸣叫声，一颗孤星低垂在西面的天空。水鸟仍在等待；渔夫也在等待。已是入夜时分。渔夫仅能模糊地看到位于其左边和右边的水鸟。终于，稻田上方那一轮初升的月亮，有部分泛起了猩红色。这是信号。伴着刺耳的尖叫声，鸬鹚们不约而同地一起拍打翅膀。渔夫的船在水面摇晃起来。从稻田和月亮所在的方向吹来一阵风，掠过水面。水鸟们将小船带离了河面，船悬在它们向上飞升的黑色翅膀中间，像一只摇篮般脆弱不堪。

“屋里的人都听到了鸬鹚们的叫声及其急速的振翅声，纷纷跑到大门口。他们眼睁睁地看着捕鱼的小船就在稻田上空被水鸟们带走了。它像一片黑色的羽毛，掠过已然升至中天的猩红色月亮，月光静静洒在水面上。从此以后，那位渔夫就杳无音信了，既无人见过他，也无人听说过他。

“至此，”格瑞斯医生说，“每个养鸬鹚的渔夫都会在捕鱼后仔仔细细地把自己的水鸟喂饱喂足了。”

我想待到太阳下山再返回城内，可格瑞斯医生没有批准。

“这就是住在由城墙合围住的城市里的一种不幸，”格瑞斯医生说，“你永远无法在郊野欣赏日出日落，而只能站在城墙上欣赏此景。如果日落前你没能从水门回到城内，那就只能在城外过夜了，因为太阳一落山，铁闸门就会被放下来。”

We waved our farewell to the little group on the shore. I too took an oar and we rowed for dear life. For, much as I would like to have stayed out all night, it's not proper! There would be some advantages in having a husband!

When we got back to the hospital we found a boy there with a note for Doctor Grace.

"It's from the house of Li, the jade merchant," she said. "They are expecting a baby there tonight. Will you go along?"

XIII THE BRIGAND'S KNIFE

"WE'LL want two donkeys," said Doctor Grace to the boy, and we flew to get ready, changing our clothes and swallowing cups of black coffee. A nurse handed Doctor Grace her out-practice bag, already packed with its sterilized instruments. The gatekeeper called two donkey boys, each with his own little donkey.

"How are you going to ride?" I asked Doctor Grace.

"I ride side-saddle," she said, "but you can ride as you please. The only real comfort is to ride astride, but so many of the older missionaries think it isn't ladylike that I yield to their wishes."

Not to be outdone in politeness, I jumped up on my donkey sidewise, with my feet dangling in a truly ladylike fashion over his side. A dilapidated bridle and cross-saddle composed the harness. Ah Fok poked the donkey on the flank, and we started off at a brisk trot. For some unaccountable reason I began to laugh. I felt too ridiculous bouncing around on the back of the little animal; it was so tiny that any man could have helped it along by kicking the ground. Ah Fok ran alongside, giving the necessary little, sharp cries that kept the donkey going and occasionally prodding him with a pointed stick, as we cantered gayly down the twilight street. Overhead the crimson sunset lingered, but in the narrow street of the city it was almost dusk. Lanterns hung before the shops. The dwelling houses

我们向岸上的人群挥手道别，他们的身影变得越来越小。我也划了一支桨，为宝贵的生活，大家奋力往回划。虽然我很想在城外待上一宿，然而那是不合适的。如此看来，有个丈夫倒确实有些益处！

一回到医院，我们就看见有个帮工正拿着一张给格瑞斯医生的便条候着。

“他是李宅派来的，那个玉石商人家。”格瑞斯医生说，“他们家今晚有孕妇要生产。你想一起去吗？”

第十三章　土匪的刀

“我们要两头毛驴。”格瑞斯医生跟帮工说。随后我们便急匆匆地去做准备：更衣，灌下好几杯清咖。一位护士将格瑞斯医生的出诊包递给她，里面已经装好各式消毒器械。门房叫来两个赶驴男孩，他们各牵了一头小毛驴。

“你打算怎么骑驴？”我问格瑞斯医生。

“我用侧坐式，”她说，“不过你可以随意。骑驴唯一真正舒服的姿势是跨骑，可那么多年长的传教士都认为（女性）跨骑不够淑女，那我就遵从他们的意见吧。”

我不想在骑姿方面表现出格，就跳上我那头毛驴，侧坐在其背上，双脚真很淑女地在一侧晃荡着。驴身上的装具由一根破烂的缰绳和一副十字形鞍鞯构成。阿福在毛驴的肋腹上戳了一下，我们就轻快地小跑起来出发了。莫名地，我大笑起来，觉得坐在这么个小动物身上一颠一颠地行进太可笑了；驴子非常瘦小，任何骑在它背上的人都能用脚蹬地，助它行走。阿福在边上跟跑，偶尔发出必要的、细小而尖锐的喊叫，催驴子赶路，不时用一根尖头棍戳它，我们就这样轻松、快乐地骑着毛驴在黄昏的街道上慢跑。头顶上血红的夕阳迟迟不肯落山，不过这条狭窄的城市街道却几乎已经全

were already closed and shuttered for the night. Across the court of a deserted temple, around a corner, and up over a bridge we went.

The bridge, like all Chinese bridges, arched up at the center, making a half circle over the surface of the water. Up we went without slowing, and off I slid. It happened very simply. As the back of the donkey assumed the steep incline of forty-five degrees I slipped gently backward over his tail. Ah Fok rushed to my rescue. Placing both his hands in the small of my back, he pushed with all his might and main to stop my avalanche. But I was too heavy; I went on sliding over the donkey's tail till I sat on the ground. It was all so funny I couldn't speak for laughing.

"Try cross-saddle," advised Doctor Grace. "They saw you start off in the proper fashion. Your intentions were good, but the only thing to do is to ride the way you can stay on."

I agreed. Those were the days of hobble skirts. Fortunately my petticoat was an heirloom of the past and possessed frills and ruffles. My dress skirt vanished from sight; it became a mere string around my waist. But my petticoat spread out in a truly gratifying manner over my legs. This manner of riding was a great improvement. The donkey was small enough for me to grasp comfortably between my knees, and I felt as secure as in a rocking chair.

"Missey can do?" asked Ah Fok, running at my side.

"Can do," I answered.

Sometimes we trotted, but more often we galloped. Over the up and down arches of the bridges we walked. The donkey boys had muscles of wire and heart and lungs of India rubber. Without the slightest effort they ran along beside the donkeys, shouting and giving little sharp jabs at their flanks.

From the comparative quiet of darkened streets we turned into one of the busy thoroughfares where the shops stood wide open. The houses were like partitions, with separating walls and a back stoop but without any front at all. Unless one has seen such a street, it is hard to conceive the variety and color that all the lighted interiors give. The eating shops were full of men sitting in groups

黑了。店铺前挂起灯笼。入夜时分，住家的宅子都已门窗紧闭。穿过一座荒废寺庙的庭院，转过街角，爬上一座桥，我们继续前进。

如同所有的中式桥梁，此桥中间拱起，在水面形成一道半圆形弧线。我们上桥没有减速，下桥我是滑下去的。这一动作出现得自然而然，颇为简单。由于驴背呈四十五度角倾斜，我就慢慢地从上面滑到了驴尾前。阿福冲过来救我，他用双手托住我那瘦小的后腰，使尽全力推着，防止我雪崩似的从驴背跌落。不过我身体太沉，一直从驴尾往下滑，直到最后一屁股坐到了地上。实在太滑稽了，我笑得说不出话来。

"试试跨坐吧。"格瑞斯医生建议，"他们看到你出发时坐姿端庄，可见你骑驴的初衷是好的，不过现在你该做的，是稳稳地骑在驴上。"

我表示同意。当年穿霍步裙[1]的时候，侧坐是合适的骑姿。幸运的是，那天我穿的衬裙是祖传的，带有花边和褶皱。这样我的外裙就从眼前消失，而仅变成了一根系在腰间的带子。不过我的衬裙以一种令人满意的方式展开，遮住我的双腿。这样的骑姿就稳当了许多。驴子很小，我跨骑着，足以舒适地夹住它，我感到自己就像坐在摇椅上一样安全。

"小姐能行？"阿福问道，他在旁边跟跑。

"能行。"我答道。

我们有时小跑，但大部分时间则是一路飞奔。上下一座座拱桥时，我们下来步行。赶驴的两个男孩有着金属丝般坚韧的肌肉和印度橡胶般富有弹性的心肺器官。他们不费力气地跟着毛驴奔跑着、喊叫着，时不时在其肋腹上快速戳一下。

从相对幽暗、静谧的街道我们转进了一条繁华大路，路两边的商铺鳞次栉比，都敞着大门。这些房舍如同一个个隔间，由墙板相隔，后有走廊相通，正面空荡开敞。除非你以前见过此类街道，否则很难想见那些掌着

[1] 也叫蹒跚裙，一种下摆很窄的长裙，令穿者行走不便，无法迈出大步，也无法跨上马车。曾在美国风靡一时。

around small square tables, shoveling in rice by the mouthful. They hold the bowls close up against their lips, open their mouths to the fullest extent, and poke in great mountains of fine white rice. Holding the bowls at their mouths, they turn around and stare at the passers-by. Men with baskets full of towels wrung out of boiling, perfumed water pass among the eaters, offering a towel to each guest. It is the custom to wipe off one's face and head and neck with these towels. The waiter passes the same towel to the next guest and so on until the towel is cold.

In the wine-shops men were filling their tiny teacups with hot wine from metal teapots. In a large eat-shop a band of musicians sat playing a weird minor song, which echoed up and down the street above the sounds of evening life. At a temple a funeral was going on, and I caught a swift glimpse of priests in robes of red and green with mitered caps. On the outskirts of the crowd hung a fringe of monks in dirty gray. The hired mourners, in a discordant chorus, wailed shrilly, and little boy acolytes, in tattered, embroidered cassocks of blue and red, beat drums. The whole party were evidently enjoying themselves very much.

Opium dens, looking like sections of Pullman sleepers, with rows of closely curtained bunks one above the other and a narrow passage running down the middle, were squeezed in between the shops.

The streets themselves were filled with a busy throng of men. Dignitaries were carried about in stately sedan chairs. Once or twice I passed a chair in which I caught a fleeting glimpse of a bejeweled woman, slowly fanning herself and peering out through the half drawn curtains with listless eyes. There were no women afoot in that crowd of animated, merry, eating humanity.

Ah Fok ran ahead, crying out, "Make way for the Illustrious Foreign-born Healer. Make way."

The clatter of the donkeys' hoofs, the shouting of the donkey boys, made a stir of interest in the mass of people. The men squeezed up against the walls to let us pass, and I heard murmurs of surprise. In the eyes of an oriental, we were

灯的店内是怎般多姿多彩、琳琅满目。吃食店里坐满了男人，他们三五成群围坐在一张张小方桌前，大口往嘴里塞着米饭。他们端着碗，使碗贴紧嘴唇，嘴巴张得极大，把碗里堆成小山似的优质精米饭拨进嘴里。端碗时，他们边吃边回头直愣愣地盯着来往路人看。有人提着装满毛巾的篮子在食客中穿梭，负责给每个客人递毛巾，这些毛巾是刚从滚烫的、撒过花露水的热水里绞起来的。吃饭时用它们擦脸、擦头和擦脖子是当地的风俗。侍者常将同一条毛巾递给一个又一个客人，直到毛巾变冷才会更换。

酒铺里，男人们正将烫热的黄酒从金属壶里倒进小酒盅。一家较大的吃食店里有一个曲艺班子，他们演奏着一支奇怪的小调，调门咿咿呀呀、来来回回地飘荡在夜生活所制造而出的各种市井声响之上。一座寺庙里，人们正操办着一场葬礼，我匆匆瞥见主持的道士们身着红绿色袍子，头戴道冠。一众身着脏兮兮灰色僧袍的和尚，如流苏般点缀在人群外围。那些受雇的哭丧者连哭带唱，节奏很不齐整，他们哭天抢地，声音激烈刺耳，旁边几个童子，穿着破烂的蓝红色带刺绣图案的长袍，敲着鼓。显然，整套办法事的班子相当自得其乐。

许多鸦片馆挤在店铺之间，它们好似铂尔曼列车上的一间间特级软席包厢，里面有成排的上下铺，都被帘子遮得严严实实，铺间有狭窄的过道穿过。

街上人头攒动、熙熙攘攘。达官显贵坐在人力抬的轿子里，威严肃穆。有一两次我经过一乘轿子时，瞬间瞥见一位穿戴得珠光宝气的女子。她悠悠地摇着扇子，从半遮掩的帘子里向外张望，眼神倦怠。那群欢快而充满活力的吃饭大军里，却见不到女性的身影。

阿福跑到前面，大叫道：“快给这位尊贵的外国郎中让路。让开。”

驴蹄的哒哒声，赶驴人的叫喊声，在人群中引起一阵好奇的骚动。人们贴到墙根让我们通过，我听见他们低声惊叹。在东方人眼中，我们两个

incomprehensible. Even our own grandmothers would have gasped! Women, alone, at that time of night, single and virtuous!

On the bridges I looked down on the dark canals, stretching like black ribbons through the city, separating the opposite houses, but linking the far parts together. Dark and mysterious they lay, in silent contrast to the night lights of the city. Over the bridge, through the bright streets, we went, till at last we left all the busy quarter of night life behind us. Ah Fok gave a vigorous jab at my donkey, and it burst into a run. Away went my stirrups; my skirts streamed out behind me. I clamped my legs around the animal's body, found I was perfectly secure, and gave myself up to enjoyment. Ah Fok was forgotten and out of sight. A long straight alley lay before me, where blank walls rose on either side. No one was in sight. Faint, dim starlight made a deeper darkness of this narrow straight alley. No lanterns hung at the doorposts, no light gleamed from under the threshold of the barred doors sunk in the walls, no sound came from the houses. The night wind blew in my face. My hairpins fell out, and my hair streamed back in the wind. Only a woman knows the sense of adventure and freedom that comes with loose, flying hair. China dropped away from my consciousness, and I was filled with the elemental delight of swift motion toward an unknown destination. But the little donkey knew where it was going. Right and left, we turned the corners galloping, with the thudding clatter of hoofs the only sound in the stillness. We seemed to be running through a city of the dead. We met no one, saw no one, heard no one.

Into the blue-black night, to which my eyes had grown accustomed, shot a thin gleam of yellow light, close along the ground. Suddenly it widened to a triangle, then vanished utterly. A door in the silent walls had opened and closed, yet I heard no footfalls nor the chatter of voices. Perhaps someone, startled by the tumultuous sound of our approach, had but peered out from curiosity. My eyes focused themselves on the spot in the wall where the break of light had occurred. Suddenly we were abreast of it, then had left it behind. A thrill of excitement tingled through me. In that moment, as we flashed by, I saw a man leaning,

西方人是高深莫测的。甚至连我们自己的祖辈（见到我）也定会惊得倒吸一口气。两个芊芊女子，无人陪伴，深更半夜，只身出行，还自命不凡！

我从桥上往下看那些黑漆漆的小河道，它们像黑色缎带伸入城市的每个角落，将相向而建的房屋分隔开，却又把远处的区域连接起来。河道幽深、神秘，河水无声地流淌着，与城市夜晚的灯光形成对比。我们走啊走，过了桥，穿过明亮的街道，直到最后将所有那些夜晚热闹的地方抛置身后。阿福用力戳了一下我的毛驴，毛驴突然飞跑起来。我的镫子掉了，裙子也向后展开。我用双腿紧紧夹住驴子，竟发现自己处于无比安全的状态，于是便纵情享受起这一刻来。我把阿福抛在脑后，他顿时消失得无影无踪。一条笔直绵长的小巷出现在眼前，它的两边耸立着白色高墙。巷里空无一人。暗淡稀疏的星光令这条笔直的窄巷更显幽暗深邃。路过的门柱上不见灯笼。一扇扇紧闭的大门陷在墙内，门槛下没有灯光透出。每间房子都悄无声息。晚风拂面，我的发卡掉了，头发迎风飞舞起来。只有女性才懂得，当其长发在风中飘逸之时，那是一种怎样的充满冒险、自由不羁的感觉。此刻，全中国都已从我的意识中消散殆尽，为赶赴某一未知目的地，我的内心完全被这种原始快感所攫获。然而，小毛驴知道它要去哪儿。我们奔驰着，忽而右转，忽而左转，寂静中唯有低沉的驴蹄哒哒声划破夜空。似乎我们穿越而过的这座城市已然死去。这一路遇不到人，见不到人，听不见人声。

我的双眼已经适应了夜色，只见靠近地面处，有一道细细的黄光射进青黑色的夜幕中。突然，光线变宽，成了三角形状，随后完全消失了。寂静之中，墙上有一扇门被人推开又关上，然而，既没有人的脚步声，也没有人的说话声。或许有人被我们经过时的吵闹所惊扰，出于好奇，仅开门向外探了下头。我的眼睛不由自主地落到墙上刚才透出光线的地方。我们突然直逼到那堵墙跟前，并很快将之甩到身后。我激动得浑身战栗。就在

slouching against the wall. He had not moved as we passed, nor had I turned my head to look at him. From some obscure reason I had pretended I had not seen him. He looked as if he did not want to be seen. The door against which he leaned was sunken in the wall about a foot. He stood in that depression, motionless and sinister. I just caught the dark blur of a man's figure and the pale patch of a face. For no reason under the sun I was excited. I looked back over my shoulder for Ah Fok, but no one was in sight, not even the hiding man. The alley stretched away behind me as dark and impenetrable and uninhabited as when I had dashed down it. Yet I felt I was not alone.

To my great relief I heard the sound of ricksha wheels, and I drew the donkey down to a walk. The thrill voices of two women talking came to me down the alley; the next moment I saw the lantern at the handlebars of a ricksha. It threw dancing, elfin shadows on the ground and made the leg of the coolie look tremendously black and thick. He was coming along carelessly at a jogtrot. The donkey halted at one side of the road, and I gathered up my hair and began rebraiding it. Two women were in the ricksha, a coolie woman and her mistress, who was sitting on the lap of the amah. Some unusual event had called them out, and they were talking in eager shrill tones, the ricksha man entering into their conversation when he saw fit. They gave a little shriek when they saw me, and craned their necks to stare back at me.

The coming of that flickering lantern made me feel suddenly forlorn. The night loomed black and threatening around me. I had no idea where I was, I didn't know how to return. The donkey had lost his initiative; he didn't seem to know any more than I did. The voices died away down the alley. The bobbing gleams of light were quite gone, so was my thrill and exhilaration. I felt utterly deserted and alone. I also felt that Edward had been very remiss to let me go off alone to Soochow! He might have known something would happen to me! Then I couldn't stand it any longer.

I dug my heels into the donkey and turned him back down the alley in the direction from which we had come, for I wanted to catch up with that lighted

飞驰而过的一刹那，我看见一个男子靠在墙上，低垂着头。我们从他跟前飞驰而过，但他并没有因此改变姿势，后来我也没再回头看他。出于某种莫名的缘故，我假装不曾见过他。他貌似不愿被人看见。他靠着的那扇门凹进墙内约一英尺深。他独自站着，神情阴郁，一动不动，心怀叵测。我只瞥见他昏暗模糊的身影和苍白的脸部。我感到一阵莫名的亢奋，回头想找阿福，却不见一人，连那个躲着的男子也不见了踪影。整条小巷在我身后一直延伸开去，与我先前冲进巷子时一样，依然纵深黑暗、不见尽头、幽寂无人。然而我隐隐感觉巷中另有其人。

远处传来黄包车的车轮声，我顿时如释重负，控制住毛驴，让它放慢速度换成走姿。巷子里传来两个女子兴奋的交谈声，紧接着我看到一盏灯笼，就挂在一辆黄包车的把手前。它胡乱地晃动着，在地上投下鬼魅般的阴影，使得拉车苦力的双腿变得出奇地暗黑粗壮。苦力拉着车漫不经心地一路小跑过来。毛驴在路的一边停住，我把头发捋到一起，重新扎起辫子。黄包车里坐着两个女子——一个女佣和她的小姐，后者坐在她那位阿妈的腿上。定是某件非比寻常的大事，促使她们深夜出门，两位女子说话声音激动，语气迫切，车夫适时插上几句。见到我，他们都发出小声尖叫，然后就伸长脖子回头盯着我看。

迎面而来的那盏灯笼烛光摇曳，令我蓦然感到凄楚。长夜漫漫，周遭危机四伏。我不知身处何地，也不知该如何折返。毛驴已经失去了起初的积极性，现在似乎和我一样不知所措。刚才的说话声在小巷里渐渐消失，晃动的灯光也完全消散，我那激动的心情也随之荡然无存，感觉自己遭到了彻底的抛弃，孑然一身，无比孤寂。我还是认为爱德华让我只身来苏州就是非常不负责任的决定！他可能早料到我会在此地遭遇变故！我再也无法忍受了。

我用鞋跟戳了戳毛驴，指挥它转身径直向来时的方向前进，因为我想

lantern and those voices. The donkey sensed my meaning, and quite resignedly he trotted along back. Around the next corner I caught sight of the friendly light shining on the legs of the ricksha man and on the spokes of the ricksha wheels and making a little arc of light on the pavement. It was a wonderful splash of light.

Suddenly something happened to it: it was dashed out of existence. A wild clamor broke out in front of me. The women screamed shrilly, their voices echoing back and forth across the alley from wall to wall, like balls bouncing to and fro. I heard the low guttural growl of a man. Then the ricksha man rushed past me, yelling. A woman screamed in mounting shriek of terror, and I heard a stir of doors opening and closing on the other side of the walls, but no one came out into the alley.

I was deathly afraid, but I couldn't stay there and hear two women murdered, so I kicked the donkey, and we clattered towards the fray. But after all it wasn't I who saved the day, it was Ah Fok, the donkey boy. Running and shouting, he turned into the alley and bore down upon us.

The mistress had been thrown out on the ground by the sudden desertion of the ricksha man. A heavy figure stooped over her, and the amah was pounding and pulling at this figure. Ah Fok and I made a goodly din in the stillness. The robber was startled. He sprang to his feet, looked up and down the alley, and saw foes approaching in both directions. Quickly he leaned against the sunken door in the wall, and vanished from our sight.

Ridiculous and infantile, more like a hopping shadow than a rescuer, Ah Fok sprang towards the prostrate woman. I was already off my donkey and kneeling beside her. The amah, in shrill excitement, pulled her to her feet.

"My rings and my bracelets," wailed the woman. "He has stolen my jewels."

With a swift movement the amah's hands went to the ears of her mistress.

"He had not time," said the woman. "I felt the blade of a knife cold against my cheek, but then the foreign woman cried out, and the man withheld his hand."

追上那辆挂着灯笼的黄包车和其上交谈着的女人。毛驴领会了我的意图，非常顺从地回头小跑起来。转过下一个弯，我看见那道友好的灯光照在黄包车车夫的腿上，也照在车轮的辐条上，它在人行道上泛起一道弧形亮光。光影洒落极为美妙。

突然，不知黄包车遭遇了什么情况：它猛地消失了。前方传来急切的呼救声。两个女子尖声大叫，声音在小巷的墙壁间回荡，如同皮球般纷乱弹撞。我听见一个男子发出低沉的吼声。然后黄包车车夫从我身边冲了过去，叫喊着。一个女子惊恐万分，喊得声嘶力竭，我听到小巷另一侧的墙上有扇门开了又关，但不见有人出来走到巷子里。

我吓得要命，但岂能坐视不管，眼睁睁听任两个女子被歹人谋害，于是我踢了踢毛驴，哒哒哒，我们冲向发生争吵的地点。不过，最终挽回事态的人并不是我，而是阿福——那个赶驴人。他大叫着一路狂奔，转进巷子，向我们直冲而来。

黄包车车夫蓦地撒手逃命而去，车上的小姐被甩倒在地。一个笨重的身影弯腰正意欲对她图谋不轨，那位阿妈正对此人又拽又打。寂静之中，阿福和我弄出相当的动静声。那个劫匪受到惊吓，跳将起来，前后打量巷子的情况，看到两个敌人正从巷子两头分别朝他逼近，就迅速靠紧墙上那扇深陷进去的门，一下子从我们眼前消失了。

阿福既可笑又幼稚，与其说他是施救者，不如说他更像个蹦跶的影子，他跳到那瘫倒在地的女子跟前，我也早已从驴背上下来，跪在她身旁。那位阿妈惊魂未定，将女子从地上扶起来。

“我的戒指和手镯，”女子大哭道，“他把我的首饰都抢走了。”

阿妈的手迅速摸了摸小姐的耳朵。

“他没有时间抢（我的耳环），”女子说，“我感到有把冰冷的刀抵着我的脸，但这个外国女人马上大叫起来，那个男的就把手收回去了。”

The amah was straightening her mistress' clothes and loudly bewailing their misfortune. Ah Fok, panting, leaned against the donkey, and I patted his hands. What funny things we do when we are upset! Neither of us spoke. I heard the sliding home of heavy bolts on the other side of the wall. At the end of the alley I saw a growing glimmer of light. It was the ricksha man, coming back with a friend. I sat on my donkey while they all had a "talkee talk." Ah Fok, satisfied as to my safety, joined in the parley, but no gate opened in the blank walls, and no head appeared to see what was up. That struck me as queer. I found I was shaking, or rather that the beating of my heart was shaking me. Also I was in a dripping perspiration. At last the Chinese turned and went off down the alley in the direction from which they had come. Ah Fok tied a leading string to the donkey's bridle. The noise of the richsha died away. In the alley it was again utterly dark and silent. A strip of starry sky roofed the space between the houses. Taking a last look at the heavy wooden door sunk in the wall, I noticed a faint glimmer of light near the threshold.

"What's that?" I asked Ah Fok.

He stooped and picked up a knife and held it out to me. It had a wide bright blade, and dusty red spots mottled its edge. I looked at it curiously. The handle was bluntly round and dark from much holding in hot, sweaty hands. I wanted to take it home as a souvenir. I wanted to show it to Edward. I wanted it very much, but so did Ah Fok. His whole body trembled with fearful entreaty. I suddenly became convinced that the robber was crouching on the other side of that barred door, listening with every nerve of his body. I almost fancied that Ah Fok turned and spoke so that his voice and words should carry to any one listening on the other side of the wall.

"Belong bad knife," he said. "Suppose Missey take homeside, some night knife can walk, can kill. Throw away."

Ah Fok held out his hands for the knife, but I still turned it over and over in my fingers, loath to relinquish it. Ah Fok, searching in his belt, drew out a box of matches. He lit two or three at once. The sudden flame made the scene weird

阿妈一边给小姐整理衣衫，一边大声哭诉刚才遭遇的不幸。阿福喘着气，靠在毛驴身上，我拍了拍他的手。我们在慌乱中做了一件多么异乎寻常的事！我和阿福一言不发。从墙的另一侧传来沉重的门闩滑动、闩落的响声。我看见巷子尽头有道光变得越来越亮。原来是那位黄包车车夫，他带着一位朋友赶回来了。我坐回驴背，这些人喋喋不休地交谈起来。看到我安然无恙，阿福十分满意，所以他也加入了这场多方会谈，但白墙上再没哪扇门被打开过，也无人从中探头查看巷里的情况。这点令我感到怪异。我发现自己瑟瑟发抖，或者说是心跳让我打战。而且我还不停冒汗，大汗淋漓。最终，那几个中国人纷纷转身，沿着来时的方向离开了。阿福把一条牵引绳系到毛驴的笼头上。黄包车声渐渐远去。巷子重又变得漆黑一片、鸦雀无声。两边房子的中间，是一长条嵌着繁星的天穹。我朝那扇陷进墙内的厚重木门看了最后一眼，发现门槛附近隐约有淡淡的光影闪动。

“那是什么？”我问阿福。

他弯身捡起一把小刀，把它递给我。刀片宽大雪亮，刃口斑驳，沾着尘土和红斑。我好奇地端详着这把刀。刀柄曾被许多只汗水涔涔、热血沸腾的手握过，显得浑圆、暗沉。我很想把它带回去当作纪念品。我要拿它在爱德华面前显摆显摆。虽然自己内心渴望拥有此刀，可阿福也想要它。他浑身颤抖，胆怯地恳求着想要回这把刀。我猛然醒悟，此时此刻，强盗必定还在那扇闩紧的大门后面蹲守，调动每一根神经倾听门外的动静。我几乎可以想见以下这幅场景：阿福回头说话，一字一句全部传进了墙另一侧某位偷听者的耳朵里。

“这刀晦气，”他说，“假如小姐带回家，不知哪天晚上（这刀就）会走路，也会杀人。扔掉。”

阿福伸手要回那把刀，但我还是拿在手上反复把玩它，不愿放弃。阿福从腰带里翻出一盒火柴，随即划着了两三根。突然出现的火苗使得周围

and uncanny, throwing a great distorted shadow of us on the smooth surface of the opposite wall. The donkey was like some monstrous beast while Ah Fok and I bent like two gnomes over the blade in my hands. At one end of the handle, cut deeply into the wood and painted red, were two Chinese characters meaning "White Wolf."

"Bah Long" (White Wolf), shouted Ah Fok.

He caught the knife from my hands and threw it over the wall. We stood immobile till we heard it clang on the pavement of the garden within the wall. From over the wall came the sound of stealthy motions and a just audible sigh of content.

Ah Fok too was satisfied. He pulled at the rope on the bridle and we walked sedately back, down that long, narrow, sinister alley where all the houses were dark and barred and silent, where no glimmer of light shone through the chinks in the walls and doorways. The way back was long and tortuous. I had a suspicion that Ah Fok was purposely twisting this way and that so that I should utterly lose what sense of direction I had, so that I should never, by any chance, find that barred door in the blind wall.

We crossed a high bridge. The dark canal was dotted with the pinpoint, white reflections of the tranquil stars overhead. With soft gurgles, the water rushed and swished against the posts of the bridge. Something like the curved blade of a knife stuck in the ooze on the shore. I was never sure about that crescent bit of light. It might have been metal, but it might have been merely the iridescent gleam of a stagnant pool that took shape and meaning from our heated imaginations.

"A White Wolf knife," I whispered, pointing at the bit of silver light.

Ah Fok shivered.

"Bah Long," he whispered, his teeth chattering. The name of the famous brigand was yet more fearful than the fear of devils. Ah Fok jabbed the donkey fiercely, and we plunged down the steep, irregular steps of the high bridge. The donkey slipped to his haunches and recovered his footing with a jerk, but Ah Fok, as if pursued by a hundred evil spirits, urged the donkey along, regardless of pitfalls. His sharp ringing cries echoed shrilly up and down the empty street. We did not slow down till we caught up with Doctor Grace.

的景象怪异可怕，火苗将我俩巨大而扭曲的影子投射到对面那面平滑的墙面上。毛驴像一只怪兽，而阿福和我则好比两个侏儒躬身盯着我手上那把小刀。木质刀柄的一端，刻着两个中国字，刻痕深邃，描了红漆，意为“白狼”。

“白狼！”阿福惊叫道。

他把刀从我手中夺走，将它抛过墙头。我们一动也不敢动，站在原地，直到听见刀触及墙内花园的地面，发出哐啷一声。墙那边有窸窸窣窣的动静，我们依稀辨出了一声如释重负的叹息。

阿福也很满意。他牵动毛驴笼头上的缰绳，我们沿着那条狭长、危险的窄巷，平静地往回走，两边的房屋昏暗、深锁、悄无声息，大门紧闭，不见一丝灯光。折返的道路漫长而痛苦。我怀疑阿福故意绕来绕去，这样我就会彻底失去之前的方向感，以后无论如何也找不到那面白墙上紧闭的大门了。

我们经过一座高桥。头上繁星静谧，暗黑的河面泛着细碎的白光，那是它们的倒影。潺潺河水冲刷、拍打着桥柱。有个弧形刀刃样的东西插在岸边的淤泥里。我无法确定那点月牙形的微光为何物。它可能只是个金属片，但也可能仅仅是来自一潭死水上的斑斓光泽，这潭死水经由我们狂热的想象获得了形式和意义。

“一把白狼刀。”我指着那道银光轻声说。

阿福打了个激灵。

“白狼。”他低声道，牙齿发颤。这个知名土匪的名字所带来的威慑力胜过了人们对鬼的恐惧。阿福猛戳小毛驴，我们顺着高桥上陡直而参差的台阶快速冲了下去。驴子打了个趔趄，臀部险些着地，猝然一拧身，才又站稳当，但是阿福，仿佛身后有上百个恶鬼在追他似的，不断催促驴子赶路，全然不顾地上有许多坑坑洼洼的地方。他那尖锐的赶驴声在空旷的街上回荡。我们一路狂奔，直到追上格瑞斯医生。

We found her dismounted, waiting in front of a massive door, with a group of amahs and coolies around her. Lanterns hung on the gateposts. A lighted doorway threw floods of light down the path to the gate. From within the house came the sound of a woman moaning.

"Where have you been?" she asked. "I was about to turn back to hunt for you."

"The donkey ran away, and I got lost," I answered, "we had quite an adventure." I explained, telling her all the details. Doctor Grace took my news seriously.

"I'm afraid we'll have to discharge Ah Fok," she said. " He came to us without a recommendation. Once before his donkey has run away in that direction. That is a very dangerous part of the city. Even in peaceful times it is unsafe, but since the terrorism of the White Wolf brigands it is really dangerous. A nest of them are reported to be in hiding somewhere over there near one of the gates. Just last week one was shot by a sentry while he was trying to escape over the wall by night. Robberies are frequent, but the people are so afraid that they do nothing."

" It wasn't Ah Fok's fault," I said. "I think I rather enjoyed it."

Something within me, utterly primitive and untamed, exulted in the close danger, in my dip into the days of lawlessness and disorder and secrecy. My blood tingled through my veins. I wanted to go back to the hidden world of violence, to cast off my tame, demure shackles and be an Amazon. I was feeling very wild and reckless. I had not known before that each individual harbors all the past of the race within his own inner consciousness, battened down, clamped under by the etiquette of civilization. It had only needed the runaway, galloping hoofs of a little donkey and the gleam of a knife along the wall to hurl me back into the æons of the past.

But Doctor Grace guessed none of this. Outwardly as quiet and well behaved as she, I walked through the gate of the House of Li, the Jeweller in Jade.

此时她已下驴，被一群阿妈和苦力围着，正在一扇巨型大门前等我们。灯笼高高挂在门柱上。门前灯火通明，将门口那条小路照得雪亮。从屋子里面，传来一个女子的呻吟声。

“你们去哪儿了？”她问道，“我都快转回去找你了。”

“驴子跑偏了，我迷了路，”我答道，“我们这一路惊心动魄。”我向她做了解释，并讲述了经历的一切。对于我说的故事，格瑞斯医生神情凝重。

“恐怕我们不得不把阿福辞掉，”她说，“他来时无人推荐。之前有一次，他的驴子也是朝那个方向跑掉的。苏州那一带非常危险。即便是和平年代，那里也不安全。自从白狼匪闹起事端后，那个区域越发凶险莫测。据传，那里某扇门附近就藏匿着一个土匪老巢。就在上周，有个人想趁夜色翻墙逃走，被一个哨兵开枪打死了。城里盗劫频发，但人们太过害怕，对之无能为力。”

“不能怪阿福，”我说，“我倒还相当喜欢刚才那段旅程呢。”

我内心有种纯粹原始、狂放不羁的东西，因为近距离接触到危险，因为多日沉醉于无拘无束、毫无秩序的诡秘生活之中，而欢喜雀跃。我血脉偾张，渴望重回那充满暴力的隐秘世界，挣脱温顺、端庄的枷锁，回归本真。我变得狂野且不顾一切。我以前从未懂得，其实每个人最深层的意识之中，都隐藏着人类所有过往，古往今来，它遭受文明社会礼仪规范的制约和封存。只需一头飞奔的小毛驴，一把白墙边的飞刀，便能一下子将我拽回那漫长的过去。

不过格瑞斯医生并未猜到我的心思。表面上我和她一般安静、一般举止得体，穿过李宅大门，我走进那位玉石珠宝商的家。

Chinese Gardens

中国园林

（多萝西·格雷著　孟祥德译）

《中国园林》（*Chinese Gardens*），作者是多萝西·格雷（Dorothy Graham，1893—1959），1938 年由达德米德股份有限公司（Dodd, Mead & Company, Inc.）出版。

多萝西·格雷是一位美国摄影爱好者，酷爱中国文化。她在考察北京、洛阳、苏州、杭州、扬州、南京、广州等地的园林的基础上，写就该书。该书具有相当的学术价值，影响颇大。作者另著有《穿过月洞门：一个美国女摄影师眼中的老北京》（*Through the Moondoor*），1926 年在美国纽约出版。

节译部分为该书第 76—81 页和第 92—107 页，全部与苏州园林相关，主要涉及留园、狮子林、西园寺、怡园、拙政园等。其文笔细腻、语言优美，展现了西方对中国园林的审美视角。

Along the Yangtse Valley where the Ming rulers first came into power, there still remain traces of the romantic gardens usually associated with the Ming tradition. Intimate gardens, precious in feeling, inimitably Chinese.

Soochow, situated amid the water-ways and rice fields of a vast alluvial plain, has been singularly fortunate in its pleasances. Seventeen centuries ago the King of Wu terraced the hill known as Li Yen Shan for Hsi Shih, the Beauty of Beauties. Throughout the succeeding ages men have been attracted to the calm loveliness of this terrain. Under the Mings, when scholarship was richly rewarded, officials retiring from government service came to Soochow to devote their leisure to the arrangement of rockeries and the cultivation of chrysanthemums.

In the examinations for political appointments, Soochow had more successful candidates than any other city in the Empire. To win honours as a scholar meant the attainment of power and wealth. Eventually there gathered in Soochow an aristocracy of learned families, maintaining their supremacy through four or five hundred years. Each generation went out to posts in the provinces and, at the end of the term, returned, enriched by administrative labours. It was the duty of the mandarin to collect taxes for the Emperor. After he had satisfied the demands of the Imperial Treasury, it was his prerogative to keep the surplus for his own use. The family, rather than the State, was the focal point for Chinese loyalty. Often a family made great sacrifices in order that a talented son might pursue his studies; and when success was assured, they expected their recompense. The mandarin's obligations compelled him to establish a *chia*, a home to shelter his progeny, his relatives and his retainers. At one time there were twenty-five hundred mandarins in Soochow, an amazing concentration of scholarship and wealth. Later, when foreign trade gave the merchant class opportunities to enrich themselves, these men, too, brought their profits to the pleasure city.

Soochow lies within grey crenelated walls, girdled by canals and intersected by an intricate system of water-ways. The plain beyond is cut into segments by paddy fields stretching to the high pale skies where tufts of clouds are swept by the upper winds. Occasionally the flatness of the sear rice stubble is broken by the arch of a stone bridge spanning a canal, a widow's *p'ailou* with a carabao browsing nearby, a bare branched persimmon tree hung with tawny fruit.

Out beyond the city lay the earliest of Ming pleasure grounds, the Garden

明初，帝王刚刚登基。在长江流域，如今尚存明传统园林，其风流隽秀痕迹依稀可见。似此私密之园，贵在情调，为中国人所独有。

苏州地处冲积平原，土地广袤，水路纵横，稻田成片；长久以来，造园弄林，得天独厚。1 700 年前[1]，吴王为西施筑台灵岩山。西施乃色中绝色。其后千百年间，当地社会安定，风物可人，人所向往。明朝治下，文人颇受优待，官员卸任后，常来苏州，造假山，种秋菊，寄托闲情。

昔日科举取士，苏州中举人数居全国城市之首。读书人一旦进士及第，则权财兼得。于是，书香门第终成权贵，四五百年间，煊赫一时。他们世代出仕各省，离任还乡时，早已政务练达。这些官员负责为帝王征缴税赋。在缴齐户部定额后，多余部分，他们优先占为己用。若论忠诚，时人先家而后国。通常情况下，子孙若有天分，举家倾其物力，供给读书；一旦取得功名，其家人即图回报。为官之道，亦在齐家，以荫蔽子孙、亲戚，乃至仆人。在苏官员一度多达 2 500 名。文人、财富如此集中，令人赞叹。后值朝廷开埠通商，商人借机发财，亦携获利，来此欢趣之都。

苏州四面城墙，墙体灰色，留有垛口；护城河环绕四周，水路纵横交错。城外平原，阡陌纵横，稻田绵延至苍茫天际。其间，风吹高天，云聚云散。四周稻茬成片，干枯齐整，间以石拱桥，横卧运河之上；或贞节牌楼，水牛傍近吃草；或秃枝柿树，上挂黄褐色果实。

拙政园在闹市之外，为明早期消遣场所。当年，御史王氏突遭罢官，

[1] 吴王生活的年代是公元前 5 世纪，距离该书出版时间 1938 年已有 2 000 多年，显然作者时间计算有误。

of the Disappointed Politician[1]. A Censor named Wang, having been abruptly deprived of office, turned his administrative talents to the creation of a garden. He experimented, draining the marshes and planting trees; where there was high ground he added earth to make a hill; where the terrain was low, he dug it out and made a lake.

His friends, travelling by litter to the interior, halted their leisurely progress at the Cho Chêng Yuan to admire and to give advice. The curve of a stream offered possibilities for discussion; the trimming of a peach bough or the placing of a wattle fence, with the cool leaves of creeping vines. The Censor Wang was reviving traditions which had lain dormant during a troubled period. The Unsuccessful in Government Garden became the example on which many later Soochow gardens were modelled.

A record of the principal scenes has been kept in a series of thirty-one paintings, a scroll by Wen Chen-ming. It does not approach the masterful manner of the Sung artists, being blurred and soft-toned. Yet the impressionistic brush-strokes suggest the oppressive burden of summer heat, the sharp break of the season in the wind-driven trees. Each vista has an explanatory verse, lines appropriate to the view. Along the Willow Shore one glimpses the ethereal mist of new tendrils in the spring. The Pavilion for Awaiting Frost shows a thatched shelter beside a bleak grove, with snow clouds scurrying across a wide sky. Every temperament has been considered. There is the Place of Smiles, the Place for Listening to the Sighing Pines, the Elevation for Remote Thought.

In the exaggerations of the artist—the height of the precipices, the desolation of marsh and lake—the onlooker is allowed to see the intention that lay behind the actuality. The Garden of the Disappointed Politician could never have had such stark crags and lonely wastes. But the Chinese exercise volition to see what they want to see; they have the propensity to ignore, to expand and to create.

The garden is an art of deception, not of realism. Subjective in influence, it is a point of departure from which the mind makes its escape.

[1] 此处 the Garden of the Disappointed Politician，以及下文中“Cho Chêng Yuan”“the Unsuccessful in Government Garden”，均指拙政园。（译者注）

遂将其为政之才尽付造园：竭泽，植树，几番尝试；高处添土为丘，低处掘地成湖。

当初，王氏好友乘轿入城，于拙政园驻足流连，观赏指点。一湾溪水之曲折，一树桃木之修剪，一篱枝条之安放，一架藤蔓之成荫，皆成话题。御史王氏意欲复兴乱世荒废之传统。拙政园终成典范之作，为后世苏州园林所宗。

文徵明依园中主景绘图三十一幅，成一册。然其线条模糊，画风绵弱，终不及宋代大家之风范。不过，园内暑气之逼人，风吹树摇中节气之突变，在其印象派笔触中一一展现。每一景，配诗一首，以为注解，诗与景合。沿柳隩，遥看春柳绒须，如烟似缕，清新缥缈。寒林傍草屋，天阔雪云飞，此待霜亭之景。世间万千心绪，一一虑及。有怡颜处、听松风处、意远台。

崖壁之高耸，池沼之苍寂，皆画家之夸张。观者于虚实背后，可窥其意图。拙政园本无悬崖峭壁，亦不会荒凉如此。但是，中国人微动意念，见所欲见；他们或实略之，或虚张之，或生造之。

园之为艺，在虚不在实。其影响在主观，可令人身处园中，而神游物外。

Soochow Gardens

The most beautiful garden in the Ming tradition is the Liu Yuan, which lies beyond Soochow on the banks of a quiet canal. Designed in the sixteenth century, it remained for several hundred years in the possession of the Liu family. During the last days of Manchu rule, it was acquired by Shang Taotai, Minister of Communications. Shang named it the Lingering Garden, a considerate act, since the Chinese pronunciation of the word to tarry differs only slightly from Liu. Shang perpetuated the name of the original maker rather than his own.

A fortune was spent upon the rehabilitation of the garden. Then, keeping pace with progress, Shang ordered the construction of the first "horse road" in the district, so that officials might drive out from Tsangman Gate and participate in the amusements commensurate with the dignity of literary men. In the courtyards of the Liu Yuan walls were left bare, waiting for impromptu verses to be composed, ready for specimens of brush-work, light as floating clouds, bold as startled dragons.

The Revolution of 1911 deprived Shang of his revenues. At his death his sons became involved in prolonged litigation and the property reverted to the city. But the old garden, spared when the T'aiping armies swept down the Yangtse Valley, remains a place of poignant loveliness.

The encircling walls of the Liu Yuan are black and high; the entrance is a gateway of dark wood. Within, one finds a courtyard in chalk white, an astonishing vacuity that is intended to divest the mind of all impression.

From this court there leads a long narrow passage, an interlude of intense whiteness, held within cool shadows. One penetrates farther and farther into austere depths of silence where footsteps echo hollowly on the grey bricks or are muted by a verdigris of moss.

After this prelude of blankness one comes suddenly upon the garden. An oval pool, obliterated by lotus; and, slanting above the pool, the great trunk of a camphor tree. There is a background of white walls, the weathered timbers of an upper storey, octagonal windows set with small panes of shell, the sweeping angle of a curved roof. A harmony of line and colour which shows the salient principle of Chinese design, the architectural setting supplying the decorative motif for the garden.

From one point one sees the rhythmic perfection of balanced line, the white walls cut by filigree, the knowing tangle of vines. Yet there are many

苏州园林

明代传统园林，留园最美。园在姑苏城外，枕运河之畔，16世纪构图建造，数百年间曾为刘氏子孙所有。晚清，园为邮传部大臣盛道台购得[1]。盛命其名为留园。此用心之举，因汉字“留”与“刘”读音相差无几[2]。盛无意盗名窃誉，而欲使造园旧主名垂后世。

修复此园花费颇巨。为赶潮流，盛着令修建该区域首条马路，以便官员乘马车出阊门，赴文人雅集。园内墙壁虚白，专待即兴诗作，挥毫其上，轻若浮云，矫若惊龙。

1911年辛亥革命夺盛氏收入。盛死后，诸子涉讼多年，该园没为官产。此前，太平军横扫长江流域之际，旧园幸免于难。如今，故园依旧，惹人怜爱。

留园四周灰墙高筑，大门为黑木结构。进得门来，却见院落四周一片粉白，空空荡荡，未免令人诧异。虚实若此，意在尽除诸相杂念。

院外一狭长廊道相通，尽头处，可见清影婆娑之中白茫茫一片。一段通道犹如一段插曲。移步而入，步步幽深。踏灰砖青苔之上，或空空回响，或闷声沉沉。

经此留白序曲，园林忽现眼前。但见池塘椭圆形状，荷叶田田，覆满水面；一香樟树干，斜依池上。（曲溪楼）粉墙掩映，二层窗木，久经风吹日晒；蠡壳窗呈八角形状，雕花屋顶，飞檐翘角。线条与色彩相映成趣，如此章法，特点鲜明，实为中国土木设计所宗。其装点主题则因境而生。

一隅观之，可见线条律动，完美平衡；几段粉墙，间以雕砖镂瓦；几处藤蔓，存意攀缘缠绕。其余方面，无不令人赞叹。空间局促如此，仍可

[1] 留园当时为盛宣怀之父盛康购得，盛宣怀后官至邮传部大臣。

[2] 实际“留”与“刘”读音完全一致。

other aspects, all astonishing. In this limited space a score of views have been suggested. By distorting the proportions of the other vistas, the designer has deprived the place of reality and projected a fantastic region that is quite unearthly.

The lotus rising from this pool cupped between the house walls and the towering rocks are savage in their profusion. They invade the scene, thrusting their virile stalks upwards. They dwarf the rocky islet with its pavilion of scarlet lacquer; they overwhelm the fretted bridge. Even the jagged pinnacles of rock high above are menaced by the encroaching lotus.

In the autumn the sun is drawn down to the cupped pool, and in the sharp pale light the seed pods of the lotus seem seared, the sap drained from the strong stalks. A blue haze seems to emanate from the enormous leaves, marked with the crevice which is the sign of withering. Blue shadows of decadence, overtones which emphasize unreality.

A maze of paths runs through the rockeries of the Liu Yuan so that one may thread a way through their piled-up confusion. Topping the highest peak is a lacquered pavilion from which one may watch the flight of birds. Another is placed to catch faint whiffs of perfume, cloves, aloes and cinnamon.

In this mild climate of the south, life is spent out of doors. At one side of the garden has been projected an open rectangular room, fifty feet in length by twenty in width, topped by tiles and finished by a moulding of unvarnished wood. Here the family gathered to drink tea and eat melon seeds, to exchange jests in mellifluous tones. The space is open to the breeze, yet affords protection from the frequent showers. It is a setting for an existence of elegant indolence, for figures in silken robes whose least gestures were weighed down by nail-protectors studded with precious stones.

Within the courts of the Liu Yuan, there are many other gardens. One is a tangle of wild olives, wax trees and cassia. Another, where the oblique sun strikes, is enlivened by the shiny leaves and the bright red berries of the bush known as "heavenly bamboo."

A recess in the long line of corridors, where the roof recedes and a diffused clarity filters through, is called Heaven's Well. This open space is intended to let a pallid clarity pierce the inner apartments, also to permit the growth of contrasting foliage against the white filigree of the wall. Magnolias with their shining leaves and waxen flowers are planted in such a place. The *olea fragrans*

得二十余景。主景之外，错乱尺寸，令该处虚实相间，超凡脱俗，宛如幻境。

池中荷花肆意丛生，其状如双手捧出，亭亭玉立于屋墙、假山之间。荷茎挺拔直上，突入眼帘，令水中乱石小岛、岛上红漆凉亭，但觉低矮；浮雕小桥，甚至参差高耸柱石，皆为之气短。

至若秋日，骄阳洒向杯状荷塘，光线亮白刺眼，莲蓬枯若焦灼，秆茎挺立依旧，但水分尽失。薄雾苍苍，似从荷盖弥漫开来；叶间缝隙渐觉，枯萎之状始显。荷影颓然暗淡，更觉气氛虚幻。

园内，蹊径纵横，蜿蜒于假山之间。穿行其中，如入乱石迷阵。假山至高处，一漆木凉亭翼然其上，亭中可观飞鸟。园中更设“闻木樨香轩”，另有丁香、芦荟、肉桂等草木。

江南气候温润，消闲多喜户外。在园一侧，一敞轩前出，长方形状，五十英尺长，二十英尺宽。青瓦作顶，素木为脊。昔日，阖家老少，常聚于此。闲嗑瓜子，慢啜香茗。你一俏言，我一趣语，细气柔声，侃侃而谈。此间空阔，轻风任拂，阵雨可避。此情此境，适高雅之士，从容闲居；丝衣罗衫佳人，若戴护指，镶金嵌玉，则举手投足之间，稍一动作，便嫌沉甸。

院落四合之内，别有小园。其一园，野橄榄、蜡树、桂花错杂；又一园，植灌木名曰“天竹”，阳光照射其上，绿叶油亮，浆果鲜红，令满园生辉。

一线长廊，曲径通幽。尽头处，上无遮蔽，亮光散漫透入，此处名曰“天井”。留此开阔空间，意在使微光穿堂入户。而室外，粉墙下，枝叶斑驳，向阳而生。天井内木兰树叶亮绿，另植蜡梅，更有桂树，为南方所喜栽。

is a favourite in the south.

In the Liu Yuan the Heaven's Well is treated with even more imagination. One such recess has a vine obscurely patterned against the wall, a tracery of tentacles like threads woven in blurred silver, weirdly significant in the dimness. It seems to be without life, the ghost of a vine, yet far above its heavy canopy of leaves extends across the sky. Another interstice in a milky dusk has three writhing trees, their claw like roots winding tenaciously about a rock. They are infinitely old, stylized symbols of age.

All these ramifications of garden and dwelling, Shang Taotai recorded on a map on a wall near the entrance. White lines on black slate show the position of the houses and the courtyards; the trees, the pavilions and the pools are sketched in realistically. The plan must have grown erratically through the years; it is the achievement of a succession of lives, given over to the deeply satisfying sensation of living.

If Shang Taotai had left a written account of his labours, it would doubtless have read very much like the record of the official who made the Yu Yuan, the Garden of Ease, in Shanghai, during the Ming dynasty.

To the west of my house [he says] lay plantations of vegetables, fields and trees. In the Chi Wei year of Chia Ching [1559] my term as an official of the Board of Rites at Peking having ended and being at leisure, I collected a few rocks and called workmen to place them. I dug a pool, built a pavilion and planted bamboos.For twenty years I continued. I sat a sit; I thought a thought; I rested a rest. But the result was still not up to my expectations.

In the Tun Chou year of the Wang Li period [1577] when I returned from Szechuan where I had held the office of Treasurer of the Province, I gave my heart to the work. I increased the size by adding fifteen plots of land. I made seventeen pools. Furthermore I bought many rice fields outside the city and devoted their revenue to beautifying the garden. My first reason was to give my mother pleasure. I also invited my friends in order to witness their enjoyment.The garden daily became more beautiful. To the east I build several high houses, in order to shut out the noise of the city. Over a doorway I placed a stone with the inscription: Yu Yuan, Garden of Ease. After a few steps one came to a second gate where I placed the ideographs Chien Chia—Beauty Penetrates Gradually.

Twenty paces to the west there is a small archway inscribed: Jen Ching Hu T'ien—Man's Place is in the Immortals' Heaven. Passing through the arch and

留园天井令人格外浮想联翩。在此休憩之所，一架葡萄攀墙缘壁，轮廓隐现。一窗触须宛若游丝，缠绕于暗银色花格之上，于一片暗绿之中，格外显眼。枯藤似无生机，然幽灵一般，枝繁叶茂，蔽日遮天。中间空隙，树影婆娑，忽明忽暗，三株藤木攀缘而上，张牙舞爪，颇似盘根错节于岩石之状。见藤木之古老，知岁月之沧桑。

近留园入口处有一墙壁，盛道台尽刻林园屋舍分布于其上。房屋庭院位置，以青石白线勾勒而出；树木、凉亭、池塘如实绘入。此园筹划经年，反复改动，实醉心于生活闲趣之人，几世为功。

造园之劳，若诉诸笔端，盛道台所记想来必不逊于《豫园记》。豫园在上海，建于明代。

《豫园记》曰："余舍之西偏，旧有蔬圃数畦。嘉靖己未，下第春官，稍稍聚石凿池，构亭艺竹，垂二十年，屡作屡止，未有成绩。

"万历丁丑，解蜀藩绶归，一意充拓。地加辟者十五，池加凿者十七。每岁耕获，尽为营治之资。时奉老亲觞咏其间，而园渐称胜区矣。园东面架楼数椽，以隔尘市之嚣，中三楹为门，匾曰'豫园'，取愉悦老亲意也。入门西行可数武，复得门，曰'渐佳'。

"西可二十武，折而北，竖一小坊，曰'人境壶天'。过坊，得石梁穹窿跨水上，梁竟而高墉，中陷石刻四篆字，曰'寰中大快'……前临奇石……

across a curved stone bridge, one steps into the Domain of Great Joy. Here is a superb rock. A pavilion with a scarlet railing hangs over the water so that one may throw flour cakes to the fishes. This is called Joy of Fishes Pavilion. Beyond it stretch rocks that have the appearance of mountains and a curving wall, carved and ornamented ... [1]

WITHIN the walled city of Soochow the lanes are thronged. The alleys are narrow slits, hung with strips of cloth that dim the sun, adorned with gilded shop signs of the merchants. The way mounts steeply over a camel-back bridge, crossing a canal where junks with tawny sails drift by, then slants down to obscure regions where ivory carvers toil and men dip lengths of cotton cloth into cauldrons of indigo dye. Through an indolent surge of humanity, vendors hurry, shouting their wares. Coolies, groaning under the weight of a catalpa-wood coffin, push forward desperately. Chair-bearers, uttering piercing cries, shoulder the poles of a palanquin curtained with black gauze that holds a painted singing-girl inside.

From this confusion and turmoil, the cacophony of varied cries, from the steaming heat and repellent odours, the officials of Soochow found surcease behind high walls. Walls of plaster stained black kept them from the ever-insistent crowds. Women in the lanes might burn joss-sticks to ward off the breath of pestilence; coolies might smoke their thick bamboo pipes in the shadow of the gate; the echo of felt-soled shoes on the cobble-stones might continue night and day. But, within, the scholars dwelt in a fantastic world of their own devising. They had, by intelligence and un-remitting study, lifted themselves from the struggles of the masses. They owed to their honorable position both isolation and forgetfulness.

A Soochow garden remote from actuality as a scene from another planet is the Forest of Lions, the noted Shih Tze Lin. Ni Tsan, the artist philosopher of the fourteenth century, gave his entire life to the placing of these weird rocks. Rocks that seem to have endured since the beginning of time, seared by fierce suns, shaped by sweeping tides, rocks that suggest infinity.

Rocks stand for longevity, and association with them is presumed to have an uplifting influence. Buddha said that each stone possesses a soul and will enter Nirvana. Yet long before the Chinese had accepted Buddhism, they had felt the potent appeal of rocks. Natural specimens, never quarried, never touched by a chisel, are valued for their contorted forms and strange erosions.

[1] Translation of Florence Aycough from *A Chinese Mirror*.（原注）

堂后轩一楹，朱槛临流，时饵鱼其下，曰‘鱼乐’……隐起作岩峦坡谷状……颇擅丹雘雕镂之美。”[1]

苏州城墙之内，道路拥挤，街巷狭长，店家挂布幔以遮阳，悬镀金招牌以装点。一拱桥状如驼背，横跨运河之上，桥身坡度不小。河中帆船挂茶色风帆，漂流而过。桥面道路下坡后，渐行渐远，或至象牙雕刻作坊，工人劳作其中；或至染布工厂，伙计将长短棉布浸入靛蓝色染缸。街道上，行人慵懒，货郎贩夫匆匆穿行，叫卖其间。脚夫苦力抬一梓木棺椁，不堪重负，呻吟、挣扎前行。轿夫肩扛抬杠，声嘶力竭，上有一轿，青纱为帘，内坐一歌女，浓妆艳抹。

昔日，四周乱糟糟、闹哄哄、热腾腾、臭乎乎一片，而苏州衙门官吏躲进高墙深院，安享一方清净。青灰泥墙外，人群络绎不绝。小巷内，妇女焚香遮臭驱赶瘟疫；苦力蹲门口墙阴下，点起粗壮竹管烟斗；薄底鞋踏在卵石表面，落地有声，日夜可闻。然而，高墙内别有天地，为文人雅士安居之所，精心营造。想当年，他们凭借才华，刻苦攻读，最终脱身于劳苦大众。其后，居职位之尊，心安理得，他们深居简出，将百姓疾苦尽抛脑后。

苏州园林狮子林，超然尘世，宛如天外之景。14 世纪书画大师倪瓒毕其生堆叠奇石。开天辟地以来，岩石历经烈日烤灼、潮水侵蚀，方成今日之形状。见岩石，知无穷。

石有长寿之寓。据传，与石久处，可受熏陶。佛说，凡石皆有灵魂，可至涅槃境界。中国人尚未接受佛教之时，早已察觉岩石魅力之大。天然石品，非开采得来，无斧凿之痕，乃风雨剥蚀而成，以奇形怪状者为上。

[1] 英文译文出自弗洛伦斯·艾思柯《中国的镜子》。该书全名为 *A Chinese Mirror, Being Reflections of the Reality behind Appearance*（《中国的镜子：透过现象看本质》）。

When a stone has personality, the Chinese find it excellent company. A famous calligraphist of the Sung dynasty, Mei Fei, anticipated the words of St. Francis of Assisi and called a rock his "big brother." A Yuan painter, Ko Chin-ssu, paid homage to a strange rock, still standing in the Half-Cocoon Garden. The Emperor Ch'ien Lung, visiting the Shih Tze Lin on his southern journey, admired the arrangement so much that he ordered it reproduced as nearly as possible for his palace near Peking.

The Shih Tze Lin rocks are limestone, obtained from the bottom of Lake T'ai. Porous, spare, grotesque, the odd shapes have been formed by the action of the waters upon their surfaces. T'ai Hu is a lake of treacherous currents and sudden storms; the restless waters working for countless aeons have produced strange conformations. An emperor of the Sung dynasty first discovered how effective these T'ai Hu rocks were in his gardens, the canals became dotted with the tall sails of junks bringing this treasure to his palace at Kaifeng.

The rarity of the T'ai Hu specimens tempted imitators; and, during the Ming period, when interest in rocks reached its height, such rocks were carved artificially and laid under waterfalls for a score of years to be tempered. But the practice was considered deplorable; the results rarely deceived connoisseurs.

The Shih Tze Lin garden is nothing but a vast accumulation of rocks. Mazes, mountains and caverns, pinnacles of rocks that fringe the pools. One is lost in their intricacies, bewildered by their proximity. Rocks crowd about one; rocks stretch into the distance, fantastic, incredible, projecting the mind to far regions.

This garden is an abstraction. Catching the essence of objects, portraying the spirit rather than the fact was the desire of the artist. Ni Tsan made pictures in imperishable rocks. The Forest of Lions is a synthesis of Chinese garden design, the final flight from actuality to the celestial places of which the scholars dreamed.

THE particular charm of Ming gardens lies in an informal alliance between the natural and the artificial. The use of curving dragon-back walls, pebbled pavements, oddly cut doors and varied windows developed the feeling of artifice to a high degree.

The circular windows with modelled designs of clay are exceptionally interesting. Animals are set within a décor of exotic foliage—startled fauns, wily squirrels, pompous elephants, superior cranes. These apertures, cut at intervals in the plaster wall, blend with the background. They appear unexpectedly when the

石有灵性，中国人引以为知己伙伴。米芾，宋代知名书法家，获奇石，以“兄”呼之。其后方有意大利阿西西的圣徒——圣弗朗西斯品石之说闻于世。元代画家柯九思见奇石下拜，该石至今仍矗立于半茧园内。乾隆南巡，游狮子林，见奇石堆砌如此，羡慕不已，遂下旨着令京郊御园仿造务肖。

狮子林所用石头为石灰石，采自太湖水底。其形透、瘦、奇、怪，乃湖水冲刷石面而成。太湖水流变化莫测，狂风暴雨常至。亿万年间，千淘万漉，太湖石方成此奇形怪状。宋徽宗见其装点花园效果颇佳，于是，大小帆船，满载奇石珍品，运往开封。一时间，运河内，云帆点点，塞满河道。

太湖石品类稀缺，仿造者难抵诱惑。明代赏玩奇石之风鼎盛之时，工匠人工刻镂后，将石置于瀑布下一二十年，经水流反复冲击。然而此举拙劣，伪造成品鲜能骗过行家。

狮子林不过湖石堆叠，颇具规模而已。其曲径、假山、洞穴、柱石，裙带池畔。其布局纵横交错，令人迷失；其外观大同小异，使人迷惑。环顾四周，但见岩石簇拥，向外连绵不尽，空灵虚幻，惹人遐思。

此园不拘物象。艺术家所追求者：领悟万物之精髓，重传神，轻写实。倪瓒以顽石入画。狮子林集中国园林设计之成就，为文人雅士梦寐以求之地，借此超脱尘世，终至羽化登仙。

游离于天工与人作之间，明代园林别具一格。墙走龙脊，卵石铺地，门户奇特，窗牖各异，颇有一股“人作”之风。

黏土预制圆窗，格外有趣。兽禽形状镶嵌其中：农牧神，人身羊首，口叼树叶，莫名惊诧，颇有异域风采。更有松鼠之狡黠，大象之傲慢，仙鹤之高冷。灰泥墙上，镂空时见，与背景相融；每当清风摇动树枝，它们

wind moves the tree branches aside.

Other rounded windows in the gardens are filled with "iron-flower" work, *t'ieh-hua*, designs cut from sheet iron by workers capable of remarkable artistry. The intricate detail of the leaf pattern is emphasized by a bird in flight or figures of lohans. The loveliest of these windows, dating from the Ming period, are in the walls of a Hangchow monastery. At night lights are placed behind the ironwork and they are called lantern windows. Such lovely designs as these are entirely unlike later reproductions, commercialized to the point of banality.

The colour scheme of the south China garden is of an admirable simplicity. The chalk-white walls are effective backgrounds for the broad fronds of the plantains, as the sharp glare of the sun alternates with the fluctuating shadows of the leaves. Usually there is the dark note of weathered wood—a tea-house, or an open gallery. The façade of the pavilion is set with windows of pearl-shell in small squares or octagons, a severe but beautiful setting for the display of foliage.

At the Si Yuan Ssu, the temple garden that lies just beyond Soochow, the shallow lake is partially framed by circular white walls. These give peculiar value to the scarlet thread of bridge zigzagging across the lake and to the island pavilion with the sharply tipped roof. The willow trees fringing the farther shore seem more diaphanous, the water clearer because of this semicircle of brilliant white.

The wall forms a gallery, for it supports a roof of tiles. Pillars of wood hold up the outer edge. The ceiling of dark unvarnished wood is dappled by the refracted light of the sun dancing on the waters.

Monks in their russet silks pace this walk, telling their beads.The processional with the gilded gods files this way when the deities are taken from their altar niches and shown the parched country-side so that they may be reminded to send rain. The autumn is caught within this space, open only to the south and west, holding the mellow quiescent sun while inimical winds are shut out. The leaves of the ginko trees, bright brittle gold, fall to the pavement and lie there untroubled.

The pavements of the Si Yuan Ssu and of all Ming gardens are of special interest. Paths that lead through shrubberies are set with small grey pebbles that have figures of birds and flowers outlined by thin curving stones. A duck with outspread wings, an opening chrysanthemum, a butterfly; these divert the eye and lead the wanderer on.

Courtyards are paved with tiny rounded pebbles, often duncoloured, the

在不经意间闪现。

其他圆窗内嵌“铁花”制品。“铁花”乃能工巧匠剪裁铁皮，设计而成。飞鸟、罗汉形状更显叶片图案精巧细致。明代以来，最可爱者莫过于杭州一寺庙内墙壁花窗。入夜，铁艺花窗为灯火掩映，是为灯笼窗。设计如此可爱，全不似后来再造者，其商业化已至庸俗地步。

在中国南方，园林色彩搭配之简令人钦佩。墙壁粉白，映衬着芭蕉阔叶，太阳之光共蕉叶之影交替晃动。通常，再配以枯木之暗黑色调，或为茶室，或为外廊。凉亭正面镶嵌蠡壳窗，或小四方形，或八角形状，与枝叶深相映衬，然不失俏丽。

西园寺，为寺园，在姑苏城外。寺内浅塘，粉墙半围，为水面小桥格外增色。小桥如红线曲折，横穿湖面，至小岛凉亭。凉亭宝顶陡峭。对岸稍远处，半圈亮白墙壁，令沿岸细柳更觉朦胧，使池水尤显清澈。

围墙上覆瓦片，因成长廊。外缘以木柱支撑。光线舞动水面，折射进来，光影斑驳，映着黑色素木屋顶。

因见僧侣着黄褐色僧衣，手持念珠，口中念念有词，携所抬镀金佛像鱼贯而出。为祈雨救灾，人们将佛像从佛龛请下来，遍示乡间旱情。秋天困顿于此地，尽日西风、南风吹拂，阳光柔和，挥之不去，却将秋风秋雨拒之门外。银杏金黄薄叶，飘零满地，无人问津。

西园寺以及所有明代园林内，路面铺陈格外有趣。小路蜿蜒于灌木丛中，取小巧卵石勾勒禽鸟之形，或花叶之状，镶嵌其中。有展翅之鸭，绽放之菊，飞舞之蝶，令人侧目，引人漫步向前。

庭院下铺小巧卵石。路面多灰褐色，呈多边形状，见暗红轮廓。图案

polygons outlined in faint rose. One pattern resembles the quatrefoil; another is a series of octagonal figures tipped by smaller squares, repeated until the impression is that of a tessellated pavement. Sometimes the design is quite obliterated by arosy-tinted plant, its infinitesimal leaves blending so perfectly that it is perceptible only as a glowing patina.

The long straight walks are paved with narrow grey brick, set in blocks of five to make alternating squares. Usually the bricks are placed at an angle, to give a herringbone effect. These walks have been worn smooth by the gliding steps of the Chinese, centuries of contact with soft-soled slippers. The grey is a cool dimcolour; moss of a vivid green creeps up between the crevices.

The tangle of shrubberies covers the area of the garden. There is never any clipped turf. Where a ragged fringe of grass appears,it is the Book Girdle Grass, growing from tiny bulbous roots. This got its name from the practice of a Han scholar who kept his slave girls kneeling on a bit of grass each morning, until each in turn had improvised a poem.

Soochow is a city of water-ways. Under the lattice windows of the houses, sampans, slipper boats and junks with tall ribbed sails drift by. The canals are eternally tranquil, catching glints of the mild sky, darkened by the shadows of high-arched bridges. They seem a basic theme of peace, gliding through existence.

Scholars brought the streams into their gardens, setting them deeply within narrow channels faced with rugged rocks. The thread of stagnant water lies far below the surface of the ground, so that the shadows of the rocks are imprisoned in the fissures. Sometimes the water was opaque with algae and glinted like a ribbon of bright metallic green.

The Yi Yuan, one of the most lovely of the old gardens, has a water-way with precipitous banks and dark sluggish depths. After a sinuous course, it reaches a deep-set lotus pool. A tea-house of weathered wood has been poised on the brink, shaped like the bow of a ship, with the obliquely projecting balusters that are seen on the poops of old sailing galleons. The scholar at his case could go sailing on the sea of his imagination. The wind in the sails was simulated by the sound of lutes, as was the sighing of the breeze and the low rhythmic sound of wave slapping against the prow.

In the Yi Yuan there are the ancient stone tables on which the lutes were placed when the singing-girls plucked at the strings and evoked plaintive

或类四叶，或为八角，棱角尖儿饰以小方块，如此重复，终成花街铺地之状。间或枝叶纤细，淡着粉红，疏影摇曳其上，融洽之至，令人但觉浮光轻掠。

若步道既长且直，则以细窄青砖尽铺路面。另外，五砖一组，砌成方块，间隔搭配。至于路面，通常两砖成斜对角铺开，呈人字形。数百年间，软底便鞋，踢踏其上，路面早已磨平。青砖颜色暗冷，苍苔翠绿，于砖缝间悄然而出。

满园灌木丛生。草皮不曾修剪。眼前青草一丛，参差不齐，名曰“书带草”，球状小根长成。相传汉代一文人，每日清晨令其奴婢跪青草之上，轮流作诗，诗成乃罢。“书带草”因而得名。

苏城水巷纵横。花格窗下，舢板、轻舟、帆船漂流而过。其中，帆船高悬风帆，帆骨如肋。运河常年静流，风和日丽之时，水光潋滟，高拱石桥倒影，暗覆水面。一派祥和景象，在岁月间溜过。

文人士大夫引流水入园，深灌狭窄水渠；水渠之侧，山石嶙峋。临渠下望，可见滞水一线，山石之影遂困于缝隙之中。偶尔，水藻泛滥，不见水底；水面泛光，如铜锈翠带轻拂。

古典园林中，怡园可爱之至；园内一水路相通，夹岸山石峻峭，流水暗滞幽深。蜿蜒前行后，至一深水莲池。池边，一枯木茶舍空悬，状如船头；栏杆斜出，为古代帆船船尾所常见。文人居此，神思当远航想象之海。风帆吹动，微风轻叹，波浪拍打船头，声音低沉，不紧不慢；风声水声，如闻琴声。

怡园内有旧石桌，可放琴筝。歌女拨动琴弦，琴声哀怨嘈切。邻院广植翠竹，微风若有若无，竹叶便窸窣作响，待细叶枯萎发白之际，摇摇欲坠，

dissonances. In one of the near-by courts a forest growth of bamboo has been planted so that the shivering leaves may magnify the least stir of wind. Blanched leaves have been left on the ground, withered and fragile, to respond sibilantly to the least whisper of air.

Bamboos are ranged along the pebbled walks in infinite varieties. There is the purple species with the mark of the tortoise along the stem, the golden feathery bamboo, dazzling in the light, the phoenix-tailed, the kind-hearted, the dripping leaf and Buddha's heart. Bamboos thrust their lilting shadows against the dragon-backed wall; they drift in great masses over the wattle fences. Bamboos droop beside the latticed façades of pearl-shell; they rear their plumed foliage by the gallery where the women stroll, looking out through openings in the form of leaves or narrow lipped vases. Across bamboo thickets, the kingfishers dart, winged streaks of iridescent blue.

The sound of bamboos in the Yi Yuan is omnipresent, simulating the sea. The garden might be on an island, cut off from the city by an expanse of wide lagoon.

The garden is neglected now. The race of scholars is nearly extinct. In a cage stands a dejected crane, as if weary of waiting for some Immortal to fly with him to paradise.

THE Fu Yuan is also a water garden, a place of deep pools and cavernous rivulets. Algae cover the stagnant water; the early sun slanting upon it makes a dazzling sheen, a bright metallic gilding that is unusual. The thickets bordering the lake are overhung with clematis; the marsh sedges are mingled with frail scarlet lilies. Framing this vista is a gateway of dark wood, panelled with translucent pearl-shell.

A gently ascending mount is the central point of the garden. Here an enormous rectangular tea-house has been placed, open on all four sides. One looks down on the sinuous glittering streams, on the ancient trees and wisteria vines with writhing silvered fibres. Monks from an adjacent temple come to make their morning meditations here. Young gentlemen of leisure in pastel silks arrive to sip tea and play finger games. Barrel-shaped garden seats of stone have been placed where the vistas are finest. There are also porcelain stools in the same characteristic form, in dull green, turquoise and deep eggplant colour.

The Fu Yuan is like a web, spun in filaments of radiant green. The oblique sun on the winding water-ways makes threads of vivid light. The flecked leaves

气息微动，即作丝丝之声以为回应。

各色翠竹，沿卵石步道齐栽。有紫竹，枝干龟纹；有金羽竹，光泽耀目。另有凤尾竹、慈竹、斑竹、佛肚竹。竹影轻摇，映在龙脊墙面，丛丛簇簇，荡漾于编条篱栅之上，低垂于蠡壳花窗之侧；而游廊边，佳人闲步处，羽叶向上挺立。透过竹叶间隙，或细颈瓶状花窗、门洞，向外可窥。翠鸟穿林渡竹，疾飞如箭，羽翼条纹，翠色斑斓。

怡园之内，竹声无处不在，如闻海浪。林园或在小岛之上，四周大片水域，与城区隔水相望。

怡园现已荒废。书香世家几近绝迹。只见一鸟笼内，立一仙鹤，垂头丧气，似乎久等仙人同飞天国不至，而心生倦怠。

复园亦多水之园，池塘幽深，溪流坑坑洼洼。池水滞留处，荇藻上覆水面。朝晖斜映，泛金属异光，令人目眩。湖边灌木，上垂铁线莲，沼泽莎草，间杂睡莲。睡莲红艳娇柔。黑木门户，镶嵌蚌壳，似透非透，尽衔远处景象。

一缓坡土丘，为该园中心。上置一茶室，方形敞轩。下可俯视曲水流光，或观古木，更见紫藤，枝干如银白纤维盘绕。附近寺院僧侣常来此坐参早禅。少年闲士，着淡雅丝绸，来此品茗，或拇战嬉戏。园内石凳，状若木桶，安放之处，乃风光至胜之地；亦有瓷凳，为清一色常见款式，或暗绿，或松绿，或茄紫。

复园如网，绿芒细丝织就。河道曲折，斜照轻泄，活泼灵动，如丝如线。树叶斑驳，辉映其间，起舞嬉戏，巧弄图案。复园华美，光阴缠绵，于曜

shine brilliantly; the interplay of dancing foliage makes intricate changing patterns. Tropic in its luxuriance, the Fu Yuan is a garden of tangled light, shiftingmutations in dazzling green. It is called the Fu Yuan, the Returned Garden, because it was restored about the middle of the eighteenth century, following the plan of an earlier garden of the Ming period. Sometimes it is identified as the Garden of the Disappointed Politician, but its location would seem to preclude that claim.

Fortunately the Fu Yuan was the headquarters of the T'aiping rebels during the campaign when they swept down the Yangtse Valley, and so escaped destruction at their hands. At that time (about 1850) a large portion of Soochow was devastated. Other walled cities were completely destroyed, their inhabitants put to the sword. It is estimated that twenty million people perished. Passing along the quiet canals of this fertile plain, one can still see ghostly, deserted cities, with ruined houses and streets choked by tall grasses. British sportsmen from Shanghai come in their house-boats to hunt quail and pheasant in the courtyards of official yamens, to flush teal from the ponds which once adorned a mandarin's garden[1].

In 1845 Vetch sent botanists from England to explore the Yangtse Valley. These men brought back quantities of specimens, Chinese in origin. In 1875 another expedition covered the same territory. No new plants were found and many of the former ones could not be located. The T'aiping War had so thoroughly devastated the land that even plant life had been exterminated. Today in Nanking it is impossible for vegetation to grow in some areas, so solidly is the ground packed with ruins of brick and rubble.

Ming gardens that are now forgotten existed in the cities of Kashing, Nanking, Yangchow, Huchow. All the lower Yangtse region, prosperous, sheltering a scholarly aristocracy, was laid waste. The inhabitants who escaped the T'aiping rebels were killed by the armies of the Imperialists, marching under the Ever-Victorious Gordon. Life has ebbed back to many of the cities of the plain. But the gardens were not often restored.

They can be numbered now in dozens, instead of thousands. THE Twilight Garden of the Anhuei Guild lies within a rambling house in a densely populated section of Soochow. It was a meeting-place for men who had been born in An-

[1] teal 疑为“鸳鸯”，a mandarin's garden 疑为“拙政园”，因当时拙政园俗称“满洲园”(the Manchu Garden)，且拙政园内至今仍饲养鸳鸯。私家园林内，野鸭恐难饲养。（译者注）

然绿意之间，变幻多姿。复园之“复”，有“复归”之意，18世纪中叶，仿明代早期造园之法修复。或称“复园”为“拙政园”，但其园址不同，此说故不成立。

太平天国运动期间，太平军横扫长江流域，征用复园为太平军大营，复园因而幸免于难。1850年前后，苏城大部面目全非。至于其他城市，则城池尽毁，城内百姓惨遭杀害。据估算，两千万民众死于刀兵。现如今，由水路仍可见：平原沃野经行处，市井萧条鬼唱歌。房屋街道，几成废墟，为蒿草吞没。英国好猎者从上海坐住家船过来，在官府衙门院内猎杀鹌鹑、野鸡，在池塘轰起野鸭。曾经，官宦人家，于花园内饲养野鸭，以供观赏。

1845年，维奇从英国派遣植物学家考察长江流域。他们带回大量中国原产植物样本。1875年，他们故地重探。结果，一无所获，而原有植物，许多已不知所踪。太平天国运动令该地满目疮痍，甚至很多植物因此灭绝。时至今日，南京某些地方堆满废砖弃瓦，密不生草。

原存于嘉兴、南京、扬州、湖州之明代园林，今已无从记起。曾几何时，江南富贵繁华之地，士绅庇荫其间，如今触目荒凉。当地百姓侥幸逃过太平军一劫，却被朝廷官兵所杀。指挥官兵长驱直入者，正是常胜军头目戈登。如今，该平原许多城市烟火生机渐起，但园林常常未得修复。

现今园林仅存数十，而非数千。安徽会馆之惠荫园，据苏城人烟阜盛之域，屋院散落，乃安徽同乡聚会之所。世道兴盛之日，园内宴饮宾客；世道衰落之时，会馆庇护穷困。年长财阔之辈掌管会馆事务，聚议良策。

huei province. In prosperous times, banquets were given here; in days of distress it sheltered the poorer members. A committee of the aged and the affluent met to give good advice. When death overtook the Anhuei men, their bodies were laid in thick-boarded coffins filled with charcoal and stored in an inner room until an auspicious date was determined and they could be transported to Anhuei to be buried in their native soil.

Few Anhuei men remain in Soochow, and the shell of the house has been deserted for many years. The endless white corridors are stained with damp. Towards the rear, closely held within the walls of a long narrow court, is a mysterious dark garden.

In the dim tranquility jagged rocks tower to preposterous heights. Water lies within cavernous depths, black with deposits of fallen leaves. Overhanging the rivulet is a gigantic fig tree, its branches spreading like malignant growth, its leaves like mammoth bats. The deep stream wanders to the far end of the court where a bridge of chiselled stone crosses it, and a path leads up to rocky pinnacles, lost in the crepuscule.

Such a fantasy might have originated in the mind of a Chinese Poe, with a predilection for regions remote and damned. Decay and oppressive darkness, a brooding sense of futility marks the Anhuei Hai Kuan. One mouldering wall is set with black tablets, traced with spectral white ideographs—the verses of poets long dead and forgotten.

It is rare to find a garden from which so deep a melancholy emanates. The past is reverenced by the Chinese, but not regretted. Neglect is often noticeable, but not the morbid quality of the Anhuei Guild.

THE He Yuan is the cassia garden, made for the autumn flowering of those trees. The fragrant small clusters of the cinnamon bloom are the symbol of waning sweetness, a reminder that summer has fled. The time of fetid heat has passed, when red tapers were lighted to keep the pestilence away. Plague and the season of parching have gone by; the sullen air has been stirred by the typhoon wind, by beating rain and fast-scudding clouds.

Then come diminishing days, the Cassia Moon, the Season of White Dew. Mornings are sharp with frost, yet a strong sun mounts in a high pale sky. The cassia with its pervasive fragrance marks a transitory peace, the bright perfection of autumn, a tranquility that may be shattered like brittle glass. It passes quickly and is recalled with nostalgic longing. The ephemeral quality caused an eighth

若有安徽同乡去世，则以厚板棺椁装殓，内置木炭，停放内室，待择吉日，运抵安徽，下葬故土。

安徽籍士仍留居苏州者，已为数不多，房屋外壳失修多年。长廊粉墙潮痕斑斑。向院深处，更见一狭长小院。院墙四合，内嵌一园，神秘幽暗。

于此黯然静谧之中，参差岩石巍然耸立，高低错落怪诞。潭水幽深昏暗，落叶浮沉其间。一株巨型无花果树，斜依水上，枝杈横生，树叶似展翅蝙蝠。深流蜿蜒至院落尽头，一石雕小桥横卧水上。过桥后，一小径通往乱石阵中，消失在苍茫之间。

中国若有爱伦·坡，亦当心生奇幻如许，亦钟爱冥远之地。腐朽、压抑、黑暗，给安徽会馆蒙上一层森然颓废气息。一段墙壁，内嵌黑色石碑，上刻白色碑文。碑文如幽灵一般，若隐若现。诗句主人，早已仙逝，无从忆起。

沉郁之气弥漫如该园之深者，少之又少。中国人尚古，而不惜古。古迹荒弃之风虽常显著，然断不至安徽会馆之病态如此。

鹤园为桂花之园，营造此园专为秋日花开。桂花盛开时，香蕊簇簇，小巧玲珑，然甜美迹象，盛极转衰，提醒人们夏日已然遁去。恶臭炎热之时已过，无须焚香驱疫。瘟疫并焦晒溽热之季一去不返。沉郁之气，为台风、骤雨、飞云所扰动。

此后，白昼渐短，始逢“桂月”[1]、白露节气。霜晨料峭，然晌午时分，骄阳上悬苍天。桂花香彻，不过祥和转瞬即逝之兆。秋光之盛，娴静易碎，脆如玻璃。其逝去也瞬乎，其追忆也怅然。转瞬如是，无怪乎 8 世纪有诗

[1] “the Cassia Moon”应指农历八月。一因桂花常于农历八月间盛开，二因农历月份常表达为 moon，如八月为 the eighth moon。

century poet to write:

You cannot pour the wine star's wine,
Nor taste the cassia of the moon ...

The He Yuan is a garden given over to autumn. The stark white walls of the successive courts are cut by windows of filigree white. Between these are placed pomegranate trees with tarnished leaves and orange-red fruit. Loquats are espaliered against the whiteness; thick silvery branches, heavy leaves of russet, pale fruit of astringent yellow are twisted into a conventional design. Quinces, called tree melons, glow like lanterns in their tawny foliage.

In a farther courtyard two great rose vines make a tracery against a high wall. Their ancient roots protrude above the ground; the spread of their flattened branches reaches twenty feet in height with more than seventy feet in width. Yet the effect on the wall is of an intricately fine etching—delicate tendrils and tiny copper leaves, veined ruddy leaves that flutter to the pavement.

人写道：“酒星非所酌，月桂不为食。”

鹤园乃纵情秋色之园。院复一院，围墙雪白，接连成片；墙壁镶嵌白色细格窗户，断断续续。粉墙掩映之间，格窗衬托之下，或植石榴，其叶暗绿，果实橘红；或架枇杷，枝干茂密，色泽暗银，叶阔赤褐，果实涩黄泛白。后者树形，扭曲弯折，成传统造型。木瓜，亦名“树木之瓜”，于茶色枝叶之间，曜若灯笼。

更深处，一庭院内，两架蔷薇藤蔓，构成花格形状，掩映于高墙之下。树根颇有年头，伸出地面；枝干扁平，蔓延开来，高足二十英尺，广七十余。然而，触须娇美，枝叶或小巧玲珑，泛黄铜微光；或色泽红润，纹理可辨，向平铺路面招摇婆娑。一枝一叶，反照墙面，宛如精雕细刻。

The Land of the Dragon

龙之国度

（威廉·斯宾塞·帕西瓦尔著　余利霞、骆碧筠译）

威廉·斯宾塞·帕西瓦尔（William Spencer Percival，1827—1888）是英国国王派驻上海的文官。《龙之国度》（*The Land of the Dragon*）是他在中国任职期间沿长江乘船度假、狩猎之游记，书中生动描述了他每一次出行的有趣冒险经历，1889 年在伦敦由赫斯特和布莱克特有限公司（Hurst and Blackett Limited）出版发行。摘译的第七章是作者乘坐住家船前往太湖岛屿度假康复的经历，以日记形式呈现，详细讲述他在拥挤河道上的奋力突围，在太湖某些岛上与当地人发生冲突，与狂风暴雨的对抗，船只搁浅撞破船底的遭遇，修补漏洞的辛苦，等等。读来极为扣人心弦，使读者仿佛与作者一起回到了 100 多年前，体会当年的风土人情。

CHAPTER VII

Country Roads—Leave for the Tai-Hu Lake—Creek Boating—Stormy Weather Toongdoong-Sin Island—The Religious Performance—Imprisoned—Escape from the Joss-house—A Deputation of Natives—Our Troubles at Toongdoong-Sin explained—Prospecting for Winter Shooting—A Brilliant Sunset—A Photographer's Difficulties—No Escape from the Natives—The Boat Springs a Leak—Make a Dry Dock—Homeward Bound—Outside Soochow—The Monastery Hill —Home at Last.

READING through the foregoing jottings, it occurs to me that, to anyone who has not lived in China, it may appear strange that you can go nowhere or do anything without a boat.

To a very great extent this is true. Round Shanghai foreigners have, with much difficulty, obtained from the Chinese authorities permission to make a very few miles of roads outside the boundary of the foreign concession. Five miles east, and five miles west is the limit. You must go and return by the same road. Day after day the same weary drive is all the carriage exercise to be had, which in a very short time becomes monotonous in the extreme.

Two or three years ago the municipal council endeavoured to buy from some of the natives a narrow strip of their land, at an absurdly high value, so as to make a new road, and vary a little the sameness of the present drive. But the Taotai stepped in and, under threats of some most awful punishment if his orders were disregarded, prohibited the Chinese from selling their land to foreigners for making new roads. His argument was that we had roads enough, and even more than we ought to have; that, whatever price we offered, the Chinese soil should not be further invaded; and that, so long as he could prevent it, we should not get any more ground. So the scheme fell through, for if any of the natives had sold their land after receiving such orders from the Taotai, they would have had a very bad time for several years to come.

Round Peking there are a few miserable excavations that are called roads, many inches deep in dust in summer, and with a depth of twelve to twenty-four inches of mud in winter. In all the country round Shanghai there is not even so good a highway as this.

The roads between the towns and villages all over this part of the Empire are simply raised earth-banks, with a small rut on either side out of which the

第七章

乡村道路——前往太湖——舟行小溪——暴风雨——洞庭山岛——宗教仪式——被囚——逃离寺院——一队当地人——释惑洞庭山之困——展望冬天狩猎——辉煌落日——摄影者的难题——躲不开的当地人——船漏了——建造干船坞——返程回家——姑苏城外——凤凰山——归家。

在前面的记录中提到，没有船只你哪儿也去不了，什么也做不成，我认为没有在中国生活过的人也许会觉得这很奇怪。

这在很大程度上是真的。在上海的外国人费尽周折才从中国官方获得许可在租界以外修建几英里的道路。东西各五英里是极限。每天在同一条道上往返。日复一日，只能在同一条路上驾着马车，很快就单调乏味极了。

两三年前，市政委员会用高得出奇的价格可劲想从当地人手中购买一块窄窄的土地，以便建造一条新路好改变一下目前一成不变的驾车体验。但是道台大人插手干预，禁止中国人把土地卖给外国人修建新路，并威胁如若违背他的指令，将遭受极为可怕的惩罚。他的理由是：我们已有足够的道路，甚至多于我们该有的；无论我们给什么价，中国土地都不应该再被侵占；只要他可以阻止，我们就不会得到更多的土地。所以这一规划无疾而终，因为在道台大人下达了指令后，如果当地人还将土地卖给外国人，未来几年他们的日子会非常难熬。

北京周遭挖了几条被称为马路的可怜的土道，夏天上面有几英寸厚的灰尘，冬天则有深达 1—2 英尺的泥巴。上海周边连这样的道路都没有。

大清的这一地区所有的乡镇间道路只是高出地面的土堤，两边各挖出一条小沟；土堤穿越田野，只高出田地几英寸，雨天就会被水淹没。土堤

bank has been dug; they are raised a few inches above the level of the fields they cross, and during rainy weather are continually under water. They vary from three feet wide in their broadest parts to one foot or even less in the narrowest. For miles and miles through the country, from town to town, from village to village, these miserable paths run on, allowing just sufficient space for a string of men to follow one another in single file.

Everything in the way of produce is carried slung from the shoulders of the men, each man's load being equally balanced at the end of a long bamboo, which he will carry many miles in the course of a day. On this narrow highway the chair of the mandarin is safely conveyed by his sure-footed bearers; the gilded litter of the bridal procession and the still more imposing funeral train trail their long lengths between the neatly defined crops without break or damage, each to its intended terminus. So it has been for centuries past, and so, in all probability, it will continue for centuries to come.

If a foreigner living in Shanghai wishes for change of air and to go to the seaside, he must make a sea-voyage of over six hundred miles to a very small town named Chefoo, at the entrance of the Gulf of Pechili. This is the nearest change he can get from the broiling heat of a Shanghai summer.

If this does not please him, he must make a still longer trip to Japan, to Nagasaki, Kobi, or Yokohama, the latter about a thousand miles away. Failing this, he is driven back upon his house-boat, and takes himself off to the rivers and creeks, of which there are hundreds running through the country in all directions, and which are used by the natives in place of roads. This alternative is frequently taken by foreigners. You carry your house with you; can stop where you like, and ramble where you will. You carry with you your own cook and boy, and the boat being well provisioned before leaving, you are altogether independent of the country people. It is a wonderfully free and easy life, one that day by day changes like a kaleidoscope; you are continually meeting with a variety of incident that makes living in a houseboat quite the reverse of monotonous. This wild Bohemian independence is most enjoyable, is full of incident;fresh scenes and fresh experiences follow one another in rapid succession; your own resources are being continually drawn upon to bring you out of a difficulty; you soon discover how to depend solely upon your own exertions, and you undoubtedly learn how to handle a boat under every contingency, and never feel at a loss what to do, whether she is lying over on her side, hove to, or drifting on to a lee shore.

最宽的地方3英尺，最窄的地方只有1英尺，甚至更窄。穿村过镇，这些可怜的道路绵延出去很长很长，只够人们一个跟着一个鱼贯而行。

所有物产均是人们肩挑，担子重量很好地均分在一根长竹竿的两端，人们挑着担子一天会走好几英里的路。在这样狭窄的道路上，步履稳健的轿夫抬着官员的轿子稳当地前进着，乱糟糟的送亲队伍和庄严的送葬队伍走在整齐的庄稼之间，奔向各自的目的地，庄稼却完好无损。这样的情形已延续几百年，很有可能未来几百年仍将如此。

若住在上海的外国人想要换个环境去海边度假，就得坐船行驶六百多英里到一个位于渤海湾入口处的小镇烟台，这是他逃离上海酷热的最近选择。

若烟台无法令他开心，就得远赴日本的长崎、神户或横滨，后者距上海大约1 000英里。如果到不了日本，他只得乘坐住家船前往河流与小溪，上海周边四面八方有几百条这样的河流与小溪，这就是当地人出行的道路。外国人也经常乘坐住家船。把家带在身边，凭喜好停船，由着性子闲逛。带上自己的厨子兼伙计，走前船上会配备足够的食物，完全不必依赖乡民。这是一种令人高兴的自由、轻松的生活，每天都像万花筒一般变化万端，每天都会遇到各种意外，住家船上的生活相当精彩。这种原始的放荡不羁的自由很令人愉悦，充满意外；全新的景致，全新的体验，接踵而至；通过不断地挖掘自己的潜能以摆脱困境，一个人很快就发现如何全靠自力更生，真正学会在紧急情况下操控船只，无论是侧倾、顶风停船，还是漂到背风岸，永远不会手足无措。

My own experience of boat life has been fairly extensive, and although on several occasions boats have served me very unkind tricks, and have been within a hair's breadth of bringing my temporary sojourn here to a sudden termination, I still think a sailing boat, with fine weather and a good breeze, one of the most healthful and enjoyable recreations possible.

Here is an account of one of my own adventures, but hardly a fair sample, for most of the time we had a succession of gales of wind accompanied by severe storms of thunder, lightning, and rain, and at the same time we unfortunately fell into the hands of the Philistines.

For several weeks I had been very much out of sorts, there was nothing particular the matter, but neither I nor anyone else could explain why some days I got much better, then suddenly fell off again bad as ever. The doctor did not like my behaviour at all, so one morning he said, 'Now out of this you must go; take a trip for a fortnight or three weeks in a house-boat. If you find it does not suit you, you can come back again; but, on the other hand, if it does suit, then stay away till you are quite well.'

I had not been out of Shanghai for some time and the idea pleased me much. My wife and daughter were to accompany me to look after the invalid, so we began at once preparing for our departure. At length all was ready; but we had entirely overlooked one thing, —none of us had for a moment thought of an itinerary. Some friends recommended one place, some another. The places named had all been too much visited by Europeans. I preferred a locality foreigners had only seen at long and uncertain intervals.

Finally we fixed on a trip to the islands of the Taihu Lake. Taihu, or the large lake about ninety to one hundred miles west of Shanghai, is a vast sheet of water upwards of seventy miles long and sixty wide, with a group of most picturesque mountainous islands lying nearly in the centre. I tried to gain some information about them, but could learn nothing. No one I knew had visited them. A Chinaman who heard of my projected trip strongly urged me not to go. He assured me the inhabitants of the islands were wild men, half savage, who spoke a language no Chinese could understand. My wife and daughter (who for the future I shall call M—and L—) rather liked the novel idea, so we decided for the islands.

The lake itself is very variable in depth, in some places large flats occur, several miles in area, with not more than six or seven feet of water on them; then the bottom suddenly deepens to one hundred and fifty feet and more, so it is not

我在船上的生活经验相当丰富、全面，尽管有几次很狼狈，甚至命悬一线，差点将我在此地的短暂逗留突然变成生命的终点，我仍然认为风和日丽时，泛舟河湖可能是最健康最快乐的休闲方式之一。

下面就是我的一次历险，但不是一个好例子，因为大多数时候我们不断遭遇狂风暴雨、电闪雷鸣，吃尽了苦头。

接连几周我的身体状况一直不佳，没有什么具体的病症，但莫名其妙地，有时候我会好起来，有时又突然跟先前一样糟糕。医生一点也不喜欢我的表现，所以一天上午他说：“你必须得摆脱这一现状；坐上住家船去度假，放松两三周。如果觉得不适合就回来，但如果感觉良好，就等康复了再回来。”

我已经有一段时间没出过上海，这一提议让我很是高兴。妻女要陪同照顾，我们立刻着手准备出发。最终一切准备妥当，但我们完全忽略了一件事——没有一个人想到安排行程。有朋友推荐这儿，也有朋友推荐那儿。他们推荐的地方都是太多欧洲人光顾过的，我更想去一个外国人偶尔一观的地方。

最终我们定下前往太湖的几个岛屿一游。太湖，位于上海以西 90—100 英里的大湖，长 70 英里、宽 60 英里的一大片水域，约湖心处有几座风景如画的山地岛屿。我试图找一些相关信息，但一无所获。我认识的人都未曾涉足这些岛屿。一个中国人听说了我的计划，强烈建议我们不要前往。他向我保证，岛上的居民是野人，很粗鲁，他们说的话没有中国人听得懂。我的妻子和女儿很喜欢与众不同，因此我们决定前往这些岛屿。

太湖深浅不一，湖底有些地方是大片平地，方圆几英里水深不过六七英尺；然后突然就深达 150 多英尺，所以不难想象在大风和汹涌的波涛中

difficult to imagine that during a high wind and lumpy water navigation becomes rather hazardous.

At length we were quite ready to start, and on a beautiful morning in the spring of the year (I think the 26th or 27th of April), we shipped on board the *Retriever*, and with a fair wind headed up the Soochow Creek. It took some time to pole our way out of the boats and junks that were straggling all over the stream; but when we had left the last bridge well astern there was a clear road before us. The yulow was brought inboard, the huge batswing sail hoisted, and away we sped, bound for the islands of the west.

Wang-doo, the first place of any importance we came to, was passed during the night, and Kwing-da, a fortified city, at about eight p.m. the following morning. We made Eding at eleven, and arrived off the fortifications of Soochow at one p.m. Soochow is a most important rebel fortification, being only second to Nanking, their capital. It was besieged and taken by the Imperialists under Colonel Gordon, in 1863. The walls are several miles in circumference and about forty feet high, surrounded by a broad and deep moat, all in an excellent state of repair.

We were uncertain whether to take the northern or southerly route round Soochow, but finally decided upon going south; so, striking off into a small creek which ran out of the south-west corner of the moat, we came in about three hours to the horrible village of Mohdoh, the most abominable, evil-smelling place I ever met with. It is built after the usual manner of riverine villages, the mud huts, very small and excessively dirty, lining each bank of the creek, with a manure heap in front of each hut coming quite down to the water, waiting for the boats to carry it off into the country. The creek itself is not more than twelve to fourteen feet wide. I very soon saw there was every chance of a block, and would have turned back had it been possible to do so. But we were hemmed in both in front and rear, and our best chance was to go ahead. I therefore told the boatmen to pole away and not waste their breath in shouting, for the amount of bawling and talking all over the place was perfectly deafening. All this time the people were heaping upon us unmeasured abuse, and threats of the most dire vengeance, which did us no harm so long as they confined themselves to words.

Wherever we saw a chance of making an opening we jammed in the nose of our boat, and then forced her through. 'Go on, go on; stop for nothing,' was my constant order to the men. The abominable stench from the heaps of filth on the

航行是多么危险。

最终，我们准备好出发，在一个美丽的春日清晨（我想是4月26日或27日），我们登上“猎犬号”顺风沿着苏州河出发了。费了点劲，我们才从船只遍布的河道中划了出去；但等我们穿过最后一座桥时，前面就畅通无阻了。我们收起橹，升起巨大的风帆，加速驶向西边的岛屿。

夜间我们经过的第一个有点名气的地方是黄渡，第二天早上8点[1]到达防御坚固的新渎。11点抵达唯亭，下午1点到了苏州城墙外。苏州是一个十分重要的太平军大本营，仅次于其首府南京。1863年戈登上校[2]率领洋枪队围困并攻取了苏州。苏州城墙周长几英里，高约40英尺，外围一条又宽又深的护城河，一应维护极佳。

我们不确定该走苏州北边还是南边的线路，但最终决定取道南边，因此我们驶进一条由护城河西南角流出的小溪，约3小时后来到了令人生畏的木渎，这是我们所到过的最令人憎恶、气味难闻的地方。此处按常见的沿河村庄式样造房子，很小很脏的简陋泥屋，成排坐落在河两岸，屋前都是粪堆，一直堆到水边，等着船只来将其运往乡村。小河宽不过12—14英尺。很快我就发现河道很可能会拥堵，如果真堵上我们就得调头。结果我们前后都堵上了，我们只有前进。因此我让船夫撑船突围，不要浪费口水大喊大叫，因为无论怎么喊叫，别人也充耳不闻。此时那些人正在不停地辱骂我们，并威胁要狠狠地报复，如果他们只是嘴上骂人，就不会对我们造成什么伤害。

一看到有出路，我们就将船头挤过去，奋力通过。“快走，快走，不要停下。”我不停地指挥着船夫。河岸上污秽散发着恶臭，密匝匝脏兮兮的人群紧紧环伺，船只能否通行尚不确定，头顶烈日灼烤，桩桩件件使我们开

---

[1] 此处原文是 eight p.m.，根据上下文应为 eight a. m.。

[2] 查理·乔治·戈登（Charles George Gordon）（1833年1月28日—1885年1月26日）英国殖民时期的职业军人，于1863年在上海接手洋枪队（上海租界组织的外国人武装队伍），号称“常胜军”。

banks, the close confined atmosphere of such a dense crowd of unwashed humanity, the uncertainty of our ever getting the boat through, and the broiling heat of the sun, began to make us all feel sick and ill. Our loudah assured me that, if we forced our way through as we were doing, the people would board us, and break up everything in the boat. On the other hand, I assured him that, if we did not get out of this very quickly, we should all of us be down with fever before night. Go on he must, and stop for nothing. I would myself guarantee that no one boarded the boat.

Taking a thick and unpleasant-looking stick I stood in the bows, and when anyone tried to board us the stick soon dissuaded him from continuing the attempt.

It was awfully hot. M—and L—were shut up in the cabin. The men worked well when they saw I could be trusted to keep the boat clear, but, although the distance through the village was not more than a mile and a half, I began to get doubtful about our pulling through.

After more than two hours' continuous work the passage became a little more clear, and half-an-hour afterwards we were again in the open fields. Our lungs once more breathed the pure air of the country, but for the remainder of the day we all suffered with sickness and headache.

About seven p.m. we just caught a glimpse of the lake which was now not more than a mile from us. The loudah strongly urged anchoring for the night within a good shelter about a hundred yards from the margin. The wind was rising, with every appearance of a gale, and, as the loudah did not know the navigation of the lake, we moored close under the bank, had a quiet dinner, and a good night's rest.

Monday, May 1st.—A beautiful morning, with a mild and soft air. We took breakfast a little before six, and then put off for the islands, which were quite invisible, so we steered by compass. The lake is like an inland sea; there are many positions from which land is invisible; and from others the tops of the mountains show faintly above the horizon. We had a headwind, and in the course of an hour managed to get the boat firmly aground on one of the flats I have mentioned in less than three feet of water. All the poling we could do was useless, we could not move her; so the whole crew dropped over the side, which lightened her considerably, and, by their all lifting together, she gradually floated off into deep water, when I let go the anchor, and took the small boat to fetch the crew from the bank.

始觉得恶心、犯晕。船老大要我相信，如果我们这样强行穿过的话，那些人会跳上我们的船，砸了所有东西。可是我要他相信，如果我们不迅速离开这里，不到晚上我们就会发烧病倒。他必须继续前行，不能停下。我决定以一己之力确保没有人能登上我们的船。

我拿着一根又粗又丑的棍子站在船头，任何人想登上我们的船，棍子很快就让他放弃尝试。

天气特别炎热，妻子和女儿关在船舱内。船夫们见我能将他人拒之船外就奋力划桨，然而，尽管穿村而过的河道长不过一英里半，我却开始担心能否安全通过。

经过两个多小时的奋力前行，河道开始不那么拥堵了，半小时后我们再次进入开阔的田野中。我们又能呼吸到乡村的纯净空气了，但当日余时我们仍头疼恶心。

约晚上 7 点，我们终于能看见太湖了，就在离我们不足 1 英里之处。船老大强烈要求在离岸边约 100 码[1]的地方找个背风处抛锚过夜。起风了，极可能会变成大风，由于船老大对太湖的航行不了解，我们在靠近岸边的地方停泊，安静地吃了晚饭，睡了个好觉。

5 月 1 日，星期一——清晨很美，微风柔和。我们在 6 点前吃了早饭，起锚前往岛屿，因为根本看不见那些岛屿，所以用罗盘导航。太湖大得像一片内陆海，很多点位看不见陆地；有的点位隐隐能看见地平线上的山顶。我们顶着风，1 小时内妥妥地搁浅在我前面提过的水深不足 3 英尺的浅滩上。我们所做的一切撑船努力都是白费劲，船根本不动，因此所有伙计都跳下船，船身一下轻了许多。在所有人的合力抬举下，船慢慢地漂浮到深水里，我放下锚，驾着小舟将岸上的人摆渡上船。

[1] 码，英美制长度单位，1 码约 0.914 4 米。

The small boat was one that I had brought upon the deck of the house-boat, and would, I thought, be good for small creeks and other places where the larger boat could not go. She was a nice handy little thing, very stiff, about fourteen feet long, with a small lug-sail which could be raised or lowered with the greatest ease.

The weather by this time, about ten a.m., began to look doubtful and overcast, the clouds gathering thickly in the north, and the barometer falling, all boding bad weather, and as we could not reach the islands till nearly evening, with the wind then blowing, we put the boat back, and brought up again at our last night's resting-place, there to wait for a fair wind.

It was fortunate we did so, instead of trying to push on. In less than an hour, after we were all snug, the storm came, accompanied by the most awful lightning and thunder. The wind roared through the trees, and I doubt if the boat could have lived through it had she been on the lake. As it was, she was perfectly sheltered and did not feel it at all. It passed over in about three hours, but, as the wind continued strong, we decided to remain where we were for the night. At sunset it cleared up. L—and I had the small boat out for a couple of hours' recreation before dark.

Tuesday, 2nd.—The morning looked doubtful, but soon after six we tried the lake again. A light breeze springing up from the east favoured us, and the boat sailed well over the easy swell left from yesterday's storm. The wind increased as the time wore on, and before noon we were close on to the island of Toongdoong-sin, when suddenly the weather became overcast again; a drizzling rain came on, enveloping us in an impenetrable mist and making the islands invisible. As there was every chance of running ashore, had we gone on, we took down the sail, let go the anchor, and waited for the weather to clear, which it did in an hour or two. We then tried to work into a small creek, but failed for want of water; put out again, and worked round to the south-west end of the island, and there we found some good moorings in ten feet of water.

Our loudah went ashore with the hopes of hunting up a few fresh eggs, but returned shortly with the information that there was a very large 'joss pidgin,' and a theatrical performance going on about a mile inland. If we would like to see it, he would be our guide, and we might get the eggs on our return. M—and L—were much pleased with the idea of seeing the Chinese actually at home, away from the restraint of the barbarous European; so off we started, the boatman in front being our guide.

小舟是我带来放在住家船甲板上的，我想着小舟会适用于小溪及其他大船无法通行的地方。小船小巧便利，很牢固，长约14英尺，一叶小四角帆可以轻易地升起落下。

此时大约上午10点，天开始转多云，北边的云层越积越厚，气压降低，一切都表明要变天了。由于我们差不多傍晚才能抵达那些岛屿，随着风力加强，我们返航，再次停泊在昨晚休息处，等候顺风顺水。

万幸我们返航了，而不是强行前进。我们停泊妥当后不到1小时，下起了暴雨，夹杂着骇人心魄的电闪雷鸣。狂风呼啸着穿过树木，我想如果待在湖上，我们的船只能否经受得起如此的狂风暴雨。而此时船只因得到完美庇护丝毫没有受到影响。约3小时后雨停了，但风仍然刮得猛烈，所以我们决定待在原处过夜。傍晚天晴了，我和女儿划着小舟在天黑前出去消遣了一两个小时。

2日，*星期二*——清晨天气阴晴不定，但6点后我们再次驾船出湖。从东边吹来的微风令我们愉悦，住家船轻松地驶过昨天暴风雨留下的小小浪涌。随着时间流逝，风力逐渐加强，中午前我们靠近了洞庭山岛，天突然转成多云，下起了小雨，朦朦胧胧的雨雾将我们笼罩着，岛屿也看不见了。如果我们继续前进很有可能会撞上岸，因此我们降下船帆，抛锚停船等天晴，一两个小时后天晴了。我们试图驶进一条小溪，但因水深不够而未果；退出后，我们绕向岛屿的西南端，在此地我们发现了一处不错的停泊点，水深10英尺。

船老大上岸希望买点新鲜的鸡蛋，但很快返回告诉我们岛内约1英里的地方有一大片庙宇，那儿正在进行表演。如果我们想去看的话，他会带我们去，返程时也许能买到鸡蛋。妻子和女儿很高兴能去看一看不受野蛮的欧洲人管束的自在中国人；于是在船老大的带领下，我们出发了。

We soon wound into a lovely valley between gently-sloping hills, covered with azaleas all bursting into bloom; then we reached a table-land with a thick plantation of mulberry-trees most carefully looked after, every dead or decaying leaf being removed, and every attention paid to the trees, so that they shall produce large and healthy leaves. Above this, again, some four hundred feet above the lake, was another table-land, very much larger and spreading out into some wide valleys running towards the interior of the island, in which were several temples of a considerable size. A large theatrical stage, twenty or thirty feet high, was erected under the side of a hill, and the performance was in full swing when we appeared on the outside edge of the crowd. There was a terrible crush, and there could not have been less than five or six thousand people on the ground.

At first the people seemed rather amused at our appearance, and examined both M—and L—'s dresses, hair, boots, &c., with a little too much curiosity. Then they looked displeased, and as we gradually worked our way towards the stage they became very angry; the performers ceased their acting and pointed and shouted at us, and, what was quite unnecessary, called the attention of the people to our presence. We were evidently the chief attraction of the whole show; and their looks and gestures not being assuring, I began to wish we were well out of it. We admired the richly-embroidered dressing of the stage and passed a little pantomimic compliment to the actors, who in return shook their fists, and looked as if they would willingly eat us there and then, clothes and all, just as we stood; we all the time gradually pushing our way through the crowd, endeavouring to find an opening in the dense mass which had now surrounded us.

The whole thing was to me incomprehensible, for I had seen many of their performances before, and on two or three occasions had been behind the scenes, and this was the first time the slightest objection had been raised. There was evidently something very wrong, for the people began to jostle and push us about, all shouting and making a great row. I asked the loudah what they were saying. He replied,

'I don't know—I can't understand a word.'

'Well,' I thought, 'what the Chinaman in Shanghai told me about these islanders evidently appears to be true. They are savages who speak an unknown tongue.'

Matters gradually got worse, until at last several of them began to strike us. This was too much; for the last twenty minutes we had tried to get quietly

很快我们就转进一个美丽的山谷，两边的小山坡道和缓，长满了怒放的杜鹃花；接着我们到了一片台地，那里密植桑树，这些桑树得到精心打理，枯叶尽去，细心照顾下才能长出大而好的桑叶。往上距湖面约400英尺的地方，是另一片台地，面积大得多，延展进岛内几片宽大的山谷，那里有几座规模不小的寺院。一个大舞台，高二三十英尺，沿着山边拔地而起，我们靠近人群外围时，表演正在热火朝天地进行着。场地上人群极度拥挤，不少于五六千人。

起初我们的出现似乎逗乐了那些人，他们以超乎寻常的好奇心打量着妻子和女儿的裙装、头发、靴子等。然后他们好像不高兴了，随着我们逐步挤向舞台，他们开始很愤怒；表演者停下来指着我们大喊大叫，这种不必要的举动引起了人们的注意，他们都发现了我们的存在。我们明显成了全场的焦点，因为他们的表情和手势都使人不放心，我开始希望我们远离此处。我们欣赏着装点华丽的舞台，打着手势赞美着表演者，可他们却挥舞着拳头，似乎要当场活吞了我们；我们一直在人群中挤着，设法在围困我们的密集人群中找到出路。

我完全不明就里，因为我以前好多次看过他们的表演，有两三次还是在后台看的，从未引起什么反感。此时明显不对劲，因为那些人开始推搡我们，大喊大叫，甚是吓人。我问船老大他们在说什么。他答道：

“不知道——我一句也听不懂。”

“好吧，”我想，“上海的那个中国人跟我讲的这些岛民的事似乎是真的，他们是野蛮人，讲的话没人懂。”

情况越来越糟，有几个人开始打我们。真是够了！最后二十分钟我们本想悄悄离开的，如果他们能给我们一点点机会，我们都已经离开了；但

away, and would still have done so had they given us the slightest chance; but they crowded more than ever and again struck at us, when five or six of the most prominent leaders in the most clumsy manner ran up against my fists, and were promptly deposited on their backs. This was such an unexpected performance that caused a sudden lull in the rapidly-gathering storm; so, taking advantage of it, I said to M—and L—,

'The natives are getting very angry; we must clear out of this and reach the boat as soon as possible. You and L—keep close to me; I'll make a road, and the loudah must bring up the rear.'

No sooner said than done; but though we struggled and fought it seemed useless; an opening was no sooner made than it was closed up again by others. They were too numerous; retreat seemed impossible.

The hot sun and the suffocating crush were beginning to tell on M—and L—; they both said they thought they should faint. If they did, what on earth was to be done I had no idea, for the natives were working themselves up into a state of frenzy. One man, more angry than the others, came through the crowd with a long knife tied to the end of a bamboo and commenced to make thrusts at the loudah. I suppose they held him responsible for bringing us there.

The loudah got behind me and dodged from side to side, as the man continued to attack him. I expected every moment to get the knife into me, for, each time he made a poke, it passed within an inch or two of my ribs, first on one side then on the other. Watching an opportunity I seized the bamboo, and broke off the knife. Then a general howl of indignation arose, and we were all carried rather than pushed into a covered passage leading to one of the temples. We soon came to the place where the josses were, but through this we were hurried into another cave-like recess, down another passage, round a corner, thence to another passage, all in semi-darkness, and were finally deposited in a small room; the door was at once closed and barricaded.

So far good, we were for the time out of the crush, in a comparatively pure atmosphere, and, happily, all together.

After a short rest, which was very much needed, we set about examining our prison and discovered a small window, about four feet from the ground, partly filled and tied up with bamboo, and through the interstices we could see the clear open country beyond. Luckily, I had still the knife which was broken off the pole, and with it we soon removed the fastenings which blocked up the window, and

更多的人拥挤过来又开始打我们，此时带头的五六个最显眼的家伙笨拙地冲上来，我的双拳迅速落在他们的背上。这一出其不意的举动使迅速聚集的风暴戛然而止，于是我抓住机会对着妻子与女儿说道：

“这些当地人怒火中烧；我们必须尽快离开这儿到船上去。你和女儿紧跟着我，我挤出一条路，船老大断后。”

说干就干。尽管我们奋力挣扎，但一切似乎都是徒劳的；刚挤开一个缺口，就被人群堵上了。他们人太多了，撤退好像不可能了。

炙热的太阳与令人窒息的挤压开始让妻子和女儿感到不适；她们都说要晕倒了。如果她们真的晕倒了，我不知道究竟该怎么办，因为当地人已进入疯狂的状态。一个比其他人火气都大的男人，从人群中走出来，手拿一把绑在竹竿上的长刀朝船老大刺去。我猜他们是怪他把我们带了过去。

船老大在我身后，那个人不停地攻击他，他左右闪躲。我感觉那把刀随时会刺中我，因为它每一次都是在离我的肋骨仅一两英寸的地方插过，忽左忽右。瞅准机会，我一把抓住竹竿，折下长刀。接着一阵愤怒的吼声响起，与其说我们是被推着不如说是被架着押进了一条通向一座寺庙的封闭过道。很快我们来到庙宇，但穿过寺庙我们被赶进另一个山洞般的凹处，走上一条过道，绕过拐角，又走上另一条半昏暗的过道，最后我们被丢进一间小屋，门被迅速关上锁起。

暂时还好，至少我们摆脱了挤压，来到了相对清净的环境，而更高兴的是，我们几个都在。

稍事休息（这是必须的），我们开始查看囚室，发现了一个小窗，填塞了一些竹子，离地约 4 英尺，透过空隙我们能看到远处空旷的乡野。幸运的是，我还拿着刚刚从竹竿上折下来的刀，很快我们就用刀砍掉了堵住

there before us was an opening to the shore, quite in an opposite direction to the mob of howling fanatics.

Passing M—and L—through this opening, we quickly followed, and, under cover of every tree, shrub or mound available, made tracks as quickly as possible for the boat. It was hot and fatiguing work, but it was impossible to foresee the result if we should be discovered before we reached the boat.

As may be supposed, we lost no time; but when within two or three hundred yards of the boat we were seen, and several hundreds of the mob gave chase. We had a splendid start, and it was hardly possible they could catch us. The loudah shouted to the men in the boat to cast of the moorings, and they, seeing something was very wrong, had everything ready to shove off the moment we were on board.

We got on board, with no time to spare, and instantly the men poled out into deep water. The sail was hoisted, and with a parting cheer to our pursuers we were again free.

We sailed away as though making for the mainland, near Mohdoh, but when well out of sight we changed our course from west to south-east, and made for another island a good many miles to the south of the one we had left. The wind rose, and got so strong that we split the sail and strained the mast. On this lake the winds rise at a few minutes' notice, blow with all the force of a gale for half-an-hour, and then as suddenly drop. We grounded twice before reaching the island, but the boat behaved very well. Ran into a small creek, and made all snug for the night by half-past seven.

Wednesday, 3rd.—The morning broke cloud and threatening, so we decided to remain where we were for a few hours. Meantime L—and I took the small boat and went off exploring. We found some fine sheets of water a mile or two inland, with quantities of reeds and water-plants growing on the margin. They—i.e., these pieces of water—would be grand places for wild-fowl shooting in winter. We put up several ducks and broods of young ones from the banks. There was plenty of broken ground and scrub that would make excellent cover; some of the pools were very large, others small, but all separated one from the other by low-lying hills. Then we tried a creek and came unexpectedly to a village, the natives flocking out of their houses as soon as they saw us. Our presence seemed to please them no more than we had pleased their compatriots yesterday. They yelled and shouted something altogether unintelligible, and it was quite as well it

窗户的那些竹子，面前是一个面向湖岸的洞口，正好在那群疯狂咆哮的暴民背后。

将妻子和女儿送出洞口，我们紧随其后，在树木、灌木和土堆的遮掩下，我们尽可能快地跑向住家船。又累又热，但如果我们在上船前被发现的话，后果无法预料。

正如大家所料，我们没有耽误时间；但是在距离船只两三百码的地方，我们被发现了，数百人追了上来。我们占了先机，他们不可能抓住我们。船老大高声叫嚷，让船夫们起锚，他们看到情况不妙，准备好一切，只待我们上船就撑走。

分秒必争，我们上了船，船夫们立即把船撑向深水区。船帆升了起来，我们欢呼着逃离追赶者，又自由了。

我们驾船离开，假装朝着木渎附近的陆地而去，但等到看不见他们后，我们由西向东南改变航线，驶向另一座小岛，位于我们刚离开的岛屿南方好几英里外。起风了，而且很大，我们将帆分开并拉紧桅杆。太湖上会毫无预兆地起风，猛烈地狠刮半小时，然后又突然减弱。抵达岛屿前，我们搁浅了两次，但住家船运转良好。驶进一条小河，到7点半就一切就绪，准备过夜了。

3日，星期三——天亮了，乌云滚滚，很是吓人，所以我们决定待在原处等候几小时。其间我和女儿驾着小舟出去探险。我们发现几片深入岛内一两英里的宁静水面，边缘长满大片芦苇和水生植物。它们——这些水域——是冬天捕猎野禽的好地方。我们惊起了岸上的几只鸭子和几窝雏鸭。地上有许多洞及灌木，形成很好的遮蔽；水塘有大有小，但都被低矮的小土坡分割开来。我们驶进一条小溪，出其不意地来到一座村庄。一看见我们，村民们就从屋子里蜂拥而出。我们的出现似乎没有取悦他们，就像昨天我们没有取悦他们的同胞一样。他们喊着叫着一些完全含混不清的话，真的

was so, for I am sure it was nothing very complimentary.

We put the boat about and pulled back again, running the gauntlet of a bridge without receiving the expected shower of stones. I desired L—to keep the boat in the middle of the stream while I 'put my back' into the oars. The natives soon got tired of following over rough ground, while the boat made good headway over the smooth water. An hour-and-a-half afterwards we again found our 'home,' and did ample justice to the excellent tiffin awaiting us. This accomplished, M—, L—, and myself took the small boat to another island on the lake, completely covered with azaleas, citron-trees, and pomegranates. Here we spent the remainder of the day sketching and rambling among these most delicious groves. No natives appeared, consequently we were at peace.

Thursday, 4th.—The mists hung heavily over the mountain-tops, but about seven o'clock they commenced to disperse, and all things presaged a fine day. Turned out before six, to try for a dish of fish for breakfast. We could see shoals of them, varying from a quarter of a pound to two pounds, swimming about in the beautifully clear water. Fortune did not favour us, we got nothing, excepting a few stones from some young urchins on the bank. Shortly after, finishing the matutinal pipe, and discussing as to where we should spend the day, a deputation of natives—about twenty—came to us bringing presents of fried melon-seeds, one or two other kinds of seed which they look upon as delicacies, fish, silkworms, eggs, etc.; and, after much talk from one of them who spoke a dialect our loudah understood, they begged our acceptance of the presents they had brought, and invited us into the village to partake of some tea and chowchow which they had prepared. We accepted the fish and silkworms; the seeds, etc., were declined with thanks. A great deal of smiling, friendly gestures, and a long pantomimic performance followed.

Then we presented the women of the deputation with some pieces of ribbon of various colours, pieces of lace, and coloured handkerchiefs. They were highly delighted with them, and showed their pleasure in their own peculiar ways.

When it came to our returning with them to the village, I had my doubts as to the wisdom of such a proceeding. Visions of traps, ambuscades, and all kinds of unpleasant positions in which we might find ourselves constantly presented themselves to my mind. We had not received very friendly treatment from these people hitherto, and I could not understand why they should so suddenly wish to become friends. I spoke to the loudah about it; he said he thought it was all right,

模糊不清，难以理解，但我确定不是什么好话。

我们再次调转航向撤退，虽有一桥阻道，预想中的石头雨却没有从天而降。我让女儿掌舵，将小舟保持在小溪中间，而我则全力划桨。小舟在平滑的水面快速前进，当地人很快就厌倦了在崎岖不平的地面追逐我们。一个半小时后我们再次找到“家”，尽情享用等待我们的丰盛午餐。饭后，我带着妻子、女儿驾着小舟驶向湖中的另一座岛屿，岛上长满杜鹃花、香橼树与石榴树。整个下午，我们在这些宜人的小树林里漫步、画素描。没有当地人出现，因此没人来烦扰我们。

4 日，星期四——薄雾笼罩着山顶，约 7 点，雾气开始消散，一切都预兆好天气。6 点前我们就起床了，想要捕点鱼做早餐。我们能看到成群的鱼儿在清澈的湖水中游来游去，重量从四分之一磅到两磅不等。幸运女神没有眷顾我们，我们一无所获，只有岸上脏孩子扔过来的石头。很快，抽完晨烟一斗，讨论着今天该去哪儿，一队当地人——大约 20 个人——带着礼物来找我们，有炒西瓜子，有他们看作美味的另外一两种种子，有鱼、蚕、鸡蛋等；船老大听得懂其中一个人说的方言，交谈了许久后，他们请求我们收下他们带来的礼物，并邀请我们去村里喝茶，享用他们准备的茶点。我们收下了鱼和蚕，谢绝了瓜子等其他东西。我们微笑着，友好地打着手势，像演哑剧一样地交流着。

我们回赠访客中的女人们各色丝带、蕾丝和彩色手帕。她们很喜欢，用奇怪的方式表达高兴。

等到我们要跟着他们回村里时，我对此行是否明智产生了怀疑。陷阱、埋伏，以及各种可能身陷的不利情形，不断地出现在我脑海中。昨天这些人对我们并不友好，我不懂为什么他们突然又想与我们交好。我向船老大提及我的疑虑；他说他觉得没事，他们想与我们友好相处，如果我们去村庄，

that they intended to act fairly by us, and that if we went to the village he would have the boat ready to sail at a moment's notice, if necessary. None of us had the least desire to show the white feather, or let the natives suppose that for a single moment we were afraid of them; so we accepted their invitation, determining to keep our eyes open, and not to be taken by surprise.

We had a lovely walk through the mulberry groves which were in the most perfect state of cultivation, and the people explained, as well as they could, how the trees were planted and tended year by year; that silk, being the staple, indeed the only produce of the islands, their entire existence depended upon this one industry alone. We walked on till we arrived at the village, which was situated in a lovely valley, and was actually clean—at least, for a Chinese collection of huts. There was no work going on in the silk factories, so they could not show us the process. We partook very sparingly of the tea, etc., and then prepared to depart. They accompanied us back to the river, where we had a number of swimming matches among the small boys for empty bottles, which they treasured exceedingly. And so the day ended without the slightest hitch of any kind. But I failed to divine the meaning of it all. Why they should almost murder us one day, and treat us like friends the next, was to me wholly incomprehensible.

Before they left, the loudah inquired from the one whose dialect he understood why the people had been so angry at the joss pidgin two days before. When the matter was explained to them, they were astonished that two foreign women should have gone to that religious ceremony, and come away again uninjured. No Chinese woman would have been tolerated there for a moment. It was a ceremony for men only; they did not mind my attending, but the presence of two women would upset the whole object and result of the meeting, and in consequence they would have to commence all over again. The mystery was solved.

Towards sunset there was every appearance of wind and rain, so we drew the boat further inland and made her secure for the night.

About eight p.m. the storm broke. The continual flashes of lightning were perfectly blinding, the thunder following the flash without any intermission, and the roll so loud, so deep and vibrating that the entire island trembled. The wind and rain were equally severe, and we heard the lake outside lashing itself into fury, but we were exceedingly snug in our well-selected shelter, and passed the night in comfort. We appear to have got into the land of storms, for they follow

他会让船只做好随时开船的准备（如果需要的话）。我们一点儿不想示弱，也丝毫不想当地人认为我们怕他们，所以我们接受了邀请，决定故作镇定，不大惊小怪。

我们愉快地走在打理得极好的桑树林里，村民们解释说他们年复一年尽可能细心地种植和照料这些桑树；作为支柱，蚕丝真的是这些岛屿唯一的产品，他们的生计完全依赖这唯一的产业。我们继续往前走，到了坐落在一个美丽山谷中的村庄，真的很干净——至少对于中国人的村舍而言是干净的。蚕丝工厂目前没有开工，他们无法向我们演示生产工艺。我们喝了少许茶水等，然后准备离开。他们陪着我们回到河边，河里几个小男孩正在为争几个空瓶子而进行游泳比赛，他们十分宝贝那些瓶子。一天就这样过去了，没有碰到一丁点儿麻烦。但是我无法理解这一切。为什么他们头一天几乎要杀了我们，第二天又当我们像朋友一样，我一头雾水。

他们离开前，船老大问了那个说话他听得懂的人，为什么两天前在寺庙的那些人如此愤怒。我们解释了当时的情形，他们非常震惊于两个外国女人居然去那样的宗教仪式场合，还能毫发无伤地离开！那种场合根本无法容忍任何中国女人。那是一种只有男人才能出席的仪式场合；他们不介意我的存在，但两个女人的出现会坏了整个仪式的目的和结果；如此一来，他们只好全部重来一次。谜题解开了。

快近黄昏时，天看起来要刮风下雨，所以我们把船划向岛内更深处好安全过夜。

晚上 8 点左右下起了暴雨。闪电不断，使人眼花目眩，随之而来的隆隆雷声绵延不绝，震耳欲聋，整座岛屿都颤抖起来。风狂雨暴，听着外面湖上浪涛怒吼，我们在精心挑选的庇护处异常安心，舒舒服服地过了一夜。

one another with little intermission.

Friday, 5th. —The storm died off about midnight, but this morning the wind was, if anything, a trifle stronger. We moved the boat more to the centre of the island, to an exceedingly pretty situation under the base of a hill; there was a village in the far distance, on the opposite side of the creek, but as this was five or six hundred feet wide we feared no trouble.

There were some very fine mandarin groves on the bank. I obtained two or three photographs here, but they were not particularly successful. There was a fine range of hills to the west, and a solitary mountain, with some extremely curious caves, to the northeast.

The water about our anchorage was very clear, and we were quite sheltered by mulberry-groves. It was lovely water for rowing, and the day being boisterous, we put out the small boat, and explored the numerous creeks that ran off in all directions from the main stream.

As to the places that I had seen on these islands—i.e., the various pools and lakes—I made a mental resolution that I would visit them again in winter, when the ground would be clear and the lakes covered with wild fowl, and made notes of the whereabouts of all these waters, with their bearings from certain conspicuous points, and, when I subsequently visited them with gun and dog, the particular localities were easily found. As I had anticipated, swans, geese, ducks, and a variety of winter birds were all over the place. The main stream completely divided the island into two parts, running from south to northeast.

There is a map of these places published in Shanghai, but it is very incorrect, and would lead anyone astray who trusted to it entirely.

Saturday, 6th. —The morning was again gloomy, but cleared before noon. What should we have done without the small boat? It was a continual source of amusement. The light became bright and clear, so we took the camera to the other side of the stream, whence several interesting views could be obtained. I had some trouble with the natives who crowded round, but they were peaceable and well-behaved.

I obtained a very fair negative of a large boat with fishing cormorants. These birds have a ring passed over their heads, and when low down on their throat it tightens, thus preventing their swallowing anything. They are then tumbled into the water, where they dive about, and when a fish is caught they come to the surface, are hoisted, by means of a bamboo, into the boat, taken by the legs,

风暴持续不断，我们似乎也落入了风暴之地。

5日，星期五——午夜时分风暴停息了，但是今晨的风，如果要说些什么，那就是又大了些。我们将船又往岛内挪了挪，来到一个非常美丽的山脚下；河对岸远处有一座村庄，但河宽有五六百英尺，我们不担心有麻烦。

岸上有几片长势良好的柑橘林。我拍了两三张照片，但不是特别理想。西边是连绵的秀美山丘和一座孤山，东北面有几个奇特的山洞。

停泊处的河水极为清澈，周围都是桑树林，水美天好宜于泛舟，我们撑开小舟去探索从主河道流向四面八方的小溪。

想起在这些岛上看到的地方——各种水塘和小湖——我下定决心冬天要再来一次。那时地面光秃，一览无余，湖里野禽遍布，我记录下这些水域的周边环境，并从几个明显的地点进行定位，等我下次扛着猎枪、带着猎犬前来时，就能轻而易举地找到这些地方。如我所料，这个地方到处都是天鹅、大雁、鸭子，还有各种过冬的鸟儿。这条主河道由南流向东北，把岛分隔成两个部分。

上海出版了这儿的地图，但极不准确，如果完全信任这张地图，一定会被带偏。

6日，星期六——上午天又阴了，但不到中午就放晴了。如果没有小舟我们还能干什么呢？这叶小舟是我们源源不断的快乐源泉。光线明亮清澈，我们带着相机前往河对岸，那里有几处景色不错。边上围了一圈当地人，给我带来了一些麻烦，但他们都很温和，举止得当。

我拍摄了一张很中意的照片，是一艘鸬鹚捕鱼船。这些鸬鹚头上套了一个环，环在喉咙下部收紧，从而防止它们吞下东西。鸬鹚被扔到了河里，潜入水中，抓到鱼后浮出水面就被竹竿捞回船上，拎起双脚头朝下，喉咙

turned upside down, their throat pressed, and out comes the fish, and they are again thrown into the stream to hunt for more.

In the evening the sunset was truly grand. On the horizon the cumulus clouds were all tinted with the most gorgeous colours, reflecting their glow on to the cirrus clouds which extended to the zenith. This was a decided promise of settled fine weather after our last week of storm. As the various tints of the clouds melted away, other colours even more brilliant than the previous ones took their place, till at last the whole of the heavens, from zenith to horizon, became of a rich golden and crimson hue, which faded away only as the darkness of the night set in; and the most perfect peace reigned over the entire island.

Sunday, 7th. —Anyone would suppose from our experience during the last week that we should have taken to-day for a day of rest. And so we did during the forenoon; but, after twelve o'clock had passed, the old restless desire of wanting to be doing something came over me, so I started off with my camera to the top of a hill; but the natives followed me everywhere, none of them being more inquisitive than a dozen young mothers, whose age, I should certainly say, did not in any case exceed fourteen, and each carried a baby, fully half the size of herself. This was the first camera they had ever seen, and their curiosity was unbounded. They could not be kept away from the lens, looking down it, then wanting to see inside the box, and upsetting the whole affair. It was perfectly useless trying to get a picture at all, so I shouldered my camera, returning to the boat, with a quarter-of-a-mile of tail behind me, and left for another anchorage about seven miles further to the north.

Monday, 8th. —I always had a liking for wet photographic plates in preference to dry plates for landscape photography. In fact, at this period, dry plates had not been brought to the perfection to which they are now, and what few I had tried gave, after an enormously long exposure, very feeble and uncertain results. The inconvenience of carrying about your nitrate bath, collodion developers, &c., and a lumbering dark tent, to say nothing about the search for water on high or mountainous ground, argued volumes in favour of the dry plates. The results I obtained with the wet were so very far more satisfactory that willingly underwent the trouble of carting about the tent and all accessories. But I certainly should not do so at the present time, when I see what dry plates are capable of producing.

This morning I took L—and two of the boat coolies, with tent and camera, in the small boat, and started for an elevated deserted point of land, looking faraway

一挤鱼就吐出来了，然后又被扔进水里再去捕鱼。

傍晚的夕阳着实壮美。地平线上的积云镶上了最美丽的色彩，云彩反射映红了天顶的卷云。经历了上周的暴风雨，这无疑预示着晴朗的好天气。前一波云彩刚消失，更灿烂的云彩就取而代之，从地平线直至天顶，整个天空一片金红色，暮色降临时才慢慢消失；整座岛屿笼罩在一片宁静中。

7日，星期天——从上周的经历看，大家肯定猜测我们今天该休息一天。上午我们的确休息了，等一过中午，静不下来，想做点什么的心思占据了上风，于是我带着相机爬上了一座山顶；当地人紧随其后，十几个年轻的妈妈比谁都好奇，她们的年龄，我敢肯定，不超过十四岁，每人都怀抱一个孩子，有她们半个个头大。这是她们第一次看见相机，有着无限的好奇心。她们黏着镜头不放，双眼往内探查，还想看机箱里面有什么，烦扰不已。我根本无法拍摄，只好扛着相机返回住家船，长达四分之一英里的人群尾随身后。我们起航深入北边约7英里的另一停泊处。

8日，星期一——在风景摄影方面，相比干版技术，我总是更喜欢湿版技术。事实上，当时干版摄影技术还未达到如今的完美程度，我尝试过几次，经长时间曝光后，得到的结果不甚令人满意。但携带硝酸片基、火棉胶显影剂等，还有笨重的帐篷式暗袋很不方便，更别说在高坡或山地找水十分困难，这些都使选择干版技术更为合理。我用湿版摄影拍照，效果令人非常满意，所以我宁愿不辞辛劳地随身携带帐篷式暗袋及各种配件。如今我不会再这样了，因为干版摄影所能产生的效果已经可以接受。

上午我带着女儿和两个伙计，扛着帐篷和相机，撑着小舟前往一个荒

across the island, with some hills and the broad expanse of the lake in the distance. Here I certainly expected to be quiet, but no sooner were the tent pitched and the camera fixed, than we were discovered by the natives, who immediately began to collect in large numbers; where they came from I cannot imagine, for there was not a cottage or dwelling of any kind in sight, and the place we were on was a barren piece of rock. However, I succeeded in getting a couple of photographs, then packed up the tent and camera, and sat down for a rest and a pipe before turning down the hill.

By this time three or four hundred people had gathered round us. There had been an immense deal of talking going on among them all the time, a great deal of arguing and gesticulating; and, as I afterwards learned, they were holding a palaver regarding myself and my doings. They had never seen or even heard of a camera before, and the upshot of their argument was that I was a magician, that by means of the mysterious box with one eye I had been engaged in casting a blight over their silkworms and crops, so as to raise the price of silk in Shanghai to the advantage of the foreign merchant, and that the only way to prevent the spell from taking effect was to consign both myself and my apparatus to the bottom of one of the deepest holes in the lake. They told us to clear out, which we refused to do; and then commenced a series of petty assaults with pieces of mud and small stones, which resulted in some of them, caught in flagrante delicto, feeling the impact of an uncommonly stiff piece of bamboo.

I ordered the men to pick up the tent and camera and get down to the small boat, for it was quite clear we should soon be at open war. As soon as we began to move down-hill a rush was made; the men dropped the tent and camera, and, with some formidable sticks they had found somewhere, we made a charge and drove back the enemy. Tent and camera were again shouldered, and we retreated fighting. They did not appear to think of surrounding us, which they might easily have done, and we should have had difficulty in our strategic move. As it was, we had none, and soon reached the large boat. The news had somehow travelled over all that part of the island, and crowds of angry people came to the moorings. It was clear we could not with any safety stop there through the night; and it being now close on to five p.m., it seemed rather late to look for another island, but there was no help for it, we had to go, and the sooner we were off the better.

When we again got on to the lake the wind began, or rather had already begun, to rise, and to all appearances it meant blowing as night came on.

无人烟的高地，远眺全岛，远处有几座小山和大片湖面。我当然希望此处是安宁之所，但我们刚支好帐篷、架好相机就被当地人发现了，他们一大群人聚集过来；我想象不出他们是从哪儿来的，因为目力所及没看见任何村舍和住所，而我们待的地方是一块光秃秃的岩石。无论如何，我成功地拍摄了几张照片，收起帐篷和相机，坐下抽一斗烟，休息一会儿然后下山。

此时我们周围已经聚集了三四百人。他们一直交谈着，不停地打着手势争论着；事后才得知他们一直大谈特谈我和我的所作所为。他们以前从未见过，甚至从未听说过相机，他们争论的要点是：我是魔术师，我通过操纵一只眼的神秘箱子损害他们的蚕和庄稼，抬高上海的丝价，好有利于外国商人。阻止魔力生效的唯一方法就是将我和我的设备扔到湖里最深的洞底。他们让我们滚开，但我们拒绝了；他们开始用泥巴和小石子攻击我们，他们有些人当场就尝到了硬竹板回击的滋味。

显然很快我们会打起来，我命伙计扛起帐篷和相机下到小舟。我们刚起步下山就遭到突袭；伙计放下帐篷和相机，他们找到几根令人畏惧的棍子，我们发起反攻赶退敌人。我们再次扛起帐篷和相机，撤出战斗。他们可以轻而易举地包围我们，但似乎没想这么干，否则我们就很难战略转移了。结果我们没有遇到任何包围，很快抵达大船。但消息还是传遍了小岛，愤怒的当地人来到了锚地。明显我们无法安全地停在此处过夜了；可是已快下午 5 点了，再找个岛停泊有点晚，但是别无他法，我们得走，越快越好。

等我们再次来到湖面时，开始起风了，或许早已经起风了，所有迹象都意味着夜幕降临会一直刮风。

When darkness set in, we were miles away from our island, and a heavy swell spread over the lake. We were certainly in an unpleasant dilemma; stay out on the lake all night we must, for there would be too much danger in approaching the rocky parts of the island in the dark. Unfortunately, while the boat was pitching a good deal she got over one of the shallow flat places I have before mentioned, and commenced to bump against the bottom. Soon she sprang a leak, the water came rushing up through the floor of the cabin, and three men were kept continually baling.

At ten p.m. the wind was evidently rising, and if it came on to blow any harder we could not live through the night in a leaky boat. After a short consultation, it was decided to take all risks and run for the nearest land; it was certain destruction to stay out on the lake, while, on the other hand, we might, with great care and a good look-out, avoid all half-concealed rocks and shoals, and run into some quiet bay for the night.

As we neared a small island we could see no landing place, or even an approach to the land, nothing but rocky points everywhere. Out of this we must get as quickly as possible; for if we only touched one of those points and made another hole in her, we should sink there and then. With great care we backed out with safety, and, finding ourselves again on the broad expanse of the lake, ran for the southern point of the island, but here the approach was rather worse than better. Had to put out again to another projecting piece of land, difficult to make out in the dark, but in about an hour we found a beautifully sheltered small bay, with smooth water, where we lay for the remainder of the night.

The cabin was in an awful state. Tins of preserved meat, broken crockery, a couple of filters, bottles, camp-stools, clothing, and sundry pieces of furniture and stores, were all mixed up together in a confused heap; the boat had been so lively that all things not screwed down had been thrown from their places, and we might consider ourselves lucky if the half of them would be of any use in the future. We were all too tired to do anything more that night, so after seeing everything secure, and arranging for the men to take alternate duty at baling throughout the night, we lay down wherever a dry spot could be found, and in a few minutes forgot all our troubles in sleep.

Tuesday, 9th. — By continual baling we kept the boat fairly free from water, but, before going out on the lake again, it was quite evident we should have to repair her bottom. Throughout the night she kept up a very disagreeable half-

天黑时，我们离岛也有几英里了，湖上涌起了大浪。我们处在讨厌的两难中；我们必须留在湖上过夜，因为黑暗中靠近岛屿的岩石危险性太大。不幸的是船在一阵颠簸中冲上了一处我前面提到的浅滩，碰撞了船底。船很快裂开了个口子，水从船舱的地板涌了上来，三个伙计不停地往外舀水。

晚上 10 点，风明显加强，如果风再大点，我们就无法靠一条漏水的船安全度过此夜。短暂商量后我们决定冒险前往最近的陆地；待在湖上肯定是毁灭性的，可另一方面，我们要十分小心并在一位优秀的瞭望员的指引下才有可能避开所有半隐半现的岩石和暗礁，驶进某个安静的湖湾过夜。

靠近一个小岛时，我们看不到能登陆的地方，甚至连靠近陆地的地方也没有，到处都是尖尖的岩石。我们必须尽快远离此处，因为如果我们碰到了一块石头，再撞了一个洞，船随时会沉没。我们十分小心地将船安全倒出，再次来到宽阔的湖面上，驶向小岛的南端，但此处登陆条件更糟。虽然在黑暗中探路困难重重，但我们也只得再次出发另寻他地，约一小时后找到了一个美丽又背风的小湖湾，风平浪静，我们在此停好船过夜。

舱房里一塌糊涂。肉罐头、破瓦罐、两面滤色镜、一堆瓶子、小马扎、衣服、各色家什和物资全都搅在一起，堆成一堆；船上一片忙乱，所有没有固定的东西都被甩了出来，若有一半未来还有用，我们就很庆幸了。那晚我们疲惫不堪，啥也做不了，在保证一切平安，安排了人手轮流通宵往外舀水后，我们就找干处躺下了，几分钟后就将一切烦恼抛之脑后入睡了。

9 日，星期二——持续不断地往外舀水，我们安全无虞，但很显然，我们得修补船底才能再次出发。整个晚上船一直颠簸摇晃，令人不适；上午

rolling, half-pitching motion; towards nine a.m. the water suddenly calmed, and we tried to haul her up on the beach. Finding this quite impossible, we decided to dry-dock her; so, selecting a smooth, shingly, sandy beach, we got to work, some with one thing, some with another, to scoop out a dry dock large enough to take her in. The ground was easily worked, and in a few hours our dock was complete; then, gradually opening the bank we had left as a flood-gate, the water poured gently in. The boat floated in beautifully, when we filled in the bank again and baled out the dock. There was plenty of room in the dock to work, so we canted her over and got well at her damaged bottom. A couple of planks were so badly broken that they could not be repaired and would have to be removed. To do this we had to take some of the inside fittings of the boat to mend the outside. Then we found there were no tools on board. These we had to make out of knives, pieces of old iron, &c.; but finally we got enough to go on with, and two of the men were sent off to another island to purchase some nails, a saw, and an axe.

In three days she was all right; when we again let in the water, and she floated out on the lake, leaking a very little, which was stopped by some additional caulking inside with some old worn-out clothes.

I was quite tired of the constant labour — of one continual state of warfare, first with the natives, then with the wind and rain and storms. No one could tell whether the leak would not break out again, for at the best it was only a patch, and not a proper repair; therefore we agreed to make for the northern end of the lake and work our way home by the Grand Canal, north of Soochow.

We kept under sail all through the night, and the following day entered a stream at the north-east end that led direct to the canal.

Although the lake had treated us roughly, we were all sorry to leave it. I had been sent there as an invalid to recover a little health, and, when l came to review the treatment, I thought it had been rather a severe one for a sick man. But it had agreed with me, for I was perfectly well and strong.

The stream we were now in was a very wide, deep piece of water, fully two hundred yards from bank to bank. About three miles from its junction with the lake the banks extended, and it formed an exceedingly fine lake of clear translucent water, in which were great quantities of fish of the most cannibalistic disposition, for the larger ones were eating all smaller than themselves as fast as they could catch them.

We anchored for the night close to the bridge and village of Wangfoh. We

9点时水面突然平静了，我们试着拖船上岸，但根本行不通。我们决定将船驶进干船坞；于是我们选了一处平坦的沙滩，开始动工，大家各抄家伙，铲挖一个足够船只进入的大大的干船坞。沙滩很容易挖，几小时后船坞完工了；然后慢慢掘开留作闸门的堤坝，水缓缓注入。船利落地漂浮进干船坞，我们再次堵上堤坝，将水舀出船坞。船坞里的空间足够操作，我们倾侧船身，修复受损的船底。两块木板破损严重，无法修复，必须移除。这样我们得从船内拆下一些配件来修补外面的破损处，可是我们发现没有工具。修补工作需要刀、铁片等；但最终凑齐了所需的一切，我们派两个伙计去另一个岛上购买了些钉子、一把锯子、一把斧头。

三天后[1]船修好了；我们又把水放进船坞，船浮入湖中，但还有一点漏水，我们用些旧衣服填嵌缝隙塞住了。

我十分厌倦不断的体力付出——那种持续的战斗状态，先是和当地人冲突，接着又是和大风、暴雨对抗。谁也说不准裂缝会不会再次裂开，毕竟我们只是上了个补丁，而不是真的修复，因此我们一致同意取道太湖北端，经由苏州北面的大运河返航回家。

我们扬起风帆通宵航行，第二天进入西北方一条直通大运河的河流。

尽管太湖对待我们颇为粗暴，我们离开时还是多有不舍。我是作为病人被送往太湖康复的，当我回顾此次治疗时，我想对于一个病人而言此行相当考验人。但这样的治疗适合我，现在我既健康又强壮。

此时身处的河流既宽又深，足有200码宽。河湖交汇之处约有3英里长，水清澈透明，里面有大量食肉鱼，大鱼正在吞食能捕食到的所有比它们小的鱼。

我们在靠近光福村的桥边抛锚过夜。本来在落日前我们可轻松到达运

[1] 此处有点令人费解，three days 可能应该是 three hours，否则与后文就非常矛盾了。

could easily have reached the canal before sunset, but I wished to remain here, so as to get four or five photographs of the pagoda, bridge, and other places by the more favourable light of the morning.

Wednesday, 10th. — Secured all the photographs I wanted, and left Wang-foh at ten a.m. with a head wind. The men, when practicable, went ashore to track, 'yulowing' the whole time.

The day whiled away very monotonously, and we entered the canal at 3.30. After passing one of the usual odoriferous villages the canal widens considerably, and is a magnificent highway for boat traffic.

It is melancholy to see, even up to this day, such numerous traces of the destroying propensities of the rebel army. The canal on both sides has been banked with fine large blocks of worked granite, most of them being twenty feet or more in length; but hundreds upon hundreds of them have been torn from their beds, broken, and thrown into the water; some have been sent down the river to Shanghai, and sold to the municipal council for road-making; others have been recovered for building purposes; others destroyed and left on the land, for no earthly purpose but from a sheer love of destruction.

There are also several temples, pagodas, and monuments on the line of the canal—at least, all that remains of them, —for the temples have been burnt, and the pagodas, &c., battered by artillery, all having been the work of the insurgents.

At eight p.m. we arrived at Soochow, the passage so completely blocked with all kinds of boats that it was impossible to get through, more especially so in the dark ...

We came to an anchor on the north side of the city wall, in an open piece of water we found after some search, where we were away from all the abominations of this truly loathsome place. How we missed the grand scenery, the fresh air, and the dancing waters of Taihu! What a contrast was that to the fetid smells of Soochow, and the filthy, pea-soupy water of its creek!

Thursday, 11th. —Got under weigh soon after daylight, tracking all day against a headwind, arriving at Dzanchung at eight p.m.

Friday, 12th. —Off again at five a.m.Passed Tsing-poo at three a.m., and reached the Monastery hill ('Fungwang-San,' Phoenix Hill) at half-past seven. Heard some distant thunder, with several flashes of very bright lightning. Heavy atmosphere, and every appearance of a storm. The crew, for some reason of their own, wished to stop between four and five miles from Fungwang-San, saying

河，但我想利用早上更好的光线，拍四五张宝塔、桥及其他地方的照片。

10 日，星期三——拍了我想要的所有照片，上午 10 点我们顶风离开光福。全程摇橹前进，条件允许时，伙计们就上岸拉纤。

一天就这样单调地慢慢流逝，下午 3 点半我们进入大运河。经过几座经常臭烘烘的村庄后，运河一下子宽阔起来，真是一条航行的黄金水道。

即使到了今天，看到太平军破坏的种种痕迹还是令人伤心。运河两岸砌着大块的花岗岩，大多长 20 多英尺，但成百上千块花岗岩已从大堤上被剥离，打碎，扔进水中；有些被沿河运往上海，卖给市政委员会用于修路；另外一些被找回了用于造房；还有一些被毁，丢在地上，这么干没有任何目的，只是纯粹出于破坏欲。

运河沿线还有几座寺庙、几顶宝塔和几块纪念碑——至少废墟还在——寺庙均被火烧，宝塔等受到火炮重创，全是太平军所为。

晚上 8 点抵达苏州，航道被各种船只完全堵塞，无法通行，在黑夜里更甚……

经过一番寻找，我们在城墙北边一处停泊，此处水域开阔，躲开了此地所有令人憎恶的东西。我们多么想念太湖壮丽的景色、新鲜的空气、荡漾的水波！与苏州恶臭的空气、肮脏浑浊的河水形成了多么鲜明的反差！

11 日，星期四——天亮不久我们就出发了，全天逆风而行，晚上 8 点抵达周庄。

12 日，星期五——早上 5 点再次起航。下午 3 点过青浦，晚上 7 点半抵达凤凰山。几束耀眼的闪电划过，远远传来雷声，气压很低，暴雨近在眼前。出于自身的原因，船员们希望在离凤凰山四五英里的地方停下，说什么没

there was no water, etc., but they had to go on, for there was abundance of water everywhere. I secured one or two very successful photos. We were all glad to get on terra-firma again, for this was the evening of the third day that we had not been off the boat. We enjoyed a long walk in the evening.

Saturday, 13th. — Rain, rain, rain all last night, and a wretched morning; the roof of the house got strained on the lake and is now leaking in a dozen places, everything being damp and wet; the tea spoiled, and everyone in a bad temper. Anything would be better than the boat, so we all started off fern-hunting, for which this hill is justly celebrated. We found as many ferns as we could carry, and some very choice ones among the number. The afternoon turned out fine, and I had no trouble in taking some more photographs ... The Jesuit missionaries have built a very pretty chapel at the top of this hill, and half-way up they have a monastery from which the hill takes its name; but I fancy their rules are not very severe, for the monks may be seen continually passing up and down the creek, to and from Shanghai. It is also used as a sanatorium for the Jesuits of Shanghai and Sicawey.

Sunday,14h. —L—, who had been along the bank of the stream looking for some water-plants(Vallisneria spiralis), came and told me she had found a lovely spot for a photograph, but we should be obliged to take the small boat, as it must be a river scene. Off we went, L—, M—, and Co., and soon came to the place. It certainly was a very pretty spot, a perfect cave over the water, formed by willows, ash, and a variety of overhanging plants and flowers. L—tried to take hold of one of the branches to steady the boat, but unfortunately she fell over the side into about twenty feet of water, giving the boat so sudden a jerk that M— fell over backwards, and lay at the bottom of the boat which drifted down the stream. It was all so sudden and to me appeared so comical, that for a short time I did nothing. My Ariel, who was at this time about fourteen years old, I soon fished out, none the worse for her ducking; we then caught the runaway boat, and finally succeeded with the photo.

Monday, 15th. —Left Foongwang-San soon after daylight, and headed again for Shanghai,which we hoped to reach in the evening. We were truly sorry to bid adieu to our wild nomadic life, for it had been extremely enjoyable, with just sufficient excitement to prevent any feeling of weariness or sameness, for while on the lake we could never tell what a day would bring forth, or what troubles we should run into before sunset.

有水之类的，但他们不得不继续前进，因为到处水量充足。我成功地拍了一两张照片。再次踏上坚实的大地，我们都很高兴，因为已经三天未曾下船了。夜晚，我们好好地散了回步，很开心。

13 日，星期六——昨天整夜、今天一上午都是雨、雨、雨，真是糟透了；船顶历经太湖的日晒雨淋不堪重负，此时有十几处在漏水，一切都是潮乎乎、湿哒哒的；茶又打翻了，大家脾气都很不好。哪儿都比待在船上强，所以我们都出去寻找蕨类植物，凤凰山正是以此出名。我们找了许多，直到拿不下，其中有一些极为珍贵。下午天晴了，我又顺利地拍了些照片……耶稣会传教士在山顶建了一座很漂亮的教堂，半山腰又修了一座修道院，凤凰山据此得名；但我想他们的戒律并不严格，因为经常看到僧侣们在河上来回穿梭，往返上海。该修道院同时也用作上海和徐家汇耶稣会士的疗养院。

14 日，星期天——女儿一直沿着河岸寻找水草（欧亚苦草），她跑来告诉我她发现了一个拍照的好地方，但因为是河景，必须得撑着小船去。“妻女合伙号”结伴出发，我们很快就来到了那个地方。这儿的确好看，河边有柳树、白蜡树及各种植物和鲜花，悬垂交错，洞然天成一幅完美的图画。女儿试图抓住一根树枝来稳住小船，但不幸从侧面跌入约 20 英尺深的水中，使船突然颠簸了一下，导致妻子仰面摔倒在船里，而小船又顺流漂走。一切发生得太突然，对我来说又似乎太滑稽，以致我一时未来得及采取行动。但我很快就将女儿爱丽儿捞出水面，没有造成什么伤害，当时她约 14 岁；然后我们抓住溜走的小船，并成功地拍了照片。

15 日，星期一——天亮不久离开凤凰山，前往上海，希望傍晚能到。告别狂野的半游牧生活，我们真的很遗憾，因为这是一种非常愉快的生活，刚刚好的兴奋使人没有疲劳、倦怠和千篇一律的感觉，而且在湖上永远无法预知会有怎样的一天等着我们，或日落前我们会遭遇怎样的麻烦。

But provisions were getting low, every bottle in the boat was either empty or broken, tea nearly all spoiled; and, worse than all, yesterday afternoon the last of the cigars faded away in light blue smoke, and the tobacco gave out on Friday.

In about six hours we passed through the village of Szching, on the Sicawey Creek, and stopped for a few photos of some picturesque old houses built on piles on the east side of the stream. Soon after this we entered one of the reaches of the Wang-poo, a short distance above the Kiangnan Arsenal, ran down the river with a fair wind and tide, and by sunset had left the boat, and were once more safely anchored in the 'old house at home.'

但是物资越来越少，船上的瓶子要么空了，要么碎了，茶叶几乎都变质了；更糟的是，昨天下午最后一根雪茄在淡蓝色的烟雾中消逝，而烟草在周五就耗尽了。

约 6 小时后，我们经过了徐家汇河边的泗泾村，河东侧有一些建在木桩上的老房子，风景如画，我们停下拍了一些照片。不久我们进入位于江南兵工厂北面不远的黄浦江的一个河段，顺风顺水而行，日落时分我们已经下船，再次安全泊在“快乐老家”。

A Magician in Many Lands

魔术师游世界

（查尔斯·伯特伦著　蔡骏译）

《魔术师游世界》（*A Magician in Many Lands*）由英国劳特利奇出版公司联合美国 E.P. 达顿出版公司于 1911 年分别在伦敦和纽约出版，作者是英国著名魔术师查尔斯·伯特伦（Charles Bertram，1853—1907）。作品出版时伯特伦已去世。路易斯·霍夫曼教授（Louis Hoffmann，1839—1919）在此书序言中缅怀查尔斯·伯特伦，称其不仅表演精湛、观察敏锐，而且性情和蔼、颇有人缘。怀着对事业的追求和对东方的向往，伯特伦在众人资助下于 1899 年 1 月从英国启程，坐船一路向东游历了印度、中国、日本、美国等地。与纯粹的旅游观光不同，伯特伦的这番世界之旅还兼具巡演性质，一路又得到许多朋友的照应和招待，因此书中的旅行片段别具一格。

选译部分是书的第二十五章，记录了伯特伦从上海到苏州再返回上海的旅途和表演经历，从西方视角描述了以苏州为代表的江南饮食、水运交通、舞台表演、人情往来，乃至刑事司法的独特体验。

CHAPTER XXV

I HAD intimated to my friend Mr Shonock how delighted I should be to partake of a real Chinese dinner, and accordingly found myself one of a party of nine, five Europeans and four Chinese gentlemen, who made all the arrangements and very kindly volunteered to see us through. We arrived at the house where the banquet was to take place and, with many kow-tows, were shown into the dining-room. Upon the table, which was laid for nine persons, there were at least fifty little dishes of curious looking food-stuffs, jams, etc., and small saucers filled with a medley of non-appetising looking trifles, of the character of which I had no idea. We were each provided with a small basin three inches in diameter and a pair of chop-sticks, which I found required a deal of practice to properly manipulate with any certainty. The first course was served in a basin six inches in diameter, placed in the centre of the table, from which we helped ourselves. I judged the contents of the basin to be tripe, but it proved to be a greater delicacy, namely 'shark's fin!' Each person dipped into the basin with his chop-sticks and took therefrom a piece of fin and placed it in the little basin in front of him. I tried in turn, but my piece of fin kept slipping out of the chop-sticks. At last after many attempts I succeeded in landing a piece into my little basin, when the difficulty seemed to be to get it out again! However, after repeated efforts I managed to hold it for a moment firmly enough to enable me to bite a piece off. It tasted very like cod's tail, was glutinous but insipid and wanted salt and bread, neither of which commodities could be obtained to make it palatable. Next followed what appeared to me to be monkey-nuts, but were really dried melon-seeds. Upon these also we Europeans practised with our chop-sticks and I soon greatly improved under the tuition of our Chinese friends. Small cups of hot shumsu were then served, which reminded me of bad spirituous sherry, and to which I did not take at all kindly. A basin of birdsnest soup was then placed before us. It had the appearance of hot gum with small squares of jelly and some pigeons' eggs floating in it. Each diner was supplied with a gigantic mustard spoon, with which to ladle the soup into our small basins, which did duty for each course. The soup was not at all bad, but insipid for lack of salt. More shumsu was served, then some eggs, a year or two old and quite green, floating in brine! I had to pass

第二十五章

我曾悄悄向朋友肖诺克先生说，如果能吃到一顿正宗的中餐真是件令人高兴的事。幸而此愿成真，我成为 9 人宴席中的一员。席间聚有 5 位欧洲人和 4 位中国绅士，中国绅士们包揽了所有安排，并主动而友善地全程照应我们。在来到要举行宴席的地方后，我们又经过反复打躬作揖才被人引入餐厅。餐桌按 9 人布置，上面至少有 50 个小盘子，盛放着奇形怪状的食物、酱汁等，还有一些小碟子里面装着各色什锦小吃，但看起来并不勾人食欲，我也不辨其为何物。我们每人都有一个直径为 3 英寸的小菜盆和一副筷子，我发觉需要大量练习才能准确使用筷子。上的第一道菜用一个直径 6 英寸的盆子盛放在桌子中央，我们从盆里自行取食。我判断这个盆里的东西是牛肚，但实则是一道珍馐美味，名曰“鱼翅”！每人都将自己的筷子伸入菜盆里夹取一片鱼翅，而后将鱼翅放在自己面前的小菜盆内。轮到我时，我试着夹菜，但鱼翅老是从筷头滑落。经过多番尝试，我终于将一筷鱼翅成功收入小菜盆，而麻烦似乎在于将鱼翅再次取出！然而，经过不懈努力，我设法将鱼翅夹牢片刻从而足以咬下一口。鱼翅味同鳕鱼尾，黏腻无味，可惜没有食盐和面包佐餐，而如能获二者之一，均能使鱼翅入味顺口。接着上的菜在我看来是花生，但实际是瓜子。我们几个欧洲人借此练习使用筷子，在中国朋友的指导之下，我的用筷技术进步神速。然后端上了小杯的热黄酒[1]，我觉得这味道像是劣质的烈性雪莉酒，实在无法接受。之后一盆燕窝羹又放在我们面前。羹汤看似冒着热气的胶状物，里面浮着若干小块桃胶和鸽蛋。每名食客都有一把巨大的黄褐色勺子，用来将汤舀进自己的小菜盆里，每道菜都会用到勺子。燕窝羹味道不赖，但因少盐而显寡淡。继而又上了黄酒，然后是有一两年“历史”、碧绿湛青的

[1] 原文中“shumsu”疑为“samshu”（黄酒或烧酒）之误，根据作者身处上海以及加热饮用等习惯，推测此处为“黄酒”。

this dainty dish! Other courses followed consisting of snails, cockles and small portions of duck wrapped in dough, but all very insipid to my taste. Finally more shumsu, and our dinner was concluded! Each was then provided with a Chinese pipe, and a singing girl deputed to wait on each of us. Her duty was to keep placing in the bowl of the pipe the tiniest pinch of tobacco. With a dexterous wave of the hand a smouldering spill she held burst into a flame from which the pipe was lighted, when one whiff entirely consumed the tobacco. This operation was repeated innumerable times to the great satisfaction of the young ladies. We left, perfectly satisfied with the experience, my European friends agreeing with me that we had better repair to the club and get something to eat. I am afraid I should never be able to master the use of chopsticks. When using them I am always reminded of a gentleman who was one day entertaining an aged friend to lunch, and noticing his guest making peculiar contortions with his mouth, ventured to remark that possibly he was not enjoying his lunch. 'Oh! yes, I am,' said he,'but you see I have only one tooth, and I am trying to spear a pickled onion,' —a feat which seemed to me to be on a par with holding anything with a pair of chopsticks.

I finished up the evening by visiting a native conjuror, who gave me a private performance at his home. He was remarkably clever in his particular style, and by far eclipsed anyone I had previously seen. I tried to induce him to come to Europe, but the difficulties he put in the way made it impossible for me to make the necessary arrangements for his visit.

The proprietor of the Chinese Theatre at Soochow engaged me to give a series of performances, extending over a week. I therefore gladly accepted the hospitality of Mr Olsen the European head of the police, who sent his house-boat down the Yang-tse-Keang for me, together with an invitation to his house during my stay in Soochow.

The house-boat was attached to what is called the 'train,' that is a string of junks and barges which are towed by a powerful tug up to Soochow-city twice a week. The boat was replete with every comfort, the cabin being very daintily upholstered. My 'boy' Jairham Jugga accompanied me, and also two of Mr Olsen's Chinese servants, who cooked and looked after my creature wants. The 'train' left Shanghai and threaded its way slowly through a mass of junks, barges and

蛋品，还浮在卤水之中！我不得不略过这道精美菜品！接下来上的菜有螺蛳、乌蛤和裹在面饼内的小块鸭肉，但这些菜对我来说都味道寡淡。最后又上了黄酒，我们的宴席就此告一段落！之后每人都拿到一柄中式烟斗，并各被安排一名歌女侍候。歌女的职责是持续在烟斗内放上极小撮烟草。她们手持一支阴燃的纸捻灵巧挥舞，纸捻蹿出火苗后用火点着烟斗，燃起的烟一口气就足以全部吸光。此种操作重复了无数次，直至我们被年轻女士们侍奉到满意为止。我们离席时对此番经历颇为满意，欧洲朋友也与我想法一致，即我们最好再去俱乐部填填肚子。恐怕我永远都无法掌握用筷。使用筷子时，我总是想起这样的场景：某日，一位绅士招待一位老年朋友吃午饭，绅士注意到这位客人的嘴奇怪地歪来扭去，就壮着胆子问来客这顿饭是不是吃得不开心。“哦！不，我开心的，”他说，“但你瞧，我只有一颗牙，我正试着用这牙戳上一块腌洋葱。”——在我看来，这番壮举堪比使用筷子。

当晚最后一程，我拜访了一位当地的魔术师，他在家里为我进行了私人表演。他的表演风格颇具巧思、独树一帜，使我之前所见的其他魔术师黯然失色。我试图怂恿他来欧洲表演，但他为此行所出的难题使我知难而退，不可能安排他赴欧。

苏州的中国大戏院老板聘请我进行为期一个多星期的系列演出。因此，我欣然接受了欧籍警察局长奥尔森先生的盛情邀请，在他安排下我乘坐住家船沿长江顺流而下，还应邀在逗留苏州期间去了他家。

这艘住家船挂在所谓的“火车”上，也就是由一艘马力强劲的拖船牵引的一长串帆船和驳船，船队每周跑两次苏州。住家船上一切都很舒适，舱内装饰精致考究。我的“童仆”贾勒姆·贾加伴我同行，随船还有奥尔森先生的两名中国仆人，他们为我做饭并照料我的表演动物。“火车”离开了上海，缓慢地穿行于苏州河流中众多的帆船、驳船和邮船之间。直到傍

post-boats in the Soochow creek. It was not until 6 p.m. that the 'train' had anything like a clear course, by which time it was quite dark and pouring with rain. By some means another 'train' got across our course, and we got mixed up in a most hopeless muddle, the barges and junks drifting between each other, fouling the ropes and cables which caused a delay of more than an hour. Whilst we were waiting one of the Chinese 'boys' came into the cabin holding a red carp-like fish by the tail. 'Master!' he said, 'my make e fly.' Well I had seen many flying fish, so I thought it quite unnecessary, and I told him so, especially as it was raining. He looked surprised and said, 'my b'long number one man cook, no can fly my make e boil.' Then it dawned on me that it was meant for my supper, and very well indeed he cooked and served it. My 'boy' Jairham had disappeared into a junk ahead of the house-boat, and, after an excellent supper, I went to bed. A perfect tempest was howling around, and the water splashing unceasingly against the sides of my cabin. I had been asleep some time when I was awakened by a terrible hullabaloo. The 'train' had stopped, the boatmen were swearing at each other in Chinese—that is, I supposed it to be swearing, for the language was awful. After some time I learned that all the commotion was in consequence of the tug having broken her propeller. I could do nothing to facilitate matters, so retired again, and after six hours further delay, another tug, coming down the river, took us in tow and we proceeded on our journey.

At 8 a.m. my cook came to me and said 'my makee chop fly.' And he did and I made it fly afterwards at my breakfast !

We arrived at Soochow at 1-30 p.m. instead of 8 a.m. our scheduled time. There I found Mr Olsen on the landing-stage waiting to receive me, and was duly installed in most comfortable quarters in the Police Station. I had a splendid suite of rooms overlooking the native city, whilst Jairham made himself comfortable somewhere in the cells below amongst the prisoners.

Next day I drove to the theatre to make my arrangements, and when I arrived a play had just commenced. I had a seat in what corresponded to our stalls, and was greatly amused at what I saw. I have not the remotest idea of what the play was about, but the masks were hideous, the dresses gorgeous, and the unearthly noise made by what they were pleased to designate a band, provided a perfect pandemonium. The stage was a platform, open on three sides, quite

晚6点，“火车”才驶上一条畅通无阻的航线，这时天已经很黑了，还下着倾盆大雨。不知怎么的，另一列“火车”驶上了我们的航线，我们于是陷入一片令人绝望的混乱之中，驳船、帆船交错漂浮，绳索、线缆纠结缠绕，使得行程耽搁了一个多小时。在我们等待时，一名中国“童仆”走进船舱，倒提着一条看似红鲤的鱼，说道：“老爷！我给倷溜（熘）吧。”要知道我看过很多会溜的鱼，所以觉得全无必要这么做，我把想法告诉了他，说况且外边还在下雨。他看起来吃了一惊，说：“我是头等厨子，不能溜（熘）就给倷煮吧。”我这时才明白过来，这条鱼是给我当晚饭吃的，而他也的确将鱼烹调到位、料理得当。我的“童仆”贾勒姆消失在住家船前面的一条帆船上，而我在美餐一顿后也上床睡觉了。周遭狂风呼啸、豪雨瓢泼，雨水不停地拍落在船舱两侧。在睡了一段时间后，我突然被一阵吓人的呼呼隆隆声吵醒了。“火车”停了，船夫们在用中文互相咒骂——我想，那应该是咒骂，因为这言语实在骇人。过了一阵，我才得知所有纷乱均因拖船螺旋桨断裂而起。我于此事无能为力，只好去睡个回笼觉。又耽搁了6个小时后，另一艘拖船顺流而来，拖着我们继续航行。

早上8点，厨师来到我跟前对我说：“我给倷溜（熘）猪排。”他做到了，因为后来我还真让早饭里的猪排给“溜”了！

我们没能按计划上午8点到，而是在下午1点半抵达苏州。我看见奥尔森先生已经在那儿的栈桥上等着迎接我，我被安顿在警察局里最舒服的住处。我所住的华丽套房可以俯瞰老城，贾勒姆则住到了下面的单人间里，与囚犯们同处一地，但也自觉舒适。

第二天，我开车去戏院做些安排，我到时一出戏刚好开演。我找了一个相当于我们包厢的座位，感觉所见情景颇为有趣。我压根儿不明白这出戏讲的是什么，但所见面具狰狞可怖，行头繁复华丽，所闻之声由他们所谓的乐队奏出，嘈杂之音世间难觅，营造出一派混乱喧嚣。舞台由一个三

devoid of scenery. The performers made their 'exits and their entrances' by two curtain-covered openings at the back of the stage, whilst the furniture and properties were openly placed in position by attendants who were not supposed to be seen. Many of the players also in full view of the audience, were not supposed to be 'en evidence' until they took up certain positions on the stage.

The audience were seated in rows, with alternately a chair and then a square table. Immediately on being seated a man came along carrying an armful of hot flannels from which the boiling water had just been wrung, he handed these to the persons seated in the stalls, who promptly commenced mopping their faces with them, another attendant brought cups of tea, each cup having a small saucer which formed a lid to it. This acts as a strainer, and keeps the tea leaves in the cup, and is pushed slightly aside when it is desired to drink the tea.

The audience do not applaud, but express their satisfaction by grunting, which requires an acquired taste to call encouraging. In my own performances, I found it extremely difficult to play in such deathly silence, which however does not signify lack of appreciation. On one occasion, as I was concluding a trick in which I produced hundreds of small flags, the audience rushed on to the stage in their anxiety to obtain them. I learned afterwards that they desired them as charms to keep away evil spirits. Also during a performance they would come up on the stage unasked, and examine my apparatus, and I had the greatest difficulty in keeping my properties from them.

But I was anything but satisfied with my reception at my first performance. Silence reigned supreme and as the audience left the theatre slowly and silently, I thought to myself what a ghastly failure I have made. However the Chinese manager came and said they were delighted and that my fame would spread throughout the city. His prophecy came true, for the next night the theatre was packed to suffocation. I think the theatre in which I played was the only decent theatre in the place, for I visited two or three others, which were packed with people of both sexes, and the plays there enacted were of the most filthy and obscene description.

There is a Chinese proverb which says 'to be supremely happy, a man should be born in Soochow, live in Canton, and die in Liang-chow,' the last named city being situated at the foot of the Nau Shau highlands. Soochow is a great commercial centre, the silk industry being represented by a greater variety

面敞开的平台构成，完全没有布景可言。演员们通过戏台后部两个由门帘遮蔽的缺口“上场、退场”，而家具和道具则由助手堂而皇之摆放到位，他们其实不应为人所见。很多演员也明明白白展现在观众眼皮底下，而他们在台上就位之前也不应“显而易见”。

观众按排就座，一把椅子挨着一张方桌依次摆放。一落座，就有个伙计提着一篮热毛巾走过来，毛巾里滚烫的水刚拧干。伙计把毛巾递给坐在包厢里的客人，客人们则迅速用毛巾擦脸；另有一名服务员上茶，每个茶杯都配个小茶碟，可以当盖子用。想喝茶时，茶碟能起到过滤器的作用，可以将茶叶轻轻撇在一旁，留于杯中。

观众们并不鼓掌，而是通过咕哝声来表示满意，这种喝彩法必须经过一番研习才能深知其道。在我自己的演出中，我发现在如此死寂的环境中表演极为困难，但这并不意味着无人欣赏。有一次，我在一个小戏法结束时变出了数百面小旗子，观众们迫不及待地拥上戏台想要拿到旗子。后来我才知道，他们想把这些旗子当作护身符来驱魔除妖。还有一次演出中，观众们不请自来，上台检查我的装置，而我费了老大劲儿才让他们拿不到我的道具。

但我对第一次演出时所遭受的待遇一点儿都不满意。除了静默还是静默，当观众们慢慢地、默默地离开戏院时，我心想自己的表演必定一塌糊涂了。然而，一位中国经理过来说观众们很开心，而我将名满全城。他预言成真，因为第二天晚上戏院被挤得水泄不通。我觉得自己演出的戏院应是此地唯一上档次的戏院，因为我还看了另外两三家戏院，里面挤满了观众，上演的剧目都极为污秽下流。

中国有句俗话说：“大福之人要生在苏州，活在广州，死在柳州。”最后提到的那座城市位于南山脚下。[1] 苏州是个大商业中心，其丝绸业涵盖

[1] 原文中“Liang-chow”疑为“Liuzhou”（柳州）之误，史料记载柳州棺材因质量出众而名满天下；原文中“Nau Shau”（南山）位于柳州市西北方。

of goods than are produced anywhere else in the Empire. Under the guidance of the proprietor Mr Denigri, I had the pleasure of inspecting one of the chief Filature Works and was greatly impressed by the extremely orderly manner in which the factory was conducted, and the clever and up-to-date machinery used in the various processes.

Of course a visit to the native city was imperative; my friend Mr Olsen and I therefore arrived at one of the city gates, and were conveyed in palanquin chairs through the city, the streets of which were very narrow, but a trifle cleaner than Canton. There is an area of three miles by two and a half miles with walls around 14 miles in circumference, and enclosing forty miles of canals and nearly a million inhabitants. Formerly a city of handsome buildings, and known as Beautiful Soo, it was captured by the Taipings in 1860 and practically reduced to ruins. Through the enterprise of the late General Gordon it was recovered in 1865. Some idea may be gathered of its original splendour from the native plan engraved on a large slab of marble which has been preserved since 1247, also from some of the ruins themselves, notably the large pagoda, a marvellous structure reaching to nine stories; the splendid gardens and remains of some of the interiors, and the Namen of the Governor. M. Tsai, Minister for Foreign Affairs, offered me his hospitality, and I was also received by the Governor Kwei, son-in-law to the late Marquis Tseng. I took tea with him and his suite, and greatly amused him with some of my little table tricks. He was delighted, and laughed most heartily, but when, as we walked in the gardens together, I gave him various hints upon the subject of horticulture, and I broke a laurel leaf in halves, taking from it a dollar, he said he thought I 'b'long devil pidgin.'

On the following day the Governor's two sons and M. Tsai, on behalf of the Governor paid a return visit, and presented me with signed photographs, four fans and four chests of tea. Mr Olsen wished me to see the mixed court, at which he sits as a magistrate in the event of an European being charged. The presiding magistrate was Mr Li, to whom I was introduced and had a seat on the bench. One of the cases heard was that of a man who had kidnapped and outraged a girl, and sold her to a farmer for 140 dollars, after which he proceeded to abduct her from the farmer. His case was adjudicated upon and he was ordered to refund the

的商品种类远胜于清帝国其他任何丝绸产地。由企业主德尼格里先生指引，我有幸参观了一家大型缫丝厂，该厂经营有条不紊，各道工序所用机器精巧先进，我对此颇为叹服。

游览老城自然必不可少。因而，我和我的朋友奥尔森先生来到一个城门前，又坐着轿子穿城而过，城里的街道狭窄，但比广州稍干净些。老城3英里见长，2英里半见宽，周围有长14英里左右的城墙，墙内有总长40英里的运河和近一百万居民。苏州城内曾有漂亮的建筑，故而被称为“姑苏”。1860年被太平天国占领后，苏州几乎沦为废墟。在已故将军戈登的努力下，苏州于1865年得以重建。修复理念汲取自原城市规划所记载的辉煌历史，规划镌刻在一块巨大的大理石碑上，该碑从1247年保存至今；还有些修复理念源自遗迹本身。值得一提的是一座高达9层、令人叹为观止的大宝塔，还有华美的花园、建筑内部遗存和巡抚衙门[1]。我受到了外务大臣蔡大人[2]的热情款待，还得到了（聂缉）椝巡抚的接见，（聂缉）椝巡抚是已故侯爵曾（国藩）的女婿。我和他及其随从一起喝茶，并用一些桌面小戏法逗他开心。他倍感高兴，开怀大笑。当我们一起在花园散步时，我向他反复提及园艺话题，还将一片月桂叶掰成两半，从里面变出一块钱——然而，这时他却说他觉得我“是洋鬼子说洋泾浜”。

第二天，巡抚的两个儿子和蔡大人代表巡抚回访，送给我几张签名照片、4把扇子和4匣茶叶。奥尔森先生想让我见识一下会审法庭，如果有欧洲人受到指控，他会以法官身份出庭。经人引见，我认识了主审法官李大人，还在法官席上落座。审理的案件之一是，一名男子绑架并凌辱了一

[1] 原文中“Namen”疑为“Yamen”（衙门）之误。

[2] 此处“蔡大人”疑为蔡蓉峰，蔡和森之父，在经商失败、家道中落后通过其妻葛兰英与聂缉椝的亲戚关系，在江南制造总局谋得小官职，从而再次振兴家业。文中记载的“Minister for Foreign Affairs”职务疑有误，从字里行间看，“蔡大人”的官职应在巡抚大人聂缉椝之下，而清末外务大臣官位应在巡抚之上，且从史料来看也未见蔡姓外务大臣或次长。

140 dollars and receive 400 cuts of the bamboo. Failing paying the money he was to be bamboo'd until he did. He had already received two doses of 400 each, so on this occasion as he had not refunded the cash he received 800 strokes. After this fearful punishment he was a really pitiable object, but was lifted in front of Mr Li, who ordered him 1,000 more if the money was not paid within five days. His friends have the expense of keeping and feeding the prisoner whilst he is in prison, and the object of the recurring sentences is to put pressure upon his relatives to induce them to find the money for him.

My eight days' sojourn in Soochow was full of interest and Mr Olsen's hospitality and kindness I fear I shall never be able to repay. I returned to Shanghai in his house-boat, bearing with me charming recollections of 'Beautiful Soo.'

Then, having taken leave of all my friends in Shanghai, I embarked on the Nipon Yusen Kaisha steamer *Saikio Maru* en route for Japan.

个姑娘，还以 140 元的价格把她卖给了一个农民，之后他再次从农民那里诱拐了她。这个案件的判决结果是，男子被责令退还 140 元，还要挨四百大板。男子不退那笔钱就要被打到退还为止。他已经挨了两轮四百大板，故而他因为没有退钱已经挨了八百大板。经过这番骇人的刑罚，男子着实可怜兮兮，但还是被架到了李大人面前。李大人下令，如果五天内不还钱就再打他一千大板。男子的朋友承担了他在关押期间的收监费和伙食费，而判决会反复生效的目的是向他的亲戚施压，迫使他们为他凑钱。

在苏州逗留的 8 天里，我兴致勃勃，而对奥尔森先生的好客恩情，恐怕我永远无以为报。满载着对“姑苏”的美妙回忆，我乘坐他的住家船回到了上海。

之后，在与上海所有的朋友告别后，我登上了日本邮船株式会社的“西京丸号”轮船前往日本。

Two Girls in China

两个女子在唐山

（玛丽 · H. 克劳特著　戴莉、孙丹译）

《两个女子在唐山》（*Two Girls in China*）是美国作家玛丽 · H. 克劳特（Mary H. Krout）撰写的旅行见闻，记录了 1899—1900 年两个美国女孩玛丽和埃伦在中国游历上海、苏州、北京、香港等地的经历，1903 年由美国图书公司（American Book Company）在纽约出版。书中有 60 多幅反映清末中国人文风景的插图与照片，留下了珍贵的历史图文资料。

节译部分是书中第五章至第七章，描写了两个女孩同父母一起受其父朋友之邀，乘坐住家船从上海出发沿吴淞江进入大运河，一路游览水乡苏州城区和木渎镇等地的所见所闻，用实录笔法反映了当时中国苏州一带的风物人情和山水景致。原书出版时封面提供了中文书名：《两个女子在唐山》，因海外华人确将“唐山”作为“中国”的别称，故译者采用了原书的中译名。

V. A HOUSE BOAT JOURNEY

The week after they reached Shanghai, a friend of Mr. Spencer invited the family to go with him on a journey to Suchau and Modo in his house boat. Mary and Ellen had read about Chinese house boats but they had never seen one. They knew that people who could do so preferred to travel in this way, as the roads everywhere in China are very bad. They are cut into deep ruts by the heavy wheels of Chinese carts and wagons and are never graded or repaired in any way. When it rains in the spring and autumn they are so muddy that it is hard work to get about at all. When it has been raining for a long time the roads are like deep ditches — so full of water that men are sometimes drowned in them. The people have made canals everywhere, the largest of which is the Grand Canal. These waterways are much better than the roads for they never have to be mended. The Chinese do not like to mend anything but their clothes, their shoes, their fences and their broken dishes, all of which they do very neatly. They wear one suit of clothes the year round, wadding it with cotton in the winter. We do not think this very nice or cleanly, but it is the best that they can do, and they seem really cleaner than many of the poor in our own great cities. As the roads are so bad, thousands and thousands of Chinese travel through the country on canals and the great rivers, and a large part of what they have to sell, —grain, cotton, oil, vegetables and wool, —they take to the markets in boats, as the people do in Holland. Ellen and Mary learned, too, that millions of the very poorest people are born in boats, live all their lives there, and die in them at last. They saw thousands of boat people in Wusung creek, the boats lying side by side. A small piece of matting was curved above the middle of the boat, forming a low roof under which a man could hardly stand erect. The father, mother and children were crowded together in this narrow space. It is very cold in the winter, although around Shanghai there is little frost or snow, and as they have no fire but the handful of charcoal which they burn in a brazier over which they boil their tea and rice when they are so fortunate as to have any, they suffer very much. Sometimes they own a duck or a chicken and the poor fowl is tied fast by the leg to the boat so that it can not run away. Mary saw a cat tied in this way, its fur matted and dirty, huddled up as if it were very wretched. It probably was, for Chinese cats in the boats and hovels of the poor cannot keep clean, and they get very little to eat and no milk, which the

第五章　住家船之旅

斯宾塞一家抵达上海的第二周，斯宾塞先生的一位朋友就邀请他们一起乘坐住家船游览苏州城区和木渎镇。玛丽和埃伦读过关于中国住家船的文章，但从未亲眼见过住家船。她们知道中国各处道路状况极其糟糕，有条件乘坐住家船的人更愿意选择这种水路旅行方式。道路被中式手推车和马车沉重的车轮碾压出一道道深深的车辙，却从未以任何方式进行分级或整修。春秋季下雨时，道路泥泞不堪，通行异常艰难。如果降雨持续很长一段时间，马路就变得像深沟——水深得有时甚至会淹死人。中国人到处开凿运河，其中规模最大的是大运河。这些水道远胜于陆道，因为从来不需要修整。中国人只爱收拾自己的衣服和鞋子，修理自家的篱笆与破碗。一年到头，他们都穿同一套衣服，冬天则往衣服里塞棉花来保暖。我们觉得这么穿不是很干净、很体面，但这是百姓最好的穿着了，而且他们看上去比我们国内大城市的很多穷人更整洁。由于道路状况太差，千千万万的中国人通过运河和大江大河去往各地，他们出售的大部分货物——谷物、棉花、油、蔬菜和羊毛——都用船运送到市场，与荷兰人的方式极为相似。埃伦和玛丽也了解到数以百万计的极度贫穷的人出生在船上，一辈子生活在船上，最终在船上离开人间。她们从吴淞江并排停泊着的船上看到了成千上万的船民。船的中间是用一小片苇席搭成的拱形棚，船篷低矮，几乎无法让人直立。父亲、母亲及孩子们都拥挤在这个逼仄的空间内。冬天非常寒冷，尽管上海周边地区很少降霜、下雪。他们除了一把木炭再无其他的取火燃料；当运气好时有些茶叶和大米，就用木炭点燃火盆煮茶、做饭，生活非常艰辛。有时他们得到一只鸭或一只鸡，可怜的家禽一只脚被牢牢地绑缚在船上以防逃跑。玛丽看见一只猫就这样被绑着，毛又乱又脏，蜷缩成一团，看似特别可怜。它可能真的很可怜，因为养在船上或穷人陋舍的中国猫是没法保持清洁的，而且它们吃得极少，也没有牛奶，中国人不

Chinese do not use.

The two girls were much interested in the house boat. They had seen several lying near the bridge, not far from the hotel. Most of them belonged to foreigners, although the wealthy Chinese also have such boats comfortably fitted up with plate glass windows curtained with silk. Mary and Ellen saw that the house boat was not unlike an American canal boat except that it was made of dark, polished wood. There were decks, fore and aft. The owner and his friends sat forward, this deck being spread with rugs and furnished with wicker chairs. The Chinese crew stayed aft, sleeping under the low deck and squatting about the rice kettle and teapot which they brought out above deck. The saloon was supplied with divans covered with crimson which were curtained at night and served for beds; racks along the sides held papers and books, and there were lockers for the clothes and the rugs. It was well lighted with many small windows which were shaded with blinds that could be drawn at night or when the sun streamed in too brightly. They ate at an ordinary table which was spread with linen and china and silver, just as it would have been at home. On such a boat it is necessary for travelers to take with them everything that they may require, for very little can be bought in the cities that they may visit. It is a great deal of trouble to get ready for a house boat journey, and several days before one starts lists are made out of food, bedding, dishes, cooking utensils, linen and supplies of all sorts. These are carefully gone over to see that nothing has been forgotten. Chinese servants do not like the house boat very much; they prefer to stay quietly at home and so avoid the trouble of packing and unpacking. All the cooking is done on board, and the cook and the boy who waits at table must go with the boat. The house boat is propelled by large sails, and, when the wind is in the wrong direction, by trackers, as the men are called who drag the boat along by means of a heavy rope. They walk on the bank in a narrow, beaten path, like a towpath, pulling and shouting with all their might. The captain, or the man in charge, is called the "Laota," which in Chinese means " old great." He usually makes a great deal of noise, screaming and using very bad language, fortunately in Chinese, so the foreigners on board are none the wiser. He calls the poor, patient trackers "pigs" and other ugly names, to which they make no reply, tugging uncomplainingly at the heavy rope. When the wind favors, the trackers raise the great sail and do other work as the "Laota" directs.

Mr. and Mrs. Spencer and the two girls were the guests of Mr. Scott, who lived in Shanghai and who owned the boat. People in Shanghai, who are very kind and hospitable, often entertain their foreign visitors in this way.

用牛奶喂猫。

玛丽和埃伦对住家船很感兴趣。她们看到在离旅店不远的桥边停着几艘，其中大多数是外国人的，尽管中国富人也有这样的船，船上装着饰有丝绸窗帘的平板玻璃窗，非常舒适。她俩发现住家船除了由深色抛光的木材建造而成，其余与美国运河上的船只别无二致。船首和船尾都有甲板。船主和他的朋友闲坐于船首，甲板上铺着小地毯，摆放着柳条椅。中国船工待在船尾，睡在下层甲板之下。他们把饭锅和茶壶从舱中取出放在甲板上，蹲坐其周。会客厅中有罩着深红色座套的长软椅，晚上拉上帷幔可作睡榻。四周的架子上摆放着报纸和书籍，还有收纳衣服和毯子的储物柜。众多的小窗户让船舱内采光充足，晚上或阳光射入太强时可拉上卷帘。就餐的桌子是常见的那种，就像在家里一样，上面铺着亚麻桌布，摆放着瓷器和银器。这样的住家船上日常所需得备置齐全，因为在所到的城市很难买到补给物品。住家船之旅的准备工作十分繁杂，出发前好几天就得列出食物、寝具、餐具、厨具、亚麻织品及各种供给的清单，并仔细查看以免遗漏。中国仆役非常不喜欢靠住家船出行，他们更愿安稳地待在家里，省去打包、开包的诸多麻烦。烧菜做饭都在船上进行，厨师和侍餐男仆必须随船同行。住家船由巨帆推动，逆风时就得靠纤夫用粗大的纤绳拉船行进。他们拼尽全力躬身背纤、喊着号子沿着狭窄平整的纤道艰难前行。船长，又被称作“Laota”，在汉语中表示“老大”之意。他通常在船上大呼小叫，语言粗鲁，所幸他讲的是中文，所以船上外国人对此也不甚了解。他用“蠢货”或者其他难听的称谓来称呼那些逆来顺受的穷苦纤夫们，而这些纤夫对此只有默默忍受，拖着沉重的纤绳缓步前行。顺风时，纤夫扬起风帆，在“老大”的指使下干其他杂活。

船主斯科特先生住在上海，他邀请斯宾塞夫妇及其两个女儿来属于他的这艘船上做客。居住在上海的人非常友善好客，通常以住家船出游的方式款待其外国宾客。

They were to be gone four or five days and Ellen and Mary put on their thick gowns and boots, for it is cool on the water.

" I shall go ashore and walk in the fields with papa," Mary said, " for the walks are half the fun on a house boat journey."

They also took their books, for there would be plenty of time for reading. They did not go on board the boat at the bridge where she lay, because it would take so long to steer through the crowded junks and sampans; but they drove out into the country and waited on the river bank. Mrs. Spencer sat down on a bench by the roadside in a sheltered place out of the wind which was rather keen. Ellen and Mary went into a garden across the road in which people were allowed to walk and climbed to the steps of a wooden tower. They could see the low gray roofs and the walls which shut in the native city, and the green rice fields which stretched away in every direction. The river wound across the level plain like a yellow ribbon, and there were hundreds of boats—the little dispatch boats which moved rapidly, rowed with the feet instead of the hands, —junks and house boats. Leather gloves were fastened to some of the oars, and the hands of the boatmen were thrust into them.

Mary and Ellen laughed at this queer custom but Ellen said:

"I think after all it is a very sensible fashion. I am sure that these boatmen never lose their gloves and always know just where to find them. The only trouble is that they can use them only when they are rowing. It would be a great deal of trouble to unfasten them from the oars every time they wanted to wear them."

The large sails of the junks came slowly in sight, the heavy vessels propelled both by the wind, which was blowing in the right direction, and by the tide which was rising fast and would carry them on their way for thirty miles. Some of the sails were of matting, like those they had seen in the Inland Sea; others were of cloth, —brown, gray, blue and even dark red in color. They were so graceful, towering aloft in the clear air with their soft, pleasing colors that they reminded Mary, she said, of flocks of great birds with widespread wings. At last they heard their mother call them and they ran down the steps and across the road. Their boat was in sight, the tall gray sails filling in the fresh, cool wind, and, what pleased them most of all, their own American flag fluttering at the bow. The "Laota" was on the forward deck, shouting and gesticulating to attract as much attention from the other boats as possible, so that other crews might see and envy the wonderful foreign house boat with its shining windows and the gay red and

他们计划出游四五天。水上寒凉，埃伦和玛丽穿上了厚外衣和靴子。

玛丽说："我要上岸和爸爸一起在田间散步，住家船之旅的一半乐趣来自岸上漫步。"

她们随行也带着书籍，因为船上有充裕的阅读时间。她们没有登上停泊在桥边的住家船，因为要行驶穿过挨挨挤挤的帆船和舢板耗时太久了；她们驱车来到乡村，在河岸边等候。斯宾塞夫人择一路边长椅而坐，正好能避开刺骨的寒风。埃伦和玛丽走进马路对面供人散步的公园，拾阶登上了一座木制塔楼。她们看到围合在城内的一片片低矮的黛瓦灰墙，而绿色的稻田四向延展。河流像黄色绸带蜿蜒穿过平原，河面上百舸争流——有急速前行的小型通信快船，它们用双脚而非双手驱动，还有帆船和住家船。一些橹上系着皮手套，船夫把手插入其中摇橹。

玛丽和埃伦觉得这种奇怪的做法很可笑，但埃伦说道：

"我觉得这种方式终究还是很明智的。这些船夫肯定永远不会丢失手套而且永远知道去哪里找手套。唯一的问题是他们只有摇橹时才能用上手套。每次他们想要戴的时候得花很大工夫从橹上解下手套。"

帆船巨大的风帆渐渐映入眼帘，重型轮船由顺风和潮水共同推动，迅速上涨的潮汐能把船往前推行三十英里。一些风帆像她们在内海见到的那样用蒲草编织而成，其余的都由布料制成——棕色、灰色、蓝色，甚至还有深红色的。色彩柔和悦目的风帆优雅地高挂晴空，玛丽说这让她联想起一群群展翅的大鸟。终于她们听到了母亲的呼唤，跑下台阶，穿过马路。接她们的船已跃入眼帘，清新的凉风鼓满高耸的灰色风帆，最令她们高兴的是看到自己国家的国旗在船头飘扬。"老大"站在前甲板上，大声喊叫，打着手势，尽可能吸引其他船只的注意力，让其他船的船员看见并羡慕这

white flag, for the Chinese have a great admiration for flags.

Presently the boat was brought about close to the shore; the plank was thrown out, one end resting on the deck and the other on the low bank, and they walked across this and were soon all on board. As they did not wish to lose the tide, the plank was raised at once and they moved slowly up stream. They were delighted with everything, —the low, soft divans heaped with cushions, the pretty cabin with its warm hangings, and flounces on the shelves and table. In one corner was a small stove, firmly fastened in its place, in which a bright fire was burning.

" I like the deck best," said Mary, " although the cabin is so snug and pretty. I think that I shall sit out there. I want to see the boats, the river, the fields, and the queer people."

She went accordingly, without loss of time, and when she had seated herself in a low chair, Ah Lum, Mr. Scott's " Number One Boy," came and wrapped her up snugly in warm wolf-skin rugs. She was happy and comfortable and presently Mrs. Spencer and Ellen came on deck, too, and were deeply interested in the strange sights all about them. "This is really China," said Ellen. The boats, both going up and down stream, grew thicker and thicker. On many women and even children were tugging at the oars, while the men squatted on their heels, smoking and gossiping and eating rice, or drinking tea.

" I think the poor women in China must lead very sad lives," said Mary. "They do all the hard work, they are not allowed to rest or enjoy themselves, and the children are not so merry and happy as the children in Japan; and yet people are poor in that country, too, and have to work hard and have but little to eat."

Mrs. Spencer could not explain this, but she said that the Japanese seem to be a more hopeful and a happier race than the Chinese. They are extremely fond of children, the parents playing with them and amusing them as if they themselves were children.

They saw a man plowing a field with a rude, heavy plow drawn by a strange animal; it was big, awkward and covered with thick, dark brown hair, the long horns bent backward toward the ears.

" What is it?" asked Mary.

" It is the water buffalo," she was told, " which is used everywhere throughout the East, in China, the Philippines and India for plowing and drawing carts, as we use horses. It is really an animal that lives much of the time in water and

艘窗明几净、插着红白相间旗帜的洋船，因为中国人非常喜欢旗帜。

不久，船就靠岸了；伸出跳板，一端搭在甲板上，另一端搭在低岸上，她们很快沿着跳板上了船。不想错过潮汐，所以立马撤去跳板，船顺着水流缓缓北上。她们对一切都很满意——堆着靠垫的柔软矮长椅、挂着温馨帘子的漂亮客舱、装饰着荷叶边的架子和桌子。一只小火炉牢牢固定在船舱一角，闪动着明亮的炉火。

玛丽说："我最喜欢甲板，虽然船舱如此舒适漂亮。我觉得应该坐在舱外甲板上。我想看船只、河流、田野和奇特的中国人。"

于是，她毫不迟疑地上了甲板，当她坐在矮椅上时，斯科特先生的大管家阿林走上前，给她紧紧裹上了暖和的用狼皮制作的毯子。她感到快乐而舒适。不久，斯宾塞夫人和埃伦也来到甲板上，她们对四周的陌生景致很感兴趣。埃伦说："这是真正的中国。"南来北往的船只越来越密集。许多船上的女人甚至孩童在用力摇橹，而男人们却蹲坐着抽烟、聊天、吃饭或喝茶。

"我想中国可怜的妇女们一定过着悲惨的生活。"玛丽说道，"她们干着所有的累活，却得不到休息和娱乐。和日本儿童相比，中国儿童似乎没那么愉快，不过日本民众也很穷，他们不得不努力工作，但吃不到什么东西。"

对此，斯宾塞夫人并没有做什么解释，不过她却说日本人似乎看上去要比中国人乐观、开心。日本人极其喜欢孩子，父母像孩童般与孩子一起玩耍、逗乐。

她们看到一个人用简陋、笨重的犁在田间耕地，拉犁的牲畜长相奇怪——它又大又笨拙，长着深褐色的浓密的毛，长角朝后弯向耳朵。

玛丽问："它是什么动物？"

她被告知："这是水牛。在整个东方，在中国、菲律宾和印度，人们用它犁地、拉车，就像我们用马一样。它确实大部分时间生活在水中，喜欢

loves to wallow in the soft mud, in which, when it can, it buries itself up to the eyes. Once every day at least the buffalo must have its bath; otherwise it almost goes mad, running in a frenzy and attacking whatever is in the way. The Chinese could hardly live without their water buffalo; nothing else could take its place in the marshy rice fields, although we get on without it in our Southern States. However, we do not raise rice in quite the same way."

Just then an ugly dog that was following the man turned, glared at the house boat and barked fiercely, and the buffalo began to rear and plunge in fright. They were near the shore and could see the animal distinctly. " They have caught scent of us," said Mr. Scott. " All Chinese animals hate the scent of a foreigner. The Chinese themselves do not like it; they say we smell like sheep."

Ellen and Mary laughed, and wondered why they were not conscious of it, but upon the whole they thought it a more pleasant odor than that of the Chinese who do not bathe very often and who, rich and poor alike, eat a great deal of garlic. The plowman finally quieted the buffalo, which moved across the field, but the shaggy dog ran toward them, still growling and barking. Fortunately he could not get at them and he was soon left behind.

Then Ah Lum, Mr. Scott's "Boy," sounded the gong and tiffin was served.

In the afternoon the house boat was dragged near the bank by the trackers, the plank was lowered and they all went ashore for a walk. They enjoyed the brisk exercise in the cold, invigorating air, and Mary and Ellen came back with their hair tossed by the wind and their cheeks glowing like roses.

Dinner was quite like dinner at home, with soup and fish and a joint, and fruit and cakes for dessert. It had all been prepared in a tiny closet, which served as a kitchen, behind the saloon. Here Ah Chung, the cook, and Ah Lum also spread down their mats and slept at night. Mrs. Spencer said that many a foreign cook, with a great, roomy kitchen, could not have prepared so good a dinner as that which Ah Chung got for them in his dark little galley.

After dinner they talked and read; then the divans were covered with sheets and blankets and the thick crimson curtains were hung around them. Mary and Ellen soon went to sleep, the water rippling drowsily under their window.

浸泡在软软的泥潭中，可能的话，它会把自己眼睛以下都埋在泥里。水牛每天至少泡一次澡；否则它几乎会疯掉，躁乱狂奔，一路冲撞。没有水牛，中国人几乎无法生存；水牛在泥泽稻田的地位是无可替代的，尽管我们南部各州不用水牛也能过活。然而，我们种植水稻的方式不尽相同。”

就在那时，跟在那人身后的一只样貌丑陋的狗转身瞪着住家船狂吠，吓得水牛猛然跃起，后腿直立。他们离河岸很近，把这一切看得一清二楚。斯科特先生说：“它们闻到了我们的气味。所有中国的动物都讨厌外国人的气味。中国人自己也不喜欢，他们说我们闻着像绵羊。”

埃伦和玛丽笑了，思忖着为什么她们没有觉察到这一点，不过，总的来说，她们认为绵羊味要比中国人身上的气味好些，中国人经常不洗澡，而且不论贫富都爱吃大蒜。农夫终于让穿过稻田的水牛平静下来，但那条蓬毛狗冲向他们，还是咆哮、吠叫不停。所幸它无法扑到他们，很快就被甩在了后面。

随后，斯科特先生的管家阿林鸣锣上午餐。

下午，纤夫把住家船拉至岸边，放下跳板，他们全都上岸散步。轻快地在寒冷的空气中漫步令人精神焕发、心情愉悦。玛丽和埃伦回来时，头发被风吹乱了，双颊绯红如玫瑰。

晚餐和家常的一样，有汤、鱼和烤肉，甜点是水果和蛋糕。这一切都是在客厅后面作为厨房的一个小隔间里准备的。这里也是厨师阿钟和阿林晚上铺开垫子睡觉的地方。斯宾塞夫人说，很多享有高级宽敞厨房的外国厨师都做不出像阿钟在昏暗的小厨房里给他们准备的那么精美的晚餐。

晚饭后她们聊天、读书；然后给长软椅铺上被单和毛毯，四周拉上厚厚的深红色帷幔。柔波荡漾，在窗下吟唱着催眠曲，玛丽和埃伦很快就入睡了。

VI. MODO

The next morning it was quite cloudy and when they awoke and looked out of the window the creek was still covered with boats. The "Laota" had come in and built the fire, and they could hear Ah Lum in the little kitchen chatting to Ah Chung among his pots and pans. Breakfast would soon be ready, so they dressed quickly, put on their hats and coats and went out on the deck, where they found their father and mother enjoying the fresh air. Ah Lum came into the saloon, took down the curtains and put them away, stored the bedding in the lockers, opened the doors and windows and put everything in order for the day. The table was set and they were called to breakfast, for which they were quite ready.

They had now left Wusung creek and entered the Grand Canal. This is one of the great waterways of China. It has been used for more than a thousand years, and is seven hundred miles long. It is like a broad river with low banks, except that there is almost no current. Hundreds of small canals empty into it which are like private roads, with little water gates that can be opened and closed. Up and down these canals boats were passing to the farms beyond. The Grand Canal near the villages is spanned by sharply arched bridges under which the junks can move, some of them without even lowering their sails. Men and boys leaned over the bridges and looked down at them, chattering and laughing, and talking about them very frankly. They knew the flag, and pointed it out to each other. Mr. Scott understood the language and he said that they were not disrespectful, for the Chinese have always been friendly to Americans; but they made jokes as they always do about everything. At one village, where a small creek emptied into the canal, they saw a crowd gathered about a sampan upon the sides of which some large white birds were sitting; they had bills like geese, but their necks were long and slender.

"What are they?" asked Mary, watching the crowd of Chinese who appeared to be admiring the birds extremely. Their owner was so interested in talking about them, —telling no doubt of their wonderful exploits, —that he did not at first notice the approach of the house boat.

" Those are cormorants," said Mr. Scott. " The Chinese find them very useful for fishing. The birds are taken out on the water, the hungrier they are the better. For that matter, they seem to be always hungry. A tight collar is fastened around the neck, not tight enough to choke them, or to hurt them, but fitting so

第六章 木渎

第二天清晨，阴云密布，她们醒来望向窗外，只见河面上仍然船只如梭。“老大”已进来生起了火，她们能听到阿林在小厨房里夹杂着锅碗瓢盆声与阿钟说话的声音。早餐很快就要准备好了，所以她们迅速穿衣戴帽，披上外套走上甲板，父亲和母亲已经在那呼吸新鲜的空气了。阿林走进客厅，取下帷幔收好，把床上用品放进储物柜，打开门窗，整理好当天的一应所需。餐桌摆好了，她们被叫去吃早餐，就等着这一刻呢。

现在船已经驶出吴淞江进入了大运河。这是中国最伟大的水道之一，已经通行了1 000多年，全长700英里，就像一条两岸低平的宽阔大江，只是几乎没有潮水。成百上千条小河像私家道路般通过可开闭的水闸汇入其中。舟船沿着这些河流来来往往驶向远处的田野。靠近村庄的大运河上建有高大的拱桥，帆船可从桥下通过，一些甚至不用降低风帆。男人和男童倚在桥栏边，低头看着他们，谈笑风生，毫不避讳地谈论着他们。他们认得美国国旗，互相指指点点。斯科特先生听得懂他们说的话，他说他们并非无礼，因为中国人一向对美国人很友好，但是他们喜欢拿一切开涮。在一个村子里，一条小河汇入了运河。他们看到一群人聚集在一只舢板周围，船舷上栖息着几只白色大鸟，它们的喙像鹅，但脖子又细又长。

望着那群似乎对大鸟极为赞佩的中国人，玛丽问道：“它们是什么鸟？”鸟的主人无疑在讲述它们的不凡身手，他正说得兴起，起初都没注意到住家船驶近了。

斯科特先生答道：“那些是鸬鹚。中国人发现它们对捕鱼很有用。把鸟带到水上，让它们越饿越好。就此而言，它们似乎总是饥肠辘辘。一个项圈紧紧套在脖子上，不至于呛住或伤害它们，但扣得很紧，使得它们无

closely that they cannot swallow. When their owner reaches the fishing grounds the cormorants are let loose, and dive after the fish which they can see at a great depth. They seize a fish in their bills, but cannot swallow it because of the snug collar. They are brought back into the boat and the fish taken from them, but every time they are rewarded with a morsel which can slip down their throats. They are supposed to be very greedy, although perhaps they do not eat much more than ducks and geese, who are hunting food most of the time. But they have the name of being greedy and now we use the word 'cormorant' sometimes when we speak of a very greedy man."

The birds were not disturbed by the crowd, but they appeared dull and stupid, as if they had had more to eat than was good for them, which happens sometimes to human beings as well as to cormorants.

All the larger cities of China are enclosed in high brick walls with openings at regular intervals along the top through which soldiers can shoot arrows or fire their guns, for the Chinese nowadays have learned to use firearms. They have warships on the sea and on their rivers, and armies on the land … The city walls are about thirty feet high, — double walls of masonry filled in with earth and paved with stone on top. This pavement is about twenty-five feet wide. There are gates to the north, south, east and west, which are really heavy doors, around which are built two other walls at right angles, forming a hollow square; in this inner wall is another gate opening into the streets of the city. The gates are closed at night and should a traveler arrive too late he must wait outside until morning when the gates are opened again.

The double gates are for better defense, for, if the outer gate is broken down, there is still another to be forced, which the people may be able to defend and thus save themselves and their homes. The strong brick walls are so high that it is hard work to scale them; and, besides this, there is either a canal, as at Suchau, or a wide, deep ditch filled with water, called a moat, dug all around them; the walls cannot then be reached except by boats, which are in danger of being sunk. The double walls, the outer and inner, are filled with earth and paved on top. Grass, shrubs, and even small trees spring up in the cracks of the pavement. In the autumn people are allowed to gather the weeds, grass and dead leaves, which they use for fuel.

The house boat reached Suchau the second day and passed under the wall, but they decided to go on to Modo, and then return.

法吞咽。当主人到达渔场时，就会放出鸬鹚潜水逐鱼，它们能看见深水处的鱼。它们用喙捕鱼，但由于紧箍的项圈而无法把鱼吞下。它们被带回到船上，鱼从嘴中被取出，但每次它们都会得到一块可以从喉咙里滑下的食物作为奖励。它们被认为是非常贪吃的，尽管也许它们吃的并不比大部分时间都在捕食的鸭子和鹅多。但是它们被冠以贪婪的恶名，现在我们有时会用'鸬鹚'这个词来形容一个非常贪婪的人。"

鸬鹚并未受人群打扰，但是看起来又呆又笨，好像是吃得过撑了，人类有时也会这样。

中国所有大点的城市都围在高高的砖墙内，城墙上每隔一定距离设有垛口，士兵通过其射箭或开火枪，现在中国人已学会使用火器了。他们在江海上有战船，陆地上有军队……城墙约 30 英尺高，双重城垣由黄土黏合的砖石砌筑而成，城墙顶上是石块铺地，宽约 25 英尺。东、西、南、北各设城门，城门非常厚重，周围建有另两面与其呈直角的墙，构成一个方形空间；在这瓮城中有另一道门通向城内街道。城门在夜间关闭，如果客行者到达太晚，那只能在城外等待，直到早晨城门再启。

双重城门是为了更好地御敌，如果外城门被攻破了，还有一道门可防守，百姓可自救和保卫家园。坚固的砖墙高不可攀；此外，像苏州城那样，城墙或由一条运河环绕，或由一道又宽又深的灌水壕沟护卫，运河或壕沟被称为护城河。只有船只冒着沉没的危险才能抵达城墙。内外两重城墙内填泥土，城墙顶铺设石板路。青草、灌木，甚至小树，从路面的裂缝中破土而出。秋天，人们可以收集野草、青草和落叶作为燃料。

住家船第二天抵达苏州并进了城，但一行人决定继续前往木渎，然后返回。

Modo is little more than a village, dark and dirty, and crowded with people. It lies huddled at the foot of a steep, high hill—the only hill in that region—which can be seen for a long distance.

They did not wait to see the shops, which were rather poor, but hurried through the crowds that had begun to gather to stare at the foreigners, to the outskirts of the town, a wide, grassy space like an open meadow.

A young Chinese prince had once lived in the pleasure garden which he laid out on top of the hill, but now nothing is left but a temple — a Chinese pagoda with many stories, or terraces, rising one above the other, and narrowing at the top. A zig-zag brick pavement has been laid from the foot to the very top of the hill, and at regular distances are broad paved spaces provided with seats where people can rest. There are many graves upon the hillside; some are the graves of nobles and soldiers, with moss-grown inscriptions in Chinese letters on the headstones. They had long been forgotten, and the withered grass around them rustled softly, as if whispering their story.

It was a long, hard climb and Mrs. Spencer and the girls rested from time to time upon the stone benches. Then they started on again and were soon at the top of the hill. Mr. Scott was there before them, with their father. The pagoda from the foot of the hill appeared airy and graceful, but near at hand it was gray and grimy and falling into decay. At each corner, from the lowest terrace to the top, was hung a small bronze bell; the clapper was a thin piece of metal shaped like the leaf of a lotus, a kind of water lily which both the Japanese and Chinese consider a sacred flower. As the wind blew the bells to and fro, they gave out a faint musical chime that was sweet but very mournful. Within the temple were many altars, upon which were figures of Buddha, whom many of the Chinese worship, and about the figures were arranged vases and candlesticks of burnished brass. There were also fierce and scowling gods whom the people worship, for the Chinese think that they must keep the wicked gods in a good humor by offering them gifts, for fear they will do them harm.

The priests that live in these temples, though poor and ignorant, are often quite gentle and polite. The heads of the Buddhist priests are shaved smooth, and they wear dirty clothes of rags which they have patched together. Travelers can often lodge in the temples, and can almost always buy food of the priests. The young man who came to meet them at the entrance of the pagoda closed his hands and placed one upon the other, raised them to his forehead, and then bowed

木渎只不过是一个又暗又脏的村庄，人口拥挤。它缩挤在一座陡峭高峻的山脚下——该地区唯一的山，遥遥可见。

一行人没有逗留去逛那些破旧的商店，而是匆匆穿过那些围拢来看老外的人群，来到镇郊，那是一片像牧场般广阔而绿草丛生的地方。

一位年轻的中国君王曾住在他建于山顶的御花园中，但现在只剩下一座庙宇 —— 一座多层中式宝塔，楼台层叠，顶部收窄。一条弯弯曲曲的砖石路从山脚通到山顶，每隔一定距离就有宽阔的平台，设有座椅供人休息。山坡有很多坟墓，一些是贵族和士兵的墓地，墓碑上刻着中文的铭文，上面已是青苔斑驳。墓主早已被人遗忘，周围枯草沙沙作响，仿佛在低语他们的故事。

这次登山漫长而艰难，斯宾塞太太和姑娘们不时地在石凳上休息。然后她们再次出发，很快就到了山顶。斯科特先生和她们的父亲先行登顶。宝塔从山脚仰望显得空灵而优雅，走近它，却是灰蒙蒙的，风化剥蚀，日渐破败。从最低层到顶层的每一个檐角都挂着一个小铜铃；铃舌是一金属薄片，形似莲叶，这是一种睡莲的叶片，日本人和中国人都视睡莲为圣洁之花。铃铛随风摇曳，发出轻灵、悦耳的声音，动听却饱含忧伤。寺中有很多供奉佛像的台座，许多中国人崇拜佛像，其周围摆放着花瓶和锃亮的黄铜烛台。人们崇拜的神灵中也有凶神恶煞，因为中国人认为必须给邪恶的神灵献祭以让他们保持心情愉快，以免他们伤害百姓。

这些寺庙中的僧人虽然贫穷无知，但通常相当温和有礼。住持的头剃得干干净净，穿着用碎布缝补的灰暗袈裟。客行者通常可以借宿寺中并能买到斋饭。那个来到宝塔入门处迎接他们的年轻僧人两手打拱，高举至前

almost to the ground. This is the way in which almost all Chinese men greet each other; women simply close the hands, place them one upon the other in the same way, move them up and down and nod their heads. Ellen thought this very queer.

"They shake their own hands in this funny, topsy-turvy country," she said, "instead of shaking ours!"

The priest spoke to Mr. Scott in Chinese and then invited them to be seated upon the narrow benches near a table, and there he left them. He came back in a little while with cups and hot water. A pinch of tea or dried willow leaves was placed in each cup and the hot water poured over them, the cup, which had a lid, resting in a holder like a saucer with a hole in the middle of it. The holder was to keep the hot cup from burning the fingers, and the lid was to prevent one from swallowing the tea leaves, it being lifted just a little as one drinks. Mary's cup was bluish-white porcelain, covered with lovely flowers and vines, and Mr. Scott bought it for her from the priest as a keepsake. Ellen was also allowed to keep hers. After the tea was poured the priest brought them some Chinese delicacies, roasted pumpkin seeds, sugared peanuts and thin strips of rice flour paste that seemed to have been dried instead of baked. Had they been really hungry, this fare would not have been very satisfying. The priests had a little garden, and a few geese in a pond, but Mr. Scott said that they do not like to work; they are about the only lazy people in China.

Nothing was left of the pleasure garden but the lotus pond which was dry and in which nothing grew. It was a square basin walled with stone and had once been full of water. It must have been very pretty then with the pink and white blossoms of the lotus and the dark glossy leaves floating on its surface.

A path led to the crest of the hill overlooking a broad valley, green with rice fields, the canals that separated them glittering in the sunshine like silver. To the west they could see a chain of lakes, and far off the dark walls of Suchau.

The young Prince of Modo had chosen a beautiful site for his pleasure garden. Mr. Scott told them his story. He had been at war with his neighbor, the powerful Prince of Hangchau, who at last, when he saw that he could not conquer his enemy, pretended to make friends with him and gave him his lovely young daughter for his wife. The Prince of Modo loved his young wife very dearly. She

额，鞠躬行礼，几乎一揖到地。这是几乎所有中国男人互相问安的方式；女子只需以同样的方式双手打拱，上下略摆，颔首行礼。埃伦觉得这种方式很怪异。

“在这个奇怪而又杂乱的国家，他们用拱手作揖的方式来和别人打招呼，”她说，“而不是跟我们握手。”

僧人用中文与斯科特先生交谈，邀请他们在桌边的窄长凳上落座后便离身而去。片刻之后，他端着茶杯和热水回来了。每个茶杯里放一撮茶叶或干柳叶，注上沸水，茶杯放在一个形似碟子中间有孔的茶托上，配有茶盖。茶托可防止滚烫的茶杯烫伤手指，喝茶的时候稍稍把茶盖掀开一点，可防止把茶叶吞咽下去。玛丽的青白瓷茶杯上饰有雅致的花卉和蔓草图纹，斯科特先生向僧人买下了这个茶杯作为纪念品送给她。埃伦也被允许保留她的茶杯。上完茶后，僧人给他们带来了一些中国美食，炒南瓜子、糖衣花生和馓子，馓子似乎是晒干的而不是烘焙的。如果他们真的饿了，这点点心是不够的。僧人们有一个小花园，池塘里养了几只鹅，但斯科特先生说这些僧人不愿劳作，他们大概是中国最懒的一群人了。

御花园中的一切都已荡然无存，唯留一个干涸且空荡无物的荷花池。这是一个石砌的方形池，曾经蓄满清水。那时的荷塘必定非常美丽，池面上漂浮着碧绿、有光泽的荷叶，粉白色的荷花亭亭玉立。

一条小径通往山顶，俯瞰广阔山谷，但见一片片绿油油的稻田，河道纵横其间，在阳光下闪着粼粼波光。向西望去，湖泊星罗棋布，远离苏州的灰暗城墙。

年轻的木渎君王（吴王）[1]选了一个风景优美的地方作为他的御花园。斯科特先生给她们讲述了吴王的故事。吴王曾与邻国强大的杭州君王（越王）[2]交战。最终，越王发现战胜不了吴王，就假装与之为友，并把自己

[1] 即吴王夫差。
[2] 即越王勾践。

must have been both wise and good, for he was so anxious to please her and to make her happy. He got for her everything she wished, and made the lotus pond and the garden and built the palace that she might not regret that she had left her own family and her home. They were so contented that they quite forgot the world. The Prince did not care to fight any longer and he spent all his time with his beautiful Princess in the palace, or walking about the garden, or feeding the gold fish in the lotus pond. One day the cruel and treacherous Prince of Hangchau marched quietly into Modo with his army, put the young Prince to death, destroyed the palace, and carried his daughter back to Hangchau.

Ellen thought that this was a very sad story, and she stopped a moment by the empty lotus pond and tried to picture the young Princess with her bright black eyes and glossy black hair, and knew how she must have mourned for her husband.

The sun was setting when they started down the hill again, and it was quite dark when they went on board, the "Laota" ordering the men to hoist the sail. In the morning they were at Suchau, and ready to go ashore again for more sight-seeing, after they had had their breakfast.

VII. SUCHAU

Neither carts nor jinrikishas could be hired in Suchau, so they prepared for a long walk. Mary and Ellen were young and strong, and they did not object to this, and they were so interested in what they saw that they did not realize that they were tired until they had come back to the house boat.

Ah Chung stayed on board to have tiffin ready for them, while the "Laota" and the Chinese crew hurried away to the Chinese inns to gossip with their friends, to smoke, and to drink tea.

The streets of Suchau are like those of the native city of Shanghai, —paved with stone, narrow, dark and dirty. But some of the shops were quite splendid. At the jeweler's they saw fine gems and collections of pearls which the Chinese prize much more than diamonds. At a florist's they were shown queer dwarfed trees in pots of blue porcelain. The roots had never been allowed room to grow, and the stunted boughs, clipped and pruned, were gnarled and twisted like the boughs of very old trees. The Chinese consider these dwarf trees very ornamen-

年轻貌美的女儿[1]献与吴王。吴王极为宠爱她。她肯定既聪慧又善良，因为吴王一心想着要取悦她，让她开心。他对她有求必应，为她造荷池与花园，并修建宫殿让她不至于因为离开家人和故土而悲憾。两人沉醉于欢娱之中，完全忘记了周遭世界。吴王再也无心打仗了，而是整日与他的爱妃厮守宫中，或在花园漫步，或是喂食荷花池中的金鱼。一日，冷酷奸诈的越王悄悄地带领军队偷袭木渎，处死了年轻的吴王，摧毁了其宫殿，把他的女儿带回了杭州。

埃伦觉得这是一个非常悲伤的故事，她在空荡荡的荷塘边驻足片刻，试着想象这位年轻的妃子有着乌黑、明丽的双眸和柔滑、亮泽的黑发，并确信她一定为失去丈夫而深感哀伤。

当他们开始下山返回时，太阳正渐渐西下，他们上船时，天色已黑，“老大”命令船工升起风帆。清晨，他们抵达苏州，准备早餐过后再次上岸观光。

第七章　苏州

在苏州（城区）雇不到马车和人力车，因此他们准备走长路。玛丽和埃伦年轻、强健，对此并不反对。她们对一路所见非常感兴趣，乐此不疲，直到回到住家船上才感到累。

阿钟留在船上为他们准备午餐，而“老大”和中国船工则匆匆赶往中式客栈与朋友们聊天、抽烟、喝茶。

苏州的街道就像上海的街道一样，铺着石子，又窄又暗，也不太干净。但有些商店相当华丽。在珠宝店，他们看到了精美的宝石和珍珠藏品，中国人对珍珠的青睐远远超过了钻石。在一家花店里，他们看到了蓝瓷盆中种着奇特的矮化树。树根从来未能获得生长的空间，长不大的树枝经过修剪和打杈，打造得像古木的树枝一样虬枝劲节。中国人认为这些矮小的树

[1]　此处应为西施，非越王的女儿，斯科特先生所述有误。

tal. They buy them for their gardens or courtyards and protect them from the cold in the winter. There were also small spruce trees cut into the form of storks, lions and other animals; bits of glass were used for the eyes and in the mouths were tongues made of red cloth. The florist was so pleased with their notice that he invited them into the shop and led the way to the court in the rear, which must have been very pretty in the spring and summer, when the plum, apricot and quince trees were in bloom and the pond covered with lotus blossoms. The chrysanthemums were budding, but it was as yet too early for the blossoms. Mr. Scott showed them how cunningly the gardener had grafted the slips of chrysanthemum on a strong, coarse weed, the artemisia, because the large stem of the latter could nourish the flowers much better than the slender stalks of the chrysanthemum itself. There was no grass in this Chinese garden, and none in any garden that they saw afterwards. Grass does not grow well anywhere in China. None of the plants were set in beds as we grow them, but they were all planted in porcelain pots which we would have thought much too fine for flower pots, and these were placed in rows along the walks. One large ash tree grew in the center of the court. The gardener was very proud of it, as there are so few trees in China. The girls noticed several of the dwarf trees which were set where they could not fail to be seen; there was a rockery like a miniature mountain, with toy bridges spanning little chasms, and rivulets trickling down the miniature cliffs.

The florist offered them tea, and was much pleased when Mrs. Spencer bought some flowers which he arranged very prettily.

After they had left the florist's shop they passed the fish market, where they saw a clever plan which the Chinese have for keeping fish alive until they are ready to be eaten. A number of boxes filled with water are arranged one above the other in such a way that a running stream falls continually from the upper box into those beneath. In the lowest box, which is placed upon the ground, the fish swim about, able to breathe in the water that has thus been mixed with air. They saw another sight, however, which made them shiver, — men scaling fish before they had been killed. These men did not seem to notice or care how the poor creatures writhed and struggled.

"It is dreadful," said Mrs. Spencer.

" You will see a great deal of such cruelty," Mr. Scott told her. " The people in China do not treat dumb creatures kindly, and they can not understand why we are so considerate of them. It may be, " he added, " that they have been so cruelly treated themselves in the past that they have now ceased to feel sympathy for

木很有观赏性。他们买来装点花园或庭院，并在冬天保护它们免受寒冷。还有些小云杉树被修整成鹳、狮子和其他动物的造型；玻璃片用来装点眼睛，红布用来做舌头。花店老板见有外宾关注其店，高兴地邀请他们进店并带至后院，那里春夏时节一定非常美丽——春天，园中的梅树、杏树和榅桲树的花朵盛开；夏天，满池荷花绽放。菊花正在萌芽，但开花还为时过早。斯科特先生向他们展示了园丁如何巧妙地将菊花插枝嫁接在一种粗壮的野草艾蒿上，因为后者的粗茎比菊花本身的细茎更能滋养花朵。这个中国花园里没有草，他们后来看到的花园里也都没有草。草在中国任何地方都长得不好。没有一株植物像我们那样种在花坛中，而是全部种在我们觉得做花盆太过精美的瓷盆中，并沿着小径摆放成行。庭院中心长着一棵高大的蜡树。园丁非常引以为豪，因为中国的树太少了。女孩们注意到了几棵被安放在显眼之处的盆景树；那里有一座像微型山岳的假山，仿真小桥横跨小峡谷，小溪从微型悬崖上涓涓而下。

花店老板给他们上茶，当斯宾塞夫人买了些他制作的漂亮插花时，他高兴极了。

离开花店后，他们经过了鱼市，在那里他们看到中国人用一个巧妙的方法让鱼在被宰杀食用前保持鲜活。几个装满水的箱子一个个被叠放着，一股水流持续不断地从上面的箱子流到下面。空气通过这种方法溶入水中，鱼儿就在那个放在地面最底层的水箱里游来游去，自由地呼吸。随后，他们看到的场景令他们颇为吃惊——有人正在刮鱼鳞，这些人似乎并不在乎这些可怜的动物还在扭动。

斯宾塞夫人说："这太可怕了。"

"你将会看到很多这样残忍的场景，"斯科特先生告诉她，"中国人对待这些不会说话的动物并不十分友好，而且他们也不能够理解为什么我们外国人会对待动物如此关爱。"他又补充道："也许是因为他们过去曾遭受

anything."

As they passed a house they heard a child sobbing and crying. It was being beaten by its mother, and the blows of the stick could be distinctly heard. Mrs. Spencer wished to go into the house and stop the angry mother, who shouted and scolded.

" No," said Mr. Scott, " you must never meddle with Chinese children. Foreigners are suspected of bewitching them, stealing them, and then putting them to death. Although the Chinese themselves leave their baby daughters in the streets to die, they can be stirred up to burn and kill if they can be made to believe that foreigners harm the little ones in any way."

They went on very quickly but Mrs. Spencer could not forget the crying of the poor baby that she would have liked to rescue if she could have done so. They intended to visit a large temple in the very heart of the city, and found it rather hard to get through the crowds that blocked the way, —scores of boys and men following them. They were not unfriendly, fortunately, but the foreigners hurried on, looking neither to the right nor to the left.

When they reached the temple the curious Chinese dropped behind and did not trouble them any more. A great fair was going on in the temple court where books, crockery and birds in cages were offered for sale. Grown men were amusing themselves spinning tops, for in China even gray-haired grandfathers spin tops and fly kites when the season rolls around, for they have their seasons for such things, just as boys in our country have.

Chinese top-spinning was unlike anything that Mary and Ellen had ever seen; the tops are quite large and make a loud, humming noise, which the Chinese like to hear. The top is thrown on the ground with a quick toss from a cord that had two wooden handles like a skipping rope. While it is whirling so fast that it can hardly be seen, the cord is drawn very tight and on this the top is caught again and tossed high in the air still spinning and humming. Then it is caught on the cord once more, tossed and caught, and never once allowed to fall. The crowd that stood looking on shouted and exclaimed when some pleasing mark of skill was shown, and the spinners themselves were very proud of what they had done. While they were busy with the sport, two of the lookers-on began to dispute, becoming quite excited and angry. The two girls were a little anxious, for they did not know what might happen.

" Do not be frightened," said Mr. Scott. "A Chinese quarrel is all threats

过虐待，所以如今他们对任何事物都缺少同情心。”

当他们经过一所房子时，听到一个孩子在抽噎哭泣。他正在被母亲责打，棍子的击打声清晰可闻。斯宾塞夫人想进屋去阻止因生气而大喊大叫的母亲。

斯科特先生说：“不，你绝对不能干涉有关中国孩子的事。他们怀疑外国人会诱骗、偷走孩子，然后把孩子弄死。虽然中国人自己有时也会将女婴遗弃街头，任其自生自灭，一旦他们知道外国人用任何方式伤害孩子，他们就容易被鼓动起来烧杀洋人。”

一行人快步前行，但斯宾塞夫人无法忘记那个可怜孩童的哭声，如果她能够救他的话肯定愿意去做的。他们打算去参观位于市中心的一座大寺庙，但发现要穿过拥堵道路的人群相当困难——很多男孩和男人跟在他们身后。所幸那些人并无恶意，身为外国人的他们只顾匆匆前行，无心环顾左右。

当他们到达寺庙时，身后那群好奇的中国人落在了后面，不再烦扰他们。寺院中正在举行一场盛大的集市，出售书籍、陶器和笼中的鸟。成年男人正玩转陀螺自娱自乐。在中国，随着四季更替，即使是头发花白的老爷爷也爱转陀螺、放风筝，就像我们国家的男孩那样，他们也有自己的季节性活动。

中国的转陀螺与玛丽和埃伦所曾见过的都不同，陀螺相当大，发出中国人爱听的响亮的嗡嗡声。用一根像跳绳一样带有两个木制手柄的绳索迅捷抽打陀螺，把其抛掷在地上。当它飞速旋转以至于几乎看不见时，拉紧绳索，再次接住陀螺并将其高高抛向空中，继续旋转、鸣响。然后，再次用绳接住，反复抛接，永远不会掉落。当展露一些令人悦服的技巧时，旁观的人群高声喝彩，陀螺玩家也为自己的技巧感到非常自豪。大家正玩得兴起时，两个旁观者开始争吵，显得非常激动和恼火。两个女孩有点不安，因为她们不知道会发生什么。

斯科特先生说：“不用害怕，中国人吵架净是威胁和叫嚷。男人不经常

and noise. The men do not often come to blows." And, true enough, as the angry men slowly approached each other, screaming and waving their arms, two other men ran after them, seized the fighters by the waist and held on, as if this were necessary to keep them from tearing each other to pieces. The men who were thus held shouted and struggled for a few minutes, and then each allowed himself to be led away by his friend. There had been a great deal of screaming and threatening, but they had not come to blows and did not really mean to hurt each other. " There!" said Mr. Scott, "that is the way the Chinese fight!"

" And a very good way, I think," said Mrs. Spencer, "if they must lose their tempers. They have had some hard words, but no one is much the worse for it."

The platters and bowls, teapots and cups offered for sale were so pretty and cheap that Mary and Ellen could not keep from buying a few. They could not bargain for themselves, but they chose what they wanted and Ah Lum, who had come with them, offered what the articles were worth and paid for them. The money in use is called "cash," ten of which make but a cent. The cash are round pieces of copper, with a square hole in the center, and they are strung on heavy cords. It is a hard matter, sometimes, to carry enough cash for a long journey, a thousand of the pieces of copper being worth only one dollar in our money. It is a common thing to take the strings of cash in a cart by themselves, or with the other supplies. We think this a very strange custom, but the copper cash are worth so little that ten cents in Chinese money would fill a large pocketbook, and it is too heavy to carry in a purse.

They looked over the collection of porcelain, which was spread out on the ground, and Mary chose a large platter on which had been painted a big, dull-blue fish caught in a yellow net; on the edge of the platter were some round blue figures meant to represent waves. She also bought a bowl with a very fierce green dragon on it, one paw raised and his mouth open, showing his wicked forked tongue. Ellen selected for herself a cup covered with red lobsters, and a pretty teapot with vines and flowers in pink and blue.

In the temple they found a great many artists painting paper scrolls, such as the girls had seen in the Japanese shops. The artists worked at wide wooden tables and painted with fine, pointed, camel's hair brushes, making every stroke very clear and clean, without blotting or having to rub it out. Mary thought that many of the pictures were, as she said, " very mixed up." The figures were not well proportioned and they seemed to be walking in the air as well as on the ground, and those that should have been painted quite small, because they

打架。”所言不虚，当那两个愤怒的男人彼此慢慢靠近，叫嚣并挥舞着胳膊时，另外两个男人紧跟其后，上前拦腰抱住他们，好像这样才能阻止他们把彼此撕成碎片。那两个被抱住的男人又挣扎着叫骂了几分钟，然后被各自的朋友劝走了。吵架双方互相谩骂、恫吓，但不动真格，也不想真的伤害对方。斯科特先生说：“你瞧！那就是中国人的打架方式！”

斯宾塞夫人说：“我觉得如果他们一定要发怒的话，这是个不错的方法。他们说的话有些很尖锐难听，但也就说说而已。”

在集市出售的大浅盘、碗、茶壶和杯子精美又便宜，玛丽和埃伦忍不住买了一些。她们自己不会讨价还价，但挑选了想要的东西，陪着一起来的阿林告诉她们物品的价格并代为付钱。所使用的钱被称为“铜钱”，10个才值1美分。铜钱是圆形的铜片，中间有一个方形的孔，用粗绳串在一起。有时，携带足够的铜钱进行长途旅行是一件困难的事情，一千个铜钱仅相当于我们的一美元。常见人们把一串串铜钱放在手推车上自己推着，或与其他生活必需品放一起携带。我们认为这是一个非常奇怪的习俗，铜钱的价值如此之低，以至于价值10美分的中国货币可以塞满一个大钱袋，而且太重了，不能放在钱包里。

她们细看铺放在地上的瓷器，玛丽挑选了一只大浅盘，上面绘着一条暗蓝色的大鱼，被兜于黄色的渔网之中，盘子边缘饰有一些代表波浪的圆形蓝色花纹。她还买了一只瓷碗，上面绘有一条凶猛的绿龙，张牙舞爪，吐着可怖的叉形舌。埃伦为自己选了一只绘着红色大龙虾的杯子和一把饰有粉色和蓝色藤蔓花卉图案的精美茶壶。

在寺庙里，她们发现许多画家在长卷纸上作画，就像她们曾经在日本商店里看到的那样。画家们在宽大的木桌上用精致的尖头骆驼毛笔作画，每一笔都非常清晰、利落，没有溅墨，也不必涂擦。正如她所说，玛丽认为许多画“非常混乱”。人物比例不均衡，他们看似同时在空中和地面上行走，而那些本来应该画得很小的在远景处的人物却和在前景处的人物一

were meant to be far off, were as large as those that were in the fore-ground, for Chinese artists do not understand the principles of perspective. The favorite colors were deep blue, pink, green, black and vermillion, and there was no shading.

The girls did not wish to buy any of the scrolls, but Mr. Scott who was a good judge of Chinese pictures gave Mrs. Spencer one which he said was a very fine piece of Chinese painting. It represented a Chinese lady of high rank in a gay dress with wide, flowing sleeves; her hair beautifully dressed with flowers and jewels, her eyes very narrow and slanting, with brows shaped like willow leaves, which the Chinese consider a mark of great beauty. The finger nails were very long, to show that the lady had never worked. In one hand she held an arrow at which she was looking closely, and on her feet she wore small boots such as Chinese soldiers wore many years ago. " I think it is meant to be a portrait of Malan, a young girl who lived more than a thousand years ago," said Mr. Scott, "but whose story is known everywhere in China and has been made into a poem. Her father was a great general and was wounded in battle so that he could not march at the head of his troops. He had no sons to take his place, and when the brave daughter learned what had happened, she put on a suit of mail, mounted a horse and led the army to battle, and drove the enemy, who had come to burn the cities and kill the people, back to their own country. Her father had been taken to his home when he could no longer fight, and no one knew who the young general was that had taken his place."

"The Prince sent for Malan to come to the palace that he might reward her. He did not dream that the brave soldier was only a young girl. When she went into his presence and knelt before the throne, he wished to reward her with gifts and honors. She refused them all, and said that she prayed only to return to her aged father, who knew not where she had gone."

"As the Prince desired to please her, he let her go. Those who went with her still thought that she was some brave young soldier that the gods had sent to help them, but at her father's door she uncovered her face, and they saw at once that it was Malan."

The Spencers were quite tired with the morning's sightseeing, and spent the afternoon quietly on the house boat, resting and reading.

In the evening they took their place in a line of six other boats, and a steam launch towed them down the Canal into the Wusung, and so back to Shanghai. Mary and Ellen had never made so interesting a journey, and for a long time they talked of the odd sights they had seen.

样大，因为中国画家不懂透视原理。他们最喜欢的颜色是深蓝色、粉色、绿色、黑色和朱红色，没有明暗处理。

两位女孩不想买任何一幅卷轴画，但对中国画很有鉴赏力的斯科特先生给了斯宾塞夫人一幅。他说这是一幅非常精美的中国画，它描绘了一位穿着飘逸宽袖的艳丽裙衫的中国贵妇；她的头发用鲜花和珠宝缀饰得很漂亮，眼睛细长上弯，眉毛形似柳叶，中国人以此为美。指甲很长，表明这位高贵女子从未劳作过。她一只手拿着支箭端详，脚上穿着许多年前中国士兵穿的那种小靴子。斯科特先生说：“我认为这是一幅木兰的画像，一个生活在一千多年前的年轻女孩，但她的故事在中国各地广为人知，并被写成了一首诗。她的父亲是一位大将军，在战斗中受了伤，因此他无法在军队的前头带队行进。他没有儿子代替他的位置，当他勇敢的女儿知道发生了什么事后，她穿上铠甲，骑上战马，带领军队驰骋沙场，把前来烧毁城池、杀戮百姓的敌人逐回了老家。她的父亲无法再战时被送回故土，没人知道接替他的年轻将军是谁。”

“皇帝召木兰进宫行赏。他做梦也没想到这位勇敢的战士竟然是一个年轻女子。当她走到他面前，在御座前下跪时，他想赏赐她礼物和荣誉。她都谢绝了，说她只祈望能回到年迈的父亲身边，他还不知道她去了哪里呢。”

“因为皇帝很想让她开心，就准许其回家了。那些随行的人仍然以为她是上天派来帮助他们的勇敢的年轻士兵。但当她回到父亲家门口露出真容时，他们立马认出这是木兰。”

斯宾塞一家上午观光后深感疲惫，下午静静地在住家船上休憩、阅读。

傍晚时分，他们与另六艘船串成一列船队，由一艘蒸汽船牵引着沿运河南下进入吴淞江返回上海。玛丽和埃伦从未有过如此有趣的旅行，滔滔不绝地谈论着所见的奇异景象。

Die Baukunst und religiöse Kultur der Chinesen

中国建筑艺术与宗教文化

（恩斯特·伯施曼著　吴悦茜译）

《中国建筑艺术与宗教文化》（*Die Baukunst und religiöse Kultur der Chinesen*）由德国建筑学家恩斯特·伯施曼（Ernst Boerschmann）所著。伯施曼于 1906—1909 年，跨越了中国 14 个省份，对中国的寺庙、祠堂、宝塔等建筑进行了全方位的考察，留下了 8 000 多张照片、2 500 多张草图、2 000 多张拓片和 1 000 多页测绘记录，被称为“全面考察和记录中国古建筑的第一人”。

《中国建筑艺术与宗教文化》正是伯施曼关于中国古代建筑和文化研究的代表作。该系列共分三卷，选译部分为该系列的第三卷《中国建筑艺术与宗教文化之宝塔》（1931 年出版）中关于苏州宝塔的介绍。该部分对虎丘山上的云岩寺塔、灵岩寺宝塔、上方山宝塔、瑞光寺塔、双塔的形制、发展和保存状况以及背后的历史文化等都做了详尽的介绍。

Die Pagoden von Sutschoufu, Prov. Kiangsu

Sutschou, die Hauptstadt der Provinz Kiangsu, mit Hangtschou, der Hauptstadt von Tschekiang, von den Chinesen als Himmel auf Erden gerühmt, ragt unter den großen Städten Chinas hervor nicht nur durch vielfältigen, geschichtlichen und literarischen Glanz, es dürfte auch, noch in seiner heutigen Planung, die älteste chinesische Stadt sein. Als die alte Hauptstadt des Königreiches Wu soll sie bereits 525 v. Chr. gegründet sein von Wu Yün（伍员）oder Wu Tzesü（伍子胥）, dem berühmten Minister des Fürsten Ho Lu（阖闾）oder Kuang（光）, der 514-495 regierte. Nur vorübergehend verlegt, steht sie noch heute auf dem alten Platz, und zwar höchst wahrscheinlich noch in der Gestalt ihrer ersten Anlage. Es wird berichtet, daß diese bereits damals symbolisch gedacht war. Sie sollte Himmel und Erde wiederspiegeln, erhielt deshalb 8 Wassertore und 8 Straßentore, die in der Art der 8 Diagramme·pa kua（八卦）angeordnet waren, die viereckige Stadtumwallung sollte ausdrücklich ein Abbild der Erde sein. Die Stadt hat durch ihre Lage ein außerordentliches, landschaftliches Gepräge erhalten. In der weiten Ebene, die sie allseitig umgibt, und die mit einem dichten Netz zahlloser Wasserstraßen überzogen ist, breiten sich im Südosten ausgedehnte Seen aus, im Süden und Südwesten nähert sich der große See Tái hu（太湖）. Zwischen diesem und der Stadt erheben sich im Westen, im weiten Bogen um die Stadt, unmittelbar aus der Ebene größere Bergketten und vereinzelte kleinere Berge. Es ist kein Wunder, daß diese landschaftliche Eigenart die Chinesen dazu bewog, gerade mit jenen Bergen den Fengschui-Gedanken zu verbinden und, als der Pagodenbau aufkam, Buddhatürme auf den Bergen zu errichten und sie in die universistische Stimmung von Stadt und Gelände einzubeziehen. Mit zahlreichen alten geschichtlichen Erinnerungen und Denkmälern, mit Bergen, Tempeln und Höhlen, mit heiligen Teichen und Inschriften, Bäumen, Hainen und Felsen, entsandten die drei Pagoden von den Bergen herab ihre heilige Wirkung in die Stadt und traten in Wechselwirkung zu anderen religiösen und staatlichen Bauanlagen, vor allem zu den vier Pagoden innerhalb der Stadt selbst. Diese Türme bilden durch ihre Siebenzahl und durch ihre Stellung den Stolz und die Zier von Sutschou auch heute noch, wo sie, besonders im Táipíng-Aufstand hart mitgenommen, leider fast sämtlich stark beschädigt oder gar Ruinen sind. Überwiegend haben sie ein hohes Alter, ja es findet sich unter ihnen wohl die älteste bekannt gewordene Pagode von China. Mit einer Ausnahme, der wohl erhaltenen

江苏省苏州府的宝塔

在中国，江苏省会苏州[1]与浙江省会杭州并称为人间天堂。苏州城不仅凭借其丰富的历史、光辉灿烂的文学成就从众多大城市中脱颖而出，而且从如今呈现的城市规划来看，苏州还可能是中国最古老的城市。据说作为吴国的都城，苏州城早在公元前 525 年就由阖闾（名光）的名臣伍子胥（名员）建造而成。阖闾于公元前 514 年至公元前 495 年在位。虽然苏州城曾有过短暂的迁移，但它至今仍坐落于当时的城址之上，而且极有可能还保持着最初的城市格局。据记载，这座城市在建造之初就考量了天与地的象征关系，开设水陆城门各八座，以八卦行阵排布，四方城墙则明显是大地的映射。苏州地理位置优越，风景独特。城市周围环绕着广袤的平原，无数水道纵横交错，向东南方向延伸后，可见广阔的湖泊，南部和西南部毗邻太湖。在太湖和苏州之间，西部较大的山脉和零散的小山丘形成了一个弧形，半拥着苏城。难怪中国人会被如此独特的地形所吸引，将这些山与风水思想相关联。随着宝塔建造的兴起，他们开始在山上修建佛塔，并将它们纳入城郭和场域的万象气场中。山上的三座宝塔承载着无数的历史记忆，与碑刻、山脉、寺庙、洞穴、圣池、铭文、树木、丛林和岩石一起将其神圣的影响扩大到了城市之中，并与其他宗教建筑和公共建筑相得益彰，尤其是与城内的四座佛塔遥相呼应。这些佛塔为七层结构，风格独特，代表了苏州城的骄傲和荣耀。尽管它们在太平天国时期遭到破坏，几乎都已被严重损毁，甚至成为废墟，但它们大多有着悠久的历史，中国已知最

[1] 本书创作之时辛亥革命已爆发，辛亥革命后，江苏省宣布独立，将都督府设在了苏州府城。

Nordpagode, einer Galeriepagode, die im folgenden Kapitel besprochen wird, gehören jene 6 übrigen Pagoden zu der Gruppe der Stockwerkpagoden, die mithin schon in früher Zeit hier in Mittelchina als eigener Typ bestanden und sogar dem Bilde von Stadt und Landschaft seine künstlerische Note zu geben vermochten.

Die Pagode vom Huk í uschan (虎邱山) Tigerhügel-Berg im Yün yen tschán sze (云岩禅寺) Kloster der Wolkenklippe bei Sutschou

Der Tigerhügel, ein Berg von geringen Abmessungen, erhebt sich eine kleine Stunde nordwestlich von Sutschou, weithin sichtbar, unvermittelt aus der fachen Ebene. Ein Kanal und ein guter Fußweg führen zu ihm. Geschichtliche Erinnerungen verknüpfen sich in reicher Zahl mit dem Berg und mit allen seinen Teilen, den Felsen, Quellen, Teichen und Gräbern und mit den Baudenkmälern, sie führten auch zu der hervorragenden buddhistischen Heiligung durch Errichtung der großen Pagode. Dieser wiederum verdankt der Berg seine dauernde religiöse Bedeutung, auch als einer der vornehmsten Einflußpunkte für ein glückliches Fengschui der Stadt. Nur der Lingyenschan kommt ihm hierin einigermaßen gleich.

In der Geschichte wird der Tigerberg zuerst genannt als die Stelle, an der über dem Grab des ersten Fürsten von Wu, Ho Lu gest. 495 v.Chr., ein gewaltiger Erdhügel aufgeworfen wurde angeblich aus dem Aushub des Kanals, der jetzt zum Berge führt. Die Darstellung von Tschepe läßt es, wohl durch den unklaren chinesischen Text in der Chronik von Sutschou, auf die er sich bezieht, unentschieden, an welcher Stelle sich der Grabhügel befunden hat, wahrscheinlich lag er in unmittelbarer Nähe des Berges in der Ebene. Es ist natürlich keine Rede davon, daß der Tigerberg selber mit seinen Quellen, den großen Bauten, darunter dem Pagodenturm, eine künstliche Aufschüttung ist, vielmehr besteht er durchweg aus gewachsenem Fels. Der Name Tigerberg geht auf eine Sage zurück, nach der, einige Zeit nach der Bestattung des Ho Lu, sich ein Weißer Tiger einfand, der nun Grab, Berg, Stadt und das ganze Land Wu behütete. Ein deutliches Symbol für die wirksamen Kräfte dynastischer Erinnerungen, zumal der Berg die richtige Lage im Nordwesten der Stadt hatte, die dem Tiger vorbehalten ist. Mit jenem Ti-

古老的宝塔也位列其中。除了下一章要介绍的北寺塔属于保存完好的廊塔，其他的六座宝塔均属于层塔，这种宝塔类型早期就在中国中部地区自成一派，为城市的风貌与景观平添了艺术气息。

苏州虎丘山上的云岩寺塔

虎丘山位于苏州城西北方向，距离城区约一小时路程，它虽然是一座体积较小的山，但在宽阔的平原上仍显得十分醒目。有一条运河和一条步道皆可通往虎丘。虎丘山以及它周围的所有景观：岩石、泉水、池塘、墓地以及建筑古迹，都蕴含着丰富的历史印记。这些历史记忆又因宝塔的建造而完成了佛教圣化的过程。这要归功于虎丘山与宗教长久的历史渊源，同时它还是这座城市的风水宝地，在这方面也只有灵岩山能与虎丘相提并论了。

虎丘山在历史上是作为吴国第一位君主阖闾的坟墓所在地被首次提及的。据说它是在公元前 495 年，由开凿运河挖出的土堆积而成的一座巨大土山。根据切柏[1]的描述，由于苏州的地方志记载不清，他无法确定坟墓在山丘的什么位置，极有可能就位于虎丘山附近。当然，尽管虎丘山拥有许多的泉以及包括宝塔在内的大型工事，但它并非人造工程，更有可能完全生自基岩中。虎丘之名源于一则传说。相传在阖闾下葬不久后，出现了一只白虎，守护着阖闾的陵墓、这座山、这座城市以及整个吴国。这是王朝记忆中明确的权力的象征，因为虎丘山在苏州城中就位于白虎所代表的

[1] 切柏（Albert Tschepe, 1844—1912），德国天主教教士，汉学家。

ger geriet der gewalttätige und rücksichtslose Kaiser Tsín Schi Huang Ti 246-209 v. Chr, in einen Kampf, als er bei seinem Besuch des Südens das Grab des Ho Lu öffnen ließ, um dessen berühmte beiden Schwerter zu erlangen, Mit seinem eigenen Schwerte schlug er nach dem Tiger, der ihn bedrohte, traf ihn aber nicht. Dieser entwich, der Schlag ging in den Felsen und hinterließ bis heute seine Spur. Die genaue Symbolik liegt auf der Hand, die ganze Erzählung ist nur ein Gleichnis. Die Schwerter selber fand Schi Huang nicht. Sie werden zuweilen auch in einer Dreizahl erwähnt und blieben Sinnbilder für die Kraft des alten Reiches Wu. Die Sage hat um sie einen Kranz geschlungen. Die mündliche Überlieferung verbindet sie fälschlich mit dem Sohn und Nachfolger des Ho Lu, mit Fu Tschái, der 495-473 als der letzte König von Wu regierte.

Im Hu kíu-Kloster, in dem sich der vielbesungene Schwerterteich befindet, wurde sie mir in folgender Fassung mitgeteilt. Der Teich wurde durch Fu Tschái angelegt als Behälter für das Wasser, das der Waffenschmied bei der Anfertigung der beiden doppelspitzigen Schwerter zur Härtung verwendete. Das eine hieß Mo hie（莫邪） Ohne Falsch, das andere Yü tscháng（鱼肠） Fischherz · Fischblase. Der Guß mißlang wiederholt, bis der Schmied endlich seine beiden Söhne in die geschmolzene Masse warf und nach diesem Opfer ein vollendetes Werk schuf. Die Schwerter hatte der König stets bei sich, auch des Nachts, wenn er schlief. Bei Nahen der Gefahr begannen sie von selbst zu singen und warnten den König. Die Schwerter eignete sich dann der Fürst Kou Tsíen（勾践） von Yüe an, der dem Reiche Wu ein Ende machte und den König Fu Tschái zum Selbstmord zwang. Die Symbolik der ganzen Erzählung ist klar, durch sie wird die geschichtliche Bedeutung des Tigerberges begreiflich als Sitz der heiligen Kraft des berühmten alten Staates Wu, von dem die Stadt Sutschou ihren Glanz herleitet. Seine buddhistische Bedeutung erhielt der Berg frühzeitig. Im Beginn der Östlichen Tsín-Dynastie 317-419 befand sich auf dem Tigerhügel der Landsitz zweier prinzlicher Brüder Wang（ 王 ）, zusammen mit ihrem Ahnentempel und einem berühmten Musikpavillon. Jene wandelten 327 ihren Besitz um in ein Kloster für den Begründer Tao I（道一）, den ältesten Schüler des Buddhisten Tái. Tschu Fa Tái（竺法汰）.Es gibt dort oben einen Nickenden Felsen. Tien tóu schi（点头石）, der mit folgendem Ereignis in Verbindung steht. Zur gleichen Zeit der Klostergründung predigte Tschu Tao Scheng（竺道生） ein anderer Schüler des Fa Tái, über ein Sutra. Während der Predigt, die sehr tief war und in vollkommenem Einklang stand mit dem Sutra, nickte der Felsen beistimmend mit dem Haupte.

西北方位。残暴无度的秦始皇（公元前246—公元前209年）[1]南下时为了获取阖闾的两把名剑，命人打开阖闾的墓穴，其时与那只白虎发生了冲突，秦始皇用自己的宝剑砍向威胁他的猛虎，但未击中目标，一下砍到了旁边的岩石上，留下的印记至今仍能看到。其中的象征意义不言而喻，但这则传说只是一种比拟罢了。秦始皇并没有找到那两把宝剑，也有传说是三把，但不管数量如何，它们始终是吴王朝权力的象征。这个传说有很多版本。口头传说错误地将虎丘与公元前495—公元前473年吴国最后一位统治者夫差联系在了一起，他是阖闾的儿子和王位继承者。

虎丘中的剑池充满了神奇色彩，我所听闻的是以下版本：剑池乃夫差所建，为铁匠铸造其两把宝剑淬火时所用。那两把宝剑，一把叫莫邪，另一把叫鱼肠。[2]然而宝剑铸造一再失败，直到铁匠最终将他的两个儿子作为祭品投入熔化的金属中后，才铸成了完美的武器。吴王总是随身携带这两把宝剑，即使晚上睡觉也不离身。当危险临近时，宝剑会自行发出暗鸣来警示吴王。这把宝剑后来被越王勾践所得，他灭了吴国，逼迫夫差自刎。整个故事具有鲜明的象征意义，揭示了虎丘在历史上的重要地位，它是昔日吴国强大的象征，也展现了苏州城历史的荣耀。虎丘很早就被赋予了佛教的意义。东晋初年（317—419），晋司徒王氏兄弟的封地正位于虎丘，这里还有他们的家族祠堂和著名的戏台。327年，王氏兄弟将自己的封地改建成了一座寺院，并把它赠予了其建造者——东晋高僧竺法汰最年长的学生道一。寺旁有一块点头石，关于这块石头也有一段传说。寺庙建造的时候，法汰的另一名弟子竺道生在此讲经布道，经文非常深奥，且与佛经

[1] 此处原作者对秦始皇的生卒年份记载有误，应为公元前259—公元前210年。
[2] 此处原作者似把鱼肠剑的传说和干将、莫邪铸剑的传说混淆了。

Er liegt noch auf dem alten Fleck am Teich vor dem Kloster und trägt eine Inschrift zur Erinnerung an die Predigt des Scheng kung. Das erinnert an die fast gleiche Geschichte des Nickenden Felsen von Ling yen sze in Schantung und an den Mönch Lang kung, der nur wenig später, 351, dort predigte und ebenfalls die Zustimmung durch einen nickenden Felsen erhielt. In der Liang-Dynastie 502-556 wurde das alte Kloster auf dem Hukiuschan vergrößert, bald folgte die größte Heiligung des Berges durch die Pagode, die genau auf dem alten Platze des früheren Pavillons steht, am Endpunkt der heutigen Klosteranlage, auf dem höchsten Punkte des Berges.

Die große Pagode vom Tigerberg wurde zuerst errichtet durch den großen Sui-Kaiser Kao Tsu in der Periode Jen Schou 601-605. Sie gehört mithin zu jener wichtigen Gruppe von Pagoden, die Kao Tsu auf Grund einer großen Verteilung von Reliquien gleichzeitig in den verschiedensten Teilen Chinas errichten ließ, und auf die bereits mehrfach hingewiesen wurde. Sie ist also baugeschichtlich wie religionsgeschichtlich außerordentlich bedeutsam. Es ist zu wünschen, daß eine eingehende Darstellung dieses hervorragenden Baudenkmals erfolgte auf Grund genauer Aufnahmen und einer erschöpfenden Verwertung der besonderen Quellen.

Während der Erbauung und der Einweihung der Pagode ereigneten sich vielfache Wunder. Bei der Ausschachtung für die Fundamente fand man unter anderen Kostbarkeiten eine versilberte Buddhafigur, wahrscheinlich in einem Behälter aus gebranntem Ton, und man mauerte jene Figur mit anderen Beigaben in die Fundamente ein. Als die vom Kaiser übersandten Reliquien sich der Stelle der späteren Pagode näherten, rauschten die umfließenden Wasser zwei Tage lang in Ehrfurcht vor der Heiligkeit der Sariras und des Mönches, der sie im kaiserlichen Auftrage überbrachte. Bei der Einweihung entsprang eine neue Quelle im Berg, Buddha erschien als befruchtender Regen und als Donner. Die Sonne verfinsterte sich und strahlte dann wieder in doppeltem Glanze. Das Kloster sah damals seine erste Blütezeit.

Danach haben Kloster und Pagode sehr wechselvolle Schicksale erlebt in den häufigen politischen Umwälzungen, denen die Gegend von Sutschou stets in besonderem Maße ausgesetzt war. In den Wirren vor der Begründung der Sung-Dynastie, also bis 960, wurde die Anlage zerstört. Der erste Sung-Kaiser befahl ihre Wiederherstellung, aber erst unter Kaiser Jen Tsung 1023-1064 wurde sie mit großer Pracht ausgebaut und scheint ihre zweite Blütezeit erlebt zu

完全一致，在此过程中，岩石也点头表示同意。这块石头如今仍然位于寺前池边的旧址处，上面刻有纪念生公讲经的铭文。这让人想起与山东灵岩寺点头石几乎相同的故事，想起那位名叫朗公的僧侣，他在公元351年——比虎丘点头石故事晚些时候，到那里讲经，也同样得到了点头石的认可。梁朝时期（502—556），虎丘山上的古寺扩建，之后宝塔的建造更是让虎丘变得更加神圣，宝塔就坐落在原来戏台的位置上，在今天寺庙的最后面，位于虎丘山的最高点。

虎丘山上的大佛塔始建于隋高祖仁寿601—605年，属于高祖建造的重要佛塔之一，这些佛塔是高祖为了在各地分散存放的舍利而同时建造的，我们之前已多次提到。因此，虎丘塔在建筑史和宗教史上都具有非常重要的意义。本篇旨在通过精确的记录和对史料充分的研究，对这座杰出的建筑做深入的介绍。

在宝塔建造和落成期间发生了许多神奇的事情。在挖掘地基的时候，人们从一堆宝物中发现了一座镀银佛像，佛像可能是从一个烧制陶器的容器中被发现的，人们把这尊佛像与其他宝物一起嵌入了宝塔的基座中。当高祖派人送来的舍利子接近后来佛塔所在的位置时，周围的水流发出了整整两天的轰鸣声，以表达对神圣的舍利子和奉命护送舍利的僧人的敬畏之情。在落成典礼上，山中涌出了一股新泉，暴雨如注，雷声隆隆，佛祖现身。太阳暗淡片刻后又重新绽放出了双倍的光芒。寺庙迎来了它的第一个繁荣时期。

此后，苏州地区频繁发生政治动荡时，寺院和佛塔的命运也经历了诸多波折。在公元960年宋朝建立前的动荡时期，虎丘塔遭到了损坏。宋太祖下令重建虎丘寺，但直到仁宗时期（1023—1064）[1]，寺庙才得到了大规模的扩建，并似乎迎来了它的第二个繁荣时期。据《中国佛教史迹》记

［1］ 仁宗时期应为1023—1063。

haben. Die Buddh, Monum. geben im Anschluß an diese Zeit für die Erbauung der Pagode die Jahre 1077-1136 an. Noch kurz vor dem Sturze der Yüen-Dynastie wandte der letzte Mongolen-Kaiser Schun Ti 1333-1368 seine Fürsorge dem Tigerberg zu. Die Kaiser der folgenden Ming Dynastie sorgten mit Eifer für die Ausgestaltung der Anlagen. Ihnen muß das Kloster mit seiner Pagode sehr am Herzen gelegen haben. Schon der erste Ming-Kaiser hatte in den Kämpfen vor der Begründung der Dynastie fast ein Jahr lang vom Tigerberg aus die Belagerung und Einnahme von Sutschou geleitet. Nach einem großen Brande 1380 begann Kaiser Tschéng Tsu · Yung Lo · die Erneuerung, die aber durch einen zweiten Brand 1430 unterbrochen wurde. Nun wurden alle Kräfte für die Wiederherstellung angespannt. Aus Beiträgen der ganzen Bevölkerung und des Kaisers Ying Tsung selber während seiner ersten Regierungszeit 1436-1450 erfolgte mit größten Mitteln der Neubau, der sich auch auf den Turm bezogen haben soll. Der Bau dauerte vom Frühling 1437 bis zum Herbst 1438. Bei der Einweihung ereigneten sich wieder zahlreiche Wunder. Als der schöne neue Turm eingeweiht wurde, umflog ein großer Schwarm von Kranichen die Turmspitze: der Himmel selber segnete die Pagode ein. Fortan hielt man Kraniche im Kloster und pflegte sie. Damals sah die Anlage ihre dritte Blüte. Im Laufe der folgenden Jahrhunderte wechselten noch öfter kleinere Brände mit Wiederherstellungen ab. Kaiser besuchten wiederholt Berg und Pagode, so in der Ming-Dynastie Ying Tsung und Schen Tsung · Wan Li, in der Tsíng-Dynastie die Kaiser Káng Hi und Kíen Lung. Sie stifteten Inschriften, die sie zuweilen selber schrieben, und schenkten dem Kloster zahlreiche buddhistische Schriften mit genauen Anweisungen für Aufbewahrung und Gebrauch der Bücher, unter Festsetzung von Strafen bei Mißbrauch. 1860 kam das Verhängnis. Die Táipíng-Rebellen zerstörten das Kloster gänzlich und ließen nur den Turm stehen. Erst in den letzten Jahrzehnten wurden wieder einige Gebäude neu errichtet.

Die Pagode in der heutigen Gestalt macht trotz ihrer schweren Beschädigungen noch einen mächtigen Eindruck, ist aber zugleich in den Einzelheiten reich gestaltet. Sie steht stark aus dem Lot. Das achtseitige Mauermassiv verjüngt sich stark nach oben. Zwischen dem inneren Kern und der äußeren Mantelmauer führen Treppenstufen in Windungen in die Höhe. Der Umriß ähnelt einem Stufenbau, die klare Teilung in gleiche Stockwerke reiht aber den Turm unter die Pagoden mit regelmäßigen Geschossen ein. Die Geschosse mit je acht Öffnungen sind voneinander durch Doppelgesimse getrennt, die auf lebhaft gegliederten

载，紧接着的一次佛塔修缮时间为 1077—1136 年。元朝覆灭前不久，最后一位皇帝元顺帝（1333—1368）还关注着虎丘山。之后的明朝皇帝们更是热衷于修缮这座佛塔，可见这座寺庙和佛塔对他们来说都很重要。明太祖早在建朝前的战争中就曾据守虎丘长达一年之久，组织了对苏州城的围攻和占领。在 1380 年的一场大火后，明成祖在永乐年间命人开始重建虎丘寺，但 1430 年的第二场大火使重建工作被迫中断。之后所有力量都被动员起来进行重建，在 1436—1450 年，在全体民众和当时的统治者英宗的共同努力下，筹集了大量的资金，开始了新一轮寺庙的重建，据说也包括佛塔的修缮。建造工程从 1437 年春一直持续到 1438 年秋。在落成典礼上又发生了许多奇观。当美丽的新塔落成时，一大群仙鹤在塔顶盘旋，仿佛上天也在为宝塔祈福。从此之后，人们就把仙鹤饲养在寺院内，并对它们悉心照料，这座宝塔此时迎来了它的第三个繁荣时期。在随后的几个世纪中，寺庙又经历了多次小火灾和修缮。历朝历代的皇帝多次前来参观虎丘山和佛塔，如明朝的英宗和神宗，清朝的康熙和乾隆皇帝。他们留下了碑刻铭文，有些还是亲笔题词，此外还向寺院捐赠了大量的佛教经书，并对书籍的保管、使用和对滥用的处罚做了详细规定。1860 年，浩劫来临，太平军彻底摧毁了寺庙，只留下了佛塔。直到最近几十年，一些建筑才得以重建。

尽管屡遭损坏，但宝塔现今的形态仍然给人一种庄重宏伟的印象，此外宝塔的细节亦饱满丰富。该佛塔的倾斜度很大，八角形的塔身向上逐渐收缩，内部与外墙之间的台阶蛇形蜿蜒而上，其外形轮廓类似于级塔造型，但因为该塔的层高相同，还是将它归入层塔的范畴。每层塔身均有八个拱券，由重檐相互隔开，塔檐下方有精致的斗拱支撑。下方的塔檐上覆有瓦片，上部的塔檐位于每扇拱券窗的下方，环绕着塔身，形似宽阔的窗台，但并

Konsolen ruhen, Die unteren Gesimse waren mit Dachabdeckungen versehen, die oberen ziehen sich als breite Solbänke unter den Öffnungen ringsum, doch ohne einen Umgang zu ermöglichen. Eine derartige Anordnung von Doppelgesimsen bildet die Regel für alle Stockwerkpagoden von Sutschou und für viele anderen am Yangtze und in Tschekiang. Die Kanten des Mauerkörpers sind mit Rundstäben als Diensten eingefaßt. Vielleicht mag die Grundform des Turmes noch auf den ersten Bau der Sui-Dynastie zurückgehen, Aufbau und Einzelheiten dürften aber aus dem Neubau um 1100, also aus der Blüte der Sung-Dynastie stammen und aus der späteren Erneuerung von 1438. Der Ziegelverband ist meist deutlich sichtbar, doch sind in den Geschossen einige Felder und Gesimsteile mit weißem Putz überzogen. Die Bogenlinien der Öffnungen sind in Kleeblattformen aufgelöst. Die betonte Aufteilung durch kräftige und isolierte Gesimskonsolen verleiht dem Turm einen lebhaften Rhythmus und entspricht dem kräftigen Aufbau der Mauermassen.

Etwa unterhalb der Pagode steht neben dem Teich mit dem Nickenden Stein ein kleiner Pavillon aus Stein, vor ihm ein 8seitiger, gegliederter Sutrapfeiler aus 958, in der Nähe ein weiterer Sutrapfeiler in Form einer kleinen quadratischen Pagode. Inschriften und Zeichnungen in Stein und Felsen betonen weiter stark die Heiligung der altehrwürdigen Stätte.

Die Pagode vom Ling yen sze（灵岩寺）Kloster des heiligwirkenden Felsen bei Sutschou

Etwas drei Stunden genau westlich von Sutschou streicht in nordsüdlicher Richtung eine stark gegliederte, etwa 180m hohe Bergkette, die in ihren einzelnen Teilen verschieden benannt, durchweg aber mit Bauanlagen, Klöstern, Gräbern, mit merkwürdigen, religiös gedeuteten Naturformen versehen und mit geschichtlichen Erinnerungen vermählt ist. Der große östliche Ausläufer der Kette heißt Tianpíngschan（天平山）Berg der Himmlischen Ruhe und trägt ein Kloster der Weißen Wolken · Po yün sze（白云寺）aus dem Jahre 826, neben diesem bezeichnet eine Inschrift Po Yün tá（白云塔）einen pagodenartig gegliederten Sutrapfeiler. Eine kleine Stunde südwestlich von jenem Rücken bildet der Lingyenschan den berühmtesten und vornehmsten, südlichen Ausläufer der

没有可供通行的外廊。苏州所有的层塔都有这样的重檐结构，包括其他长江流域和浙江地区的许多宝塔。宝塔墙体的侧棱以圆柱为配进行装饰，从该塔的基本轮廓或许还能看到隋朝初建时的影子，但其结构和具体细节可能源于公元 1100 年前后宝塔的重建时期，也就是在宋朝的鼎盛时期，以及源于之后 1438 年的重修。塔身的砖砌图案大部分清晰可见，但各层的一些区格和塔檐部分覆盖上了一层白色的灰浆。拱券上方的拱线呈三叶草形状。斗拱之间间隔明显，增强了宝塔外形轮廓的律动感，也与高大的塔身结构相呼应。

大约在宝塔的正下方，靠近点头石所在的白莲池旁边，有一座小石亭，亭前有一座建于 958 年的有八面分段的经柱，旁边还有一座小型四方形宝塔式样的经柱。石亭的山石上镌刻的铭文和图案，更彰显出这座古老寺塔的神圣气息。

苏州灵岩寺宝塔

苏州城以西约 3 小时路程处，有一片高约 180 米，南北走向，连绵起伏的山脉，群山虽名称各异，但均配以建筑、寺院、陵墓，以及充满鲜明宗教色彩的景观，承载着历史的记忆。该山脉东部的一条大支脉叫天平山，山上有一座修建于公元 826 年的白云寺，旁边有一座宝塔状经幢，名为白云塔。从天平山向西南方向走大约一个小时，就到了该山脉最著名、最重要的南部支脉灵岩山。其名灵岩让人联想到山东长清县著名的同名寺院，该寺内有一座叠层塔。为了与它区分开来，我把苏州城郊的这座山称为吴

Bergkette. Sein Name Ling yen erinnert an das berühmte Kloster mit seiner Ringpagode im Kreise Tschángtsínghien in Schantung, das den gleichen Namen trägt. Zur Unterscheidung von diesem Berg wird der Berg bei Sutschou genannt Wu（吴）Lingyenschan, nach dem alten Reiche Wu, dessen Name auch heute noch für jene ganze Landschaft südlich vom unteren Yangtze gebräuchlich ist. Auf dem Berge standen die Sommerpaläste der alten Könige von Wu, Ho Lu und Fu Tsháі. Nach den Buddh. Monum. heißt das zugehörige Kloster auch Tshúng pao tschán sze（崇报禅寺）Kloster der Erhabenen Vergeltung. Den Gipfel krönt eine Pagode, ausdrücklich bezeichnet als Tschuan tá·Ziegelpagode, heute leider eine Ruine. Nach dem chinesischen Text, der von einem Gelehrten mit Namen Sun aus der Sungzeit stammt, wurde die Pagode unter der Sung-Dynastie erbaut in der Periode Tái Píng Hing Kuo 976-983, und zwar genau 978, als 9stöckiger Turm innerhalb von 76 Tagen. Sun Tschén Yin errichtete damals den Turm zum Gedächtnis an seine Schwestern, die Königinnen von Wu und Yüe. Nach 100 Jahren, in der Periode 1078-1085, wurde das Kloster umgewandelt in ein Tschán（禅）Kloster mit dem Namen Hiu feng sze（秀峰寺）Schöner Gipfel. Infolge Blitzschlages 1600 brannten alle Holzteile ab. Heute hat der Turm nur noch 8 regelmäßige Geschosse mit allseitigen Öffnungen und ist mit einer Kegelspitze abgedeckt, die vielleicht die Stelle des früheren, jetzt zerstörten obersten Geschosses einnimmt. Die oberen 6 Geschosse setzen in deutlichen, gleichmäßigen Abtreppungen gegeneiander ab. Innerer Kern der Pagode und die Treppe sind verschwunden, der Innenraum ist jetzt ein völlig hohler Zylinder.

Die Pagode von Schangfangschan bei Sutschou（苏州附近的上方山宝塔）

Etwa 1 1/2 Stunden südwestlich von Sutschou, bereits eingeschlossen von zwei Armen des großen Sees Tái hu, erhebt sich der Tsítzeschan（七子山）Berg der 7 Söhne, nämlich der 7 sehr bewegten Ausläufer eines Hauptbergstockes. Den nordöstlichen Gipfel, mit dem Namen Schangfangschan, krönt inmitten von Überresten eines gänzlich zerstörten Klosters die schöne Pagode, die zusammen mit den beiden anderen Türmen vom Tigerberg und vom Lingyenschan das große Fengschui der Stadt vornehmlich bestimmt. Der Ausblick auf die weite Ebene, das Netz der Kanäle und Buchten, den See, ferne Bergketten und Stadt ist

灵岩山,“吴”出自古老的吴国，今天整个长江下游以南地区仍然通称为“吴地”。吴王阖闾和夫差的避暑行宫也位于灵岩山上。据《中国佛教史迹》记载，山上这座寺院又被称为“崇报禅寺”。山顶的宝塔如为其加冠，人们称之为砖塔，可惜如今已成废墟。根据一位姓孙的宋代学者的文字记载，该塔建于宋太平兴国时期（976—983），准确时间为978年，耗时76天，塔高九层，乃当时孙承祐[1]为纪念他的姐姐吴越王妃所建。100年后，在1078—1085年，该寺院改建成了名为秀峰寺的禅宗寺院。1600年，寺内所有木制部件均遭雷击烧毁。今天这座塔塔身只有八层，每层高度相同，塔身每面均开有券门，塔顶呈圆锥形，这可能替代了原来被毁的顶层。上方的六层塔身均匀地间隔开，呈阶梯状叠加。宝塔的内里和阶梯都已经不复存在了，现在内部完全是一个空心的圆柱体。

苏州附近的上方山宝塔

七子山距苏州城西南方向约一个半小时路程，被太湖的两条支流所环绕，此山因有七座非常陡峭的山峰而得名，其中东北方向的一座山峰名叫上方山，山上原有的寺庙已完全被损，但在废墟之中有一座美丽的宝塔，这座塔与虎丘塔和灵岩寺塔一起构建了这座城市的风水格局。登塔远眺，远处的平原、纵横交错的运河和湖湾、太湖、远山和苏州城的美景尽收眼底，

[1] 孙承祐（936—985），杭州钱塘人，吴越王钱俶的外戚，官至泰宁军节度使、大名府知府。

herrlich, wie von allen Höhen um Sutschou, und wird nur übertroffen durch die Aussicht vom Tigerberg, der einen vollkommenen Rundblick gestattet.

Die Pagode ist ursprünglich errichtet fast gleichzeitig mit der Pagode vom Tigerberg, nämlich in der Sui-Dynastie unter Kaiser Yang Ti 605-617, dem Nachfolger von Kao Tsu, und zwar im Jahre 608. Es ist aber kaum anzunehmen, daß sie schon damals die heutige schlanke, fast zierliche Gestalt besessen oder gar noch zu der berühmten Gruppe der Pagoden des Kao Tsu aus der Periode Jen Schou 601-605 gehört hat, die fast durchweg große und besonders wuchtige Formen aufweisen. Genauere Daten liegen nicht vor. Nach dem Aufbau kann man den heutigen Turm der Sung-Dynastie zuschreiben, muß aber noch spätere, selbst neueste Erneuerungen und Änderungen annehmen.

Die nur wenig verjüngte Pagode besteht aus einem Sockelgeschoß und 6 oberen, insgesamt also 7 Geschossen, deren 5 obere durch Doppelgesimse voneinander abgetrennt sind. Die unteren Teile dieser Doppelgesimse sind reich gegliedert durch Konsolen, die sich auf den Ecken und den Mitten der Seiten aus dem flachen Relief frei entwickeln. Die Dachabdeckungen schwingen sich in großen Bogen wie Guirlanden um den Turm. Das obere, feinere Gurtgesims läuft gerade herum und ermöglicht den Austritt aus den wechselständigen Öffnungen. Jede Fläche ist durch Lisenen in Felder geteilt. Der regelmäßig und spröde aufgeteilte Turm erfährt durch die Verdoppelung der Gesimse die gleiche Belebung wie die anderen Pagoden um Sutschou. Als Spitze krönt den Turm über einem knappen Zeltdach eine hohe Gipfelstange, die mit Ringen, durchbrochenem Schirm und Juwel geschmückt ist. Diese Pagode vom Schangfangschan scheint eine unmittelbare Nachahmung gefunden zu haben in der Pagode von Nakihien in der Provinz Szetschúan. Sie ist im siebenten Abschnitt skizziert und zeigt bei hohem Erdgeschoß und 5 oberen Geschossen fast den gleichen Aufbau und Umriß, nur die Schwingung der Dachkränze fehlt.

Die Pagode vom Jui kuang sze（瑞光寺）Kloster des glückverheißenden Glanzes in Sutschou

In der Südwestecke der Stadt, unweit des Tores Pán men, steht eine etwa 50 m hohe, achtseitige Pagode mit 7 Geschossen. Sie gilt in ihrer ersten Anlage

蔚为壮观，这样的视野仅次于能够眺望苏州全景的虎丘。

上方塔的初建时间与虎丘塔相近，在隋炀帝四年，即公元608年。然而很难想象，当时的塔身已具备了如今般纤细精巧的造型，更难以想象的是，此塔还是隋文帝仁寿时期（601—605）[1]所建的著名佛塔之一，而那一时期的佛塔多呈高大壮观的外形。对比，没有更详细的资料可以解释上述问题。根据其结构推断，现今的宝塔应该建于宋朝，但不排除那是因后期甚至是近期修缮改建使然。

宝塔向上收缩不明显，由一层基座和六层塔身构成，共七层，其中上面的五层塔身被重檐分隔。这些重檐的下部由精美繁复的斗拱分隔，这些斗拱在各拐角和每侧中部自平面浮雕中延伸出来。塔顶结构呈上扬的大弧形，像花环一样围绕着塔身。上部较为精美的飞檐恣意伸展，得以从错落的拱券窗中探出。塔身外侧由线条分割成块状。结构工整而单薄的宝塔因重檐结构变得生动无比，与苏州其他的宝塔一样活力焕发。塔顶部分呈窄帐篷状，在上面竖了一根高高的刹杆，上面装饰着相轮、华盖和宝珠。四川省纳溪县的一座宝塔看上去就是仿照上方山的宝塔而建。四川的这座宝塔在第七章简单介绍过，高大的塔基和上面的五层塔身与上方山宝塔的结构轮廓基本相同，只是塔檐没有上翘。

瑞光寺

苏州城西南角距盘门不远处，矗立着一座高约50米的八角七层塔。初建时，它被视为苏州最古老的宝塔，同时也是中国最古老的宝塔之一。据

[1] 隋文帝仁寿时期应为601—604。

als älteste Pagode von Sutschou und zu den ältesten von China überhaupt. lhr erster Bau soll aus dem Jahre 241 stammen. Die Quellen geben tatsächlich dieses bestimmte Jahr, und es ist kein Zweifel, daß damals bereits eine Pagode an jener Stelle stand. Sie hatte indessen 13 Gliederungen statt der heutigen 7. Nach der Chronik stammt der heutige Turm aus der Zeit des Sung-Kaisers Hui Tsung, Periode Süen Ho 1119-1126, und wurde erbaut offenbar auf der Stelle der alten zerstörten Pagode. Der Text besagt: >Die Pagode steht südlich vom Kái yüen sze（开元寺）· Im 4. Jahre von Wu Tschí Wu（吴赤乌）238-251, also 241, erbaute der Kaiser Sun Küen（孙权）aus Dankbarkeit für seine Mutter eine Sarira-Pagode · Sche li tá mit 13 Gliederungen. Der Mönch Sing Káng（性康）· Sing aus Sogdiana · wohnte dort im Pú tsi tschán yüen（普济禅院）Dhyana-Kloster der allgemeinen Errettung. Im 2. Jahre der Periode Tíen Fu 902 Táng-Dynastie · setzten die Mönche Tschi Ming（智明）und Tsung Yüen（琮远）die Pagode instand. Sie strahlte ein vielfarbiges Licht aus. Der Kaiser ließ eine Messingtafel, die er gestiftet hatte, auf der Spitze der Pagode Sutschou anbringen. Im 2. Jahre der Periode Yüen Feng · 1079· ließ der Sung-Kaiser Schen Tsung dort feierliche Predigten halten. Wieder strahlte die Pagode ein vielfarbiges Licht aus. Damals hörte eine weiße Schildkröte der Predigt zu. Die Dharmatrommel tönte von selbst, der grüne Bambus umarmte sich selber vor Freude, die Pagode entsandte einen Glanz. Hiernach nannte man den Bau: Sze jui táng（四瑞堂）Halle der vierfachen Glücksverheißung. Im 4. Jahre der Periode Tschung Ning ·1105 · wurde die Pagode auf kaiserlichen Befehl erneuert, Sie strahlte ein fünffarbiges Licht aus und erhielt den Namen: Pagode der 10 000 Jahre himmlischen Friedens· Tien ning（天宁）. In der Periode Süen Ho 1119-1126 brachte man Kapital auf und erbaute ein siebengeschossige Pagode. Im 3. Jahre der Periode Tíen Kí · 1623 · schuf der Mönch Yüen Tsing（圆净）ein Haus der 7 Buddhas · Tsí fo ko（七佛阁）auf dem alten Fundament der Sze jui táng. Als eben die Pfeiler errichtet wurden, entsandte das Himmelsauge einen Glanz. Wang Kung（王珙）machte einen Aufsatz über das Haus des Himmelsauges. Später zeigte sich das Licht der Pagode häufig. Stets wenn des Nachts die Lampen der Sarira-Pagoden brannten, fingen die Fischer vom Tái hu, dem großen nahen See bei Sutschou, nichts in ihren Netzen. Der See war 30 li von der Pagode entfernt<. Der Widerglanz der erleuchteten Pagode im Wasser des Sees sollte, auch nach Erklärung der Chinesen, die Fische davon abhalten, in die Netze zu gehen. Dafür ist die Entfernung von mehr als 15 km allerdings zu groß. Trotzdem handelt es sich um den buddhistischen Gedanken, der eine unmittelbare Wirkung des beleuchteten Turmes auf

记载，此塔始建的时间可以追溯到公元 241 年，史料上明确记载了这一特定的年份，故当时在此地有一座宝塔是毫无争议的，但所记载的宝塔有 13 层，而不是现在的 7 层。根据苏州地方志记载，现在的宝塔建于宋徽宗宣和年间（1119—1126）[1]，显然是在被损毁的旧塔遗址上建造的。据文献记载，该塔位于开元寺的南部，吴赤乌四年，即公元 241 年，孙权为报母恩修建了一座 13 层的舍利塔，来自粟特的和尚性康就住在那里的普济禅院。唐天复二年（902），僧人智明和琮远修缮了这座宝塔，这座塔焕发出奇光异彩。皇帝命人在这座宝塔的顶部放置了一块他捐赠的黄铜牌匾。元丰二年（1079），宋神宗在此地举行了隆重的讲经活动，宝塔再次焕发出了多彩金光。其时，白龟听法，法鼓自鸣，青竹合欢，宝塔放光。由于出现了这四种祥瑞之兆，此地故被称为“四瑞堂”。崇宁四年（1105），工匠奉诏重修此塔，宝塔散发出了五彩光芒，得名“天宁塔”。宣和年间（1119—1126），人们募集资金建造了一座七层宝塔。天启三年（1623），圆净法师在四瑞堂旧址上建造了七佛阁。佛阁落成之时，天眼贺以金光。御史王珙曾题额“天眼阁”。后来，宝塔上的佛光频频出现。每当舍利塔上的夜灯点亮时，苏州城外太湖的渔民就徒劳无功了。太湖距离宝塔有 30 里远，根据当地人的解释，点灯之塔反光于湖上，故而鱼儿不再入网，但相距 15 公里未免太远了。话虽如此，其中更多是关乎佛家思想，以点灯之佛塔施法以保护生

[1] 宋徽宗宣和年间应为 1119—1125。下文同。

den Schutz lebender Wesen vor absichtlicher Tötung annimmt.

Das am Anfang des Textes erwähnte Kái yüen-Kloster wurde erbaut unter Liang Wu Ti 502-550 und liegt nördlich der Pagode, jetzt fast ganz in Trümmern. Als Überrest von ihm steht nur eine gut erhaltene, gänzlich massive, zweigeschossige Halle, eine sogenannte Wu liangtien, wie es deren mehrere in China gibt an verschiedenen Stellen des Reiches. Sie ist wahrscheinlich bei der letzten großen Erneuerung des Klosters unter Ta Ming Wan li 1601 erbaut worden und dient als Bibliothek für die buddhistischen Schriften. Die Pagode von Jui kuangsze steht genau südlich in ihrer Hauptachse. Die Pagode hat außer dem niedrigen Sockelgeschoß, über dem der Dachkranz ganz verschwunden ist, 6 Geschosse. Von diesen haben die beiden unteren je 8, die oberen vier je 4 wechselständig angeordnete Öffnungen. Die Achteckflächen jedes Geschosses sind mit leichtem Reliefwerk von Pilastern und Architraven versehen, die mitsamt allen Mauerflächen weiß geputzt sind. Die Doppelgesimse, die stark beschädigt sind, bestanden aus zwei gegliederten Konsolreihen, unten abgedeckt, oben als Solbänke, in der Art der anderen Pagoden von Sutschou. Die Bekrönung bildet ein Zeltdach mit stark in die Höhe gebogenen Traufen und gewellten Graten, die in einem Knauf endigen.

Die Pagode soll einen wichtigen Einfluß ausgeübt haben auf das Geschick des Provinzialgouverneurs, von dessen Yamen aus man einen vollen Blick auf sie hatte. Ein Gouverneur ließ gegen Ende des 19. Jahrhunderts, als ein Táifun die hohe Stange herabgeblasen hatte, die Pagode instand setzen, um das Leben seiner kranken Mutter zu verlängern. Es wurde Geld gesammelt und mit dem Bau begonnen. Jedoch die Mittel reichten nicht, der Bauunternehmer erlitt Verluste und stellte die Arbeit ein. Alsbald starb die Mutter, und der Gouverneur hatte zu seiner Trauer noch große Einbuße an Vermögen, weil er sein Amt unterbrechen mußte. Vielleicht sind es jene umfangreichen Erneuerungen, von denen du Bose spricht und die 1880 für einen Betrag von 50 000 Tael stattgefunden haben sollen, aber nicht zu Ende geführt wurden.

Schuang tá（双塔）Die Zwillingspagoden in Sutschou

Im östlichen Teile von Sutschou, schon im südlichen Viertel, stehen nahe der Stadtmauer, eng beieinander inmitten von Ruinen und wildwachsendem Ge-

灵免受蓄意的杀戮。

本卷开头提到的开元寺建于梁武帝（502—550）时期，位于瑞光塔的北面，现在几乎已成废墟，只留下一座保存完好、雄伟的两层大殿，名叫无梁殿，中国各地都有此类建筑。这座无梁殿可能是在1601年大明万历年间建造的，当时寺院进行了最后一次大规模的修缮，它是当时寺院的藏经阁。瑞光寺塔位于无梁殿主轴线的正南方。宝塔塔基较矮，塔基上的塔身共有6层，基座上方的飞檐都已完全消失。塔身的6层中，下方的两层塔身各有8个券门，上面4层各有4个间隔分布的券门。每层塔身的八角面均以壁柱和额枋上的平面浮雕装饰，它们连同所有墙面均刷上了灰白色的浆。重檐损毁严重，由双排斗拱支撑，下部被瓦片覆盖，上方则作窗台，与苏州其他宝塔的飞檐结构相似。宝塔顶部呈帐篷样式，檐角向上高高翘起，屋脊呈波浪形，延伸至顶端为一球形柱顶。

据说这座宝塔对当地官员的运势影响重大，从衙门向外可以看到塔的全貌。19世纪末，一场台风把塔顶的刹杆吹倒了，当地的一位官员为使他患病的母亲延年益寿，找人修缮这座宝塔。他筹集资金开始动工，但由于所筹的资金不够，承建的工头不堪亏损只能中断工程。不久后，他的母亲去世了，这位官员不仅承受丧母之痛，还因丁忧去职而薪俸尽失。也许这就是杜步西[1]所提到的大规模修缮工程，据说此项工程在1880年耗资五万两白银，但最终也没有完工。

苏州双塔

在苏州城东南门处，离城墙不远的地方，两座完全一样的宝塔并排立于一片废墟和荒野之中。虽然塔檐已被损坏，但其余部分，尤其是塔顶保

[1] 杜步西（Hampden Coit DuBose, 1845—1910），美国传教士，中国禁烟会的创立者、会长，苏州使徒堂创始人。

sträuch, zwei völlig gleiche Pagoden. In den Gesimsen sind sie zwar beschädigt, im übrigen aber, zumal in den Spitzen, wohl erhalten und in ihrer Durchbildung gut erkennbar. Das zugehörige Kloster ist ganz verschwunden.

Nach den Angaben von Parker und der Buddh. Monum. ergibt sich folgendes geschichtliches Bild. Das Kloster Pan jo sze（般若寺）wurde gegründet noch zu Ende der Táng-Dynastie 860-874, die Zwillingspagoden wurden erbaut durch Wang Wenhan unter dem Sung-Kaiser Táng Tsung in der Periode Yung Hi 985, danach aber scheinbar wieder neu errichtet unter Schen Tsung in der Periode Hi Ning 1068-1078. Sie sind wiederholt ausgebessert, zuletzt 1822.

Die Türme sind die kleinsten unter allen anderen von Sutschou und einander fast ganz gleich. Auf niedrigem Erdgeschoß stehen 6 obere Geschosse, stark abgetreppt ohne Schwellung, und enden in einer hohen Gipfelstange mit Ringen, die nach oben immer kleiner werden. Darüber folgt ein größerer schwebender Ring und eine letzte, wiederum gegliederte Spitze. Es sind vortreffliche Beispiele für solche Siang lun. Die oberen Gesimse sind, wie gewöhnlich in Sutschou, verdoppelt und bestehen aus einem unteren geschweiften Dachring über Konsolen und einem oberen einfachen Gurtsims, zugleich Solband für die Öffnungen. Nur das unterste Gesims zeigt keinen Dachring, wenn auch leise Verdoppelung. Die Geschosse sind niedrig und lassen die Türme eher als Ringpagoden erscheinen. Je 4 Öffnungen mit gelappten Bogenschlüssen und je 4 rechteckige Blendnischen, scheinbar mit Fenstergittern oder Inschrifttafeln, sind wechselständig angeordnet. Die Flächen sind in flache Rahmenwerke aufgeteilt und durch runde Eckdienste eingefaßt.

In dem literarischen Sutschou wurden diese auffallenden Zwillingspagoden natürlich als glückliche Vorbedeutung für ein gutes Fengschui von den Gelehrten seit je gerne in Anspruch genommen. Sie sollen wiederholt günstigen Einfluß ausgeübt haben auf die literarischen Prüfungen, die in den einst eng benachbarten Prüfungshallen der Provinz stattfanden, man bemühte sich, diese Einflüsse ständig zu verbessern. Die Geomanten fanden, daß bei diesen Prüfungshallen durch die unmittelbar neben ihnen stehenden Doppeltürme der Einfluß des Weißen Tigers Pai hu（白虎）, der den Westen beherrscht, zu stark sei und ausgeglichen werden müsse durch ein höheres Bauwerk. das den Einfluß des blaugrünen Drachen · Tsíng lung（青龙）, der den Osten beherrscht, besser zur Geltung kommen lasse. Darum wurde weiter im Osten, schon ganz nahe der Stadtmauer, der Wentscháng ko（文昌阁）erbaut, der Turm für den Wentscháng

存完好，塔的结构也清晰可见，但宝塔所属的罗汉院已消失殆尽。

根据庄延龄[1]和《中国佛教史迹》的记载，般若寺始建于唐朝末年860—874年，双塔由王文罕奉宋太宗之命于雍熙二年所建，之后可能在宋神宗熙宁年间，即1068—1078年又重建了一次。双塔历经多次修缮，最后一次是在1822年。

双塔是苏州所有宝塔中最小的，两座塔几乎完全相同。低矮的塔基之上有6层塔身，向上逐层内收，塔层间无隆起裙边，塔顶有一根高高耸立的刹杆，它由自下而上逐渐变小的相轮构成，刹杆顶端有一个稍大些的悬浮状的圆环，上面另有一个尖顶。这是此类塔刹相轮结构的典型。与苏州常见的宝塔一样，塔身上方的塔檐是重檐结构，其下层的塔檐结构呈弧形，由斗拱支撑，上层塔檐是结构简单的腰檐，同时作为拱券的台檐。只有底层的塔檐没有飞檐，有少许重檐。每层塔身的高度都很低，所以该塔看起来更像是一座密檐塔。每层塔身分布着四扇辟壶门和四扇似带窗格和铭文的直棂窗。宝塔外壁以槏柱分割，转角饰圆椅柱。

在文化底蕴深厚的苏州，这两座醒目的双子塔自然被文人墨客看作风水吉兆的象征。据说这两座宝塔曾多次对在附近贡院举行的考试产生过积极的影响，人们不断试图通过双塔振兴文运。风水师们发现，双塔紧邻考场，使得掌管西方的白虎影响力太强，必须通过一座更高的建筑来平衡，使掌管东方的青龙更好地发挥它的影响力。因此，人们在东边紧挨城墙的地方修建了一座文昌阁，这是用来供奉掌管文运的文昌帝的塔楼，它同时也是城市的钟楼。文昌阁建于1589年，并于1704年，康熙年间对它进行了一

[1] 庄延龄（Edward Harper Parker, 1849—1925），英国著名汉学家，发表过大量关于中国方言、宗教、民族、文化的论著。

Gott der Literatur. Er dient zugleich als Glockenturm der Stadt. Die Erbauung erfolgte 1589 eine große Ausbesserung 1704 unter Káng Hi. Es waren offenbar die Literaten, die diesen Bau durchgesetzt hatten, um den beiden buddhistischen Türmen ihre Herrschaft zu nehmen. Denn Wentscháng war der berufene altchinesische Schutzgott der Literaten. Weiterhin verband man mit diesen Bauwerken einen Literatenscherz. Die Zwillingspagoden verglich man mit Schreibpinseln, zu denen der Tuschstein gefehlt hatte, der in Gestalt des quadratischen, massiven und schwarzen Wentscháng-Turmes geschaffen wurde. Dieser hieß nun im Volksmunde die Tuschpagode. Näheres über ihn findet sich in der Abhandlung über die Kúeising-Fengschui-Türme. Gerade für Zwillingspagoden erfand das Volk häufig solche kleinen Geschichten, denn das Außergewöhnliche der verdoppelten Form reizte die chinesische Phantasie zu harmlos ausschweifender Erdichtung. Die gedankliche Verbindung von Bauformen mit Schreibgerät findet sich noch bei anderen Gelegenheiten. So enden die Pfosten der Páilou einiger Konfuziustempel in den Provinzen Hunan und Hupei bewußt in Formen von Schreibpinseln. Die Schuang tá wurden somit aus dem rein buddhistischen Gedankenkreis in den Bereich chinesischer Geomantik einbezogen, ebenso wie alle anderen Pagoden von Sutschou, insgesamt also 7 buddhistische und als 8., Der Turm des Wentscháng. Selbst die größte und bedeutendste, die Nordpagode von Sutschou, geriet in diese altchinesischen Vorstellungen. Sie wird als Galeriepagode im nächsten Kapitel behandelt.

Räumlich und stilistisch zu den Pagoden von Sutschou scheinen die beiden Pagoden von Sungkiangfu zu gehören, etwa zwischen Sutschou und Schanghai. Sie stehen am Sche·Gebirge·Zosai·südwestlich der Stadt, wo sich jetzt ein Observatorium befindet, und sollen aus der Sung-Dynastie stammen. Die eine war um 1914 eine vollkommene Ruine von 21 m Höhe und dürfte heute verschwunden sein, die andere ragt noch in unseren Tagen, wenn auch stark beschädigt, in klarer Gliederung empor, bekrönt von der reichen Gipfelstange mit Abzeichenringen und umgestülpter Schale. Sie ist 29 m hoch, hat 7 Geschosse, wechselständige Türöffnungen, verdoppelte Konsolengesimse und dürfte in ihrer äußeren Ausbildung ursprünglich am ehesten dem Turm vom Schangfangschan bei Sutschou geglichen haben, nur daß das Verhältnis bei weitem schlanker ist. Die Dachkränze luden aber, wie Reste längerer Sparren zeigen, recht weit aus nach dem Muster von Jui kuang sze tá in Sutschou.

次大规模的修缮。这次修缮工作显然是由文人们发起的，为了从佛刹双塔处拿回（文运）掌控权，因为文昌是中国古代主掌文运的星宿。此外，人们还用这些建筑做了一个文雅的比喻。他们把双塔比喻成缺了砚台的两支毛笔，而方形、厚重、黑色的文昌塔就像砚台。现在文昌阁在民间亦被称为墨阁。关于文昌阁更详细的信息可以在关于魁星 – 风水 – 塔的文献资料中找到。独特的双塔形态激发了人们很多无伤大雅的丰富想象，人们为之编造很多这样的小故事。像这样把建筑结构和文房工具联系起来的例子也非个例。湖南、湖北一些孔庙牌楼的立柱就特意做成了毛笔形状。这样看来，正如苏州地区的其他宝塔一样，双塔也完全跳出了纯粹的佛教思想，将中国的风水学说纳入考量。这里一共有七座佛塔、一座文昌阁，其中最大和最重要的苏州北寺塔也符合中国的传统想象，我们将把它作为廊塔的代表在下一章中加以阐述。

松江府的两座宝塔在空间构造和风格上似乎都属于苏州宝塔的派系，松江府介于苏州和上海之间。这两座宝塔位于松江府西南的佘山上，建造时间据说可以追溯到宋朝，现在那里有一个天文台。其中的一座 21 米高的宝塔在 1914 年前后已成为废墟，现在可能已经消失殆尽，另一座虽遭严重损毁，但如今依然屹立于世，其层次清晰可见。华丽的塔刹由相轮、刹杆和露盘构成。该宝塔高 29 米，有 7 层，拱券间隔分布，有双层斗拱，初建时塔的外形可能最接近于苏州的上方山宝塔，只是从比例上看，它修长得多。从长椽残留的痕迹来看，屋顶的檐角远远挑出，与苏州的瑞光寺塔样式相似。

译后记

《苏州外文史料译编（第一辑）》于 2022 年 11 月正式出版面世。虽然译著销量有限，但不经意间，这本小书总会给我们这些译者带来些许惊喜和一丝成就感。记得有一次，一位同事周末带着孩子在苏州一家颇有名气的旧书店里“淘宝”，意外发现我们的译著赫然位列其中，这位同事特地拍照发在朋友圈内并给了一个大大的“赞”。还有一次，我无意中在微信上发现一个名为“英美在维度”的英语学习视频号，视频博主竟然以译著中的第一篇译文《姑苏景志》为例，连续做了 9 期视频，分析讲解其中的语言点和苏州历史文化。2023 年 4 月，我们翻译团队应邀前往中国矿业大学外国语言文化学院就外语学科如何与地方文化研究相结合进行了经验分享。在 2023 年年底召开的苏州历史文化研究会年会上，会长李峰教授更是特别点名表扬了我们的这本译著，认为本书给苏州历史文化研究提供了新的视角和珍贵史料，并鼓励我们继续做下去。也正是这样一个又一个的小惊喜，以及学界前辈、同仁们的殷切期望，让我们有了不断前行的动力，《苏州外文史料译编（第二辑）》亦能如期与读者见面。

在《苏州外文史料译编（第二辑）》的整个翻译、讨论、校对过程中，团队成员们依旧秉承“红脸出汗”的原则，对译文中出现的每一个细小问题都“争执不休”，力争为读者呈现准确、通畅的译文。和第一辑相比，第二辑在语种上除了英语之外，还增加了德语；在内容上也更加丰富，共收录译稿七篇，具体如下：潘慎文（A. P. Parker）的《苏州历史摘录》（*Notes on the History of Suchow*，英文单篇连载，卞浩宇、严佳译），古列尔玛 · F. 阿尔索普（Gulielma F. Alsop）的《我的在华岁月》（*My Chinese Days*，英文节译本，徐冰、徐舟涟译），多萝西·格雷（Dorothy Graham）的《中国园林》（*Chinese Gardens*，英文节译本，孟祥德译），威廉·斯宾塞·帕西瓦尔（William Spencer Percival）的《龙之国度》（*The Land of the Dragon*，英文节译本，余利霞、骆碧筠译），查尔斯·伯特伦（Charles Bertram）的《魔术师游世界》（*A Magician in Many Lands*，英文节译本，蔡骏译），玛丽·H. 克劳特（Mary H. Krout）的《两个女子在唐山》（*Two Girls in China*，英文节译本，戴莉、孙丹译），恩斯特·伯施曼（Ernst Boerschmann）的《中国建筑艺术与宗教文化》（*Die Baukunst und religiöse Kultur der Chinesen*，德语节译本，吴悦茜译）。这些史料，既有对苏州历史、名胜古迹、园林艺术以及民间传说的介绍，又有对当地水陆居民生活、交通方式的细致描述，还有西人在苏州度假、冒险经历的叙述，读来颇为有趣，引人入胜。熊月之先生曾指出，外语文献对于复原、再现、了解地方历史具有重要的参考价值，能够起到“存史之真、补史之缺、纠史之偏、详史之略”之功效，我们也希望读者能够从这些译文中了解更多“遗失”在域外的苏州记忆。

虽然整个整理、翻译和出版的过程费时耗力，一路走来也颇为曲折艰辛，个中辛酸唯有自知，但我们始终坚信，“阳光总在风雨后，乌云上有晴空”！希望我们的所有付出和努力能够换来读者的满意和认可，这也许就是我们最大的心愿了。

最后，特别感谢苏州市职业大学曹毓民书记、温贻芳校长对我们整个项目的关心以及提供的经费支持。曹书记曾多次表扬团队工作，并希望大家通过翻译，在讲好苏州故事的同时进而赢得“文化他信”；温校长也多次对团队付出的努力给予高度肯定和鼓励！此外，还要感谢苏州大学出版社李寿春副总编、沈琴编辑以及各位审读专家为本书出版付出的辛苦努力！

译文如有不当之处，敬请读者批评指正！

卞浩宇

2023 年 12 月于姑苏和茂苑